Edward Pickering is a writer and journalist who was former deputy editor of *Cycle Sport* magazine. He has also written for *Cycling Weekly*, the *New York Times* and *Loaded*, and was the co-author of Robbie McEwen's autobiography, *One Way Road*. When not cycling, he indulges his other passion, taiko drumming.

THE RACE AGAINST TIME

Edward Pickering

CORGI BOOKS

TRANSWORLD PUBLISHERS
61–63 Uxbridge Road, London W5 5SA
A Random House Group Company
www.transworldbooks.co.uk

THE RACE AGAINST TIME
A CORGI BOOK: 9780552167352

First published in Great Britain
in 2013 by Bantam Press
an imprint of Transworld Publishers
Corgi edition published 2014

All photographs © Phil O'Connor except:
Boardman and Windcheetah © Leo Mason;
Boardman on Lotus in Barcelona © Neal Simpson/EMPICS Sport

This book is a work of non-fiction.

A CIP catalogue record for this book
is available from the British Library.

Addresses for Random House Group Ltd companies outside the UK
can be found at: www.randomhouse.co.uk
The Random House Group Ltd Reg. No. 954009

The Random House Group Limited supports the Forest Stewardship Council® (FSC®),
the leading international forest certification organisation. Our books carrying the FSC
label are printed on FSC®-certified paper. FSC is the only forest-certification scheme supported by the leading environmental organisations, including Greenpeace. Our paper
procurement policy can be found at www.randomhouse.co.uk/environment

Typeset in Minion by Falcon Oast Graphic Art.
Printed and bound by CPI Group (UK) Ltd, Croydon, CR0 4YY.

Contents

Prologue

The Clash of Champions

Newtownards, Northern Ireland, Sunday, 22 April 1990

A nagging wind whips across Strangford Lough, a narrow finger of the Irish Sea which reaches inland behind the Ards Peninsula east of Belfast. The cold air is making the competitors of the Lee Ards Super 25 time trial shiver as they line up one by one to set off, a chilly minute's wait separating each one.

Ahead of them: a 12.5-mile ride down the A20, a winding road which hugs the shore of the lough, the grey tarmac separated only in places from the colourless waters lapping at the verge by a foot-high wall. A dead turn in the road at Kircubbin, then retrace route back to Newtownards. The course record for the 25 miles, set by British time-trialling legend Dave Lloyd five years previously, is well under the hour mark at 54.17, but most of the riders today aren't in Lloyd's class. A handful of decent racers and local amateurs are recording times of around an hour for the 25 miles – a good time in the blustery conditions, but no different from the hundreds of riders taking part in dozens of similar events the length of the United Kingdom.

However, there is a reason this race has been billed by the organizers as the 'Clash of Champions'. The field is mainly pack fodder – it comprises sixty-eight middle-markers, hobbyists, weekend warriors and also-rans – but also includes the British 25-mile champion Chris Boardman and the Scottish 25-mile champion Graeme Obree, the two best time triallists in Britain (a quirk of geographical bureaucracy means that though Boardman holds the 'British' title, in real terms it's actually the English and Welsh title). Today is the first time trial head-to-head between the two riders.

A clash of champions.

Obree is the sixtieth rider to take to the start line. He's a freak. You can't help but stare at the weird position he's adopted on the bike: he's turned the handlebars up, like a 1970s schoolkid, and he lies flat on them, his arms tucked in beside his body. When he races, his mouth gapes open, gulping in air like a whale eating plankton. He rolls a large gear slowly, in contradiction of coaching wisdom handed down over the generations, which advises turning a higher gear at a faster cadence. It almost looks like he doesn't really know how to ride a bike. You'd laugh, except for one thing – he's fast.

Ten minutes after Obree, Boardman's off. He's a freak, too. The twenty-one-year-old already has five years of international racing experience, but the fragmented rivalry between the competing disciplines of road racing and time trialling means that he's respected but not universally popular. To the time-trialling fraternity, he is a once-in-a-generation talent; to road racers, he is a time triallist who occasionally wins road races through brute force and ignorance. Boardman's position on the bike is also unusual; he's an early adopter of the triathlon handlebars introduced into mainstream cycling culture by Greg LeMond in the Tour de France just nine months previously. Boardman is fast, too. The general consensus is that it's only a matter of time before he achieves time trialling's holy grail – beating the British record for 25 miles, which stands at 49.24, set twelve years previously by Alf Engers.

Just 100 yards into the race, Boardman stops and is off his bike. His starting effort, an aggressive sprint up to race speed, is so strong that his rear wheel has been pulled off-centre. It takes him a good half a minute to locate the problem, loosen the nuts either side of the wheel, centre it, tighten the nuts again, get back on and restart his race. Normally this would not be a problem – after all, Boardman had won the national title by over a minute the previous June. There's plenty of time to take the 30 seconds back.

At Kircubbin, where a few dozen metres of dark pebbly shingle form what passes for a beach on the edge of the lough, Boardman reaches the turn 16 seconds down on his Scottish rival. There are a dozen miles left and he needs to ride each one a fraction over a second faster than Obree.

A neutral watching the race would probably have predicted a win for the Englishman. Boardman looks the part: his geared Cougar bike is sleek and aerodynamic-looking, with a rear disc wheel; he wears an aero helmet with a tinted visor, and on his wrist there's a large digital watch (Boardman's been experimenting with new-fangled scientific training methods involving pulse measurement). He's not right at the cutting edge, however – he's still using old-fashioned toe clips and straps on his pedals. He might be using 1990s training methods, but he's still got one foot – or two, actually – in the 1980s.

Obree, on the other hand, looks like a bloke who has turned up on the off chance to give time trialling a go. His concessions to aero clothing are a cycling cap stretched over an old-style leather-banded crash hat and a pair of sports socks worn over his shoes. His bike, built from a Jim Docherty frame, has a single fixed gear, and that tucked position on the upturned handlebars looks ungainly and awkward.

But Obree, incredibly, is matching Boardman's speed back north towards the finish in Newtownards. When the Scot thunders through the finish line, he stops the clock at 53.41 – a time 36 seconds better than Dave Lloyd's old course record. Ten minutes and 17 seconds later, Boardman crosses the line. He's actually lost a second since Kircubbin.

It's Boardman's first significant defeat in a time trial for over a year. For two seasons he has had his boot on the throat of domestic competition, taking his first national title – the hill climb – at the end of 1988, then three more the following year: the track pursuit, 25-mile and hill climb. Nobody has been close to him, until today.

As iconic cycling battlegrounds go, the A20 on a grey day in April is hardly comparable to Alpe d'Huez or the Champs Elysées, where tens of thousands of fans cheer on the riders of the Tour de France. But this first race on the road between the two stars of British time trialling was the beginning of an intense rivalry, one that pitted two very different men against each other and which would result in their vying for world pursuit championships and world hour records. Boardman would also go on to wear the yellow jersey in the Tour de France on three occasions.

The Lee Ards Super 25 was not just a clash of champions, but a clash of cultures which was more than just the cycling equivalent of an orthodox puncher taking on a southpaw. Obree and Boardman were binary opposites, and as with any rivalry, the achievements of one were enhanced and given meaning by the presence of the other. The Greek myths were built on this idea – that there is no hero without a villain, no good without evil, no order without chaos. Aether, the god of brightness and light, was the son of Erebus, the god of darkness. One could not exist without the other.

This rivalry pitted the establishment man Boardman against the outsider Obree. Boardman was born into the sport. The son of a champion time triallist father and keen cycle-touring mother, he took up cycling at thirteen, and within three years was representing the national men's team on the track. He grew up with an extended surrogate family of clubmates and international cyclists, the golden boy of British track racing, time trialling and, later, road racing. Obree, on the other hand, discovered that cycling was an excellent method of escaping as fast as possible from a brutal and unhappy childhood in Ayrshire. He spent his life on the periphery. For a start, he'd chosen a different sport from his peers, and even within Scottish cycling, which itself was out on a limb, Ayrshire was outside the mainstream. He was never one of us, always one of them. Boardman versus Obree was not quite Toff versus Tough, but Boardman's middle-class background was certainly more comfortable than the rough matrix of small-town working-class Ayrshire.

This rivalry was the team player against the individualist. Boardman surrounded himself with a tight-knit circle of confidants, and spent almost his entire racing career working with the same physiologist, Peter Keen, an avant-garde thinker whose experimental approach to new training methods had the perfect guinea pig in the analytical, empirical Boardman. Boardman's support team was so integral to his success that when talking about his achievements he invariably uses the personal pronoun 'we' rather than 'I'. We won the world championship. We took the hour record. Obree was a loner, albeit one capable of being very sociable. He trained alone, built his own bikes alone, and bounced between different advisers, teams, agents and managers without hanging on to any of them for very long. The cliché is that cycling is a team sport for individuals. For Obree, it was an individual sport for individuals.

This rivalry was a collision of contrasting characters. Boardman is a calm, unflappable, stoic, laconic, unemotional man who seems to go through life experiencing neither dizzying highs nor terrifying lows. He describes disappointments and triumphs in broadly similar and unexpressive terms. For most people, sport is a gladiatorial arena of ecstasy or despair, but Boardman would pronounce himself no more than 'satisfied' to have been crowned world champion, or to have taken the yellow jersey in the Tour de France. Obree is excitable, engaging, amusing, prone to mood swings and depression, with a mind that seems to be in a permanent state of superficial activity. While Boardman stuck to a careful, controlled and balanced path down the middle of the road, Obree swung wildly across both lanes. He was capable of enjoying the great triumphs of sporting success, but just as capable of pitching into a bleak, dark, incomprehensible slough of despondency.

The rivalry was a battle of the head against the heart, logic against spirit. When Boardman raced, he almost always seemed to have one eye on his pulse monitor. He knew from experience what his body could do, and once he hit the limit of what was sustainable, he carefully held it there. The reduction of this most intuitive and romantic of sports to a set of three digits on a handlebar-mounted computer infuriated the traditionalists. By contrast, Obree pedalled until he could taste blood, until he was on the verge of blacking out. Boardman's mentor Keen had him relying heavily on revolutionary new energy drinks and sports nutrition products. Obree, whether he hammed it up for the cameras and journalists or not, seemed to subsist on a diet of jam sandwiches and cornflakes.

Both riders were extraordinarily innovative. Boardman, who had married and had the first of six children at the age of twenty, couldn't follow the traditional route to becoming an international road professional, which involved hard years of penury and misery working up through the amateur ranks in a foreign country, so he invented a new one. He broke the world hour record in Bordeaux velodrome on the same day the Tour de France had a stage finish in the town – a red-and-yellow billboard speeding round the banked track in front of the managers of the twenty best professional road teams in the world. Obree was a radical bike designer. Until the 1980s, racing cyclists had more or less used the same position that James Starley, the inventor of the bicycle, would have used on his very first model. Three new positions were developed in the 1980s and 1990s: the triathlon-style handlebar position made popular by Greg LeMond when he won the 1989 Tour using it, the 'tuck' and the 'Superman'. The last two were invented by Obree.

Cycling is a sport in which insularity and self-obsession are common among its practitioners, and Obree and Boardman would insist that their primary concern was themselves. Both riders talked down their rivalry, which is a surefire sign that it was a major factor in their careers. My Chambers dictionary defines a rival as 'a person pursuing an object in competition with another', which is good enough for me. It was a happy coincidence that these two riders came along at the same time, from the same nation. Both were good at the same things and both were revolutionary in their training methods and approach to equipment. As Boardman has pointed out, they took very different paths but ended up at the same place. Both excelled in domestic time trialling, then swapped world hour records and track pursuit titles before Boardman adapted his talents to international road racing and the Tour de France.

It was a classic, many-faceted rivalry in which the differences in character, approach and style made it natural and easy for people to pick a favourite. Obree and Boardman were cycling's equivalent of Steve Ovett and Sebastian Coe, or Jimmy White and Steve Davis. And as with these famous rivalries, there was an inverse relationship between success and popularity. Obree found far less success over his cycling career than Boardman, but his chaotic, emotional approach was more popular among cycling fans, while Boardman was respected, even admired, but hard to love.

Cycling fans would recognize a parallel in the story of Jacques Anquetil and Raymond Poulidor, whose rivalry in the Tour de France during the 1960s captured the imagination of France. The more Anquetil beat Poulidor, the more popular the latter became in the eyes of the public, and the less Anquetil understood it. The hapless Poulidor, who managed to snatch defeat from the jaws of victory so often that his nickname was 'the Eternal Second', was no match for Anquetil, a hugely efficient and organized rider whose primary weapon was the time trial. But the public saw no contradiction whatsoever in applauding Anquetil politely for his victories, and cheering Poulidor to the rafters for his losses. There was the champion, and there was the people's champion.

Boardman and Obree's careers played out against a backdrop of the most revolutionary changes seen in a whole century of bike racing. When both started out, racing evening time trials in the early 1980s, cycling was not noticeably different from how it had been thirty, even fifty years previously. A bit of technological advancement and better roads had made the riders of the 1980s faster than their forebears, and colour photography and light television cameras had made them more accessible to the public, but the training methods and philosophies were much the same.

In the early 1990s, however, the sport underwent a cataclysmic process of modernization. New materials such as carbon-fibre made bikes lighter. Scientific training methods made riders faster (and so did some extremely effective performance-enhancing drugs, but we'll come to those later). Professional riders' salaries went up as the sport opened to new markets. Australian, American and Eastern European riders joined the ranks, and the line between professional and amateur, already eroded by years of under-the-table payments, was erased. In short, science was starting to take over the sport, especially in Britain. The Obree and Boardman rivalry was a microcosm of the global rise of a more organized, methodical approach to cycling.

Obree was one of the last of a breed. For years, British cyclists were successful independently, in spite of the underfunded national coaching system, and Obree was firmly entrenched in that tradition. Boardman was the first of a new breed. He was a child of the British cycling system, although he and Keen were changing it from a position slightly on the outside, but from the success they had with their new takes on coaching, training and racing it is possible to draw a straight line to the Olympic velodrome successes of Beijing and London, and to Bradley Wiggins winning the Tour de France.

This is a story of science versus art. Tradition versus modernity. Scot versus Englishman. Establishment versus unorthodox. Middle class versus working class. Control versus emotion. Jam sandwiches versus polymer-based energy drinks. But first and foremost it is the story of two men, each of whom wanted to be the fastest cyclist in the world.

1

Uncle Chris

I wonder what's in Chris Boardman's head as he watches a group of riders training behind a motorbike in Manchester velodrome. Sometimes you see football pundits, retired professionals, watching a match on television, and it's clear where they want to be. Involuntary kicks, strangled shouts and intense stares show that they miss the action, want still to be part of it; their bodies betray their minds' desire to be on the pitch, among the players.

The velodrome was the scene of three of Boardman's greatest triumphs. He's won a world championship and set two world hour records on the varnished pine boards below us. On each occasion, the place was a shrieking cauldron of emotion – Boardman may have been from Merseyside, but Manchester was his home track.

Yet if he misses being a racing cyclist, or is feeling nostalgic about his triumphs, he's hiding it very well. We're sitting in the seats above a steeply banked corner, around which the cyclists are whizzing once every 20 seconds or so, the buzzing of the motorbike engine growing, then shrinking, as the driver paces the group around. Boardman's not taking much notice of them.

That's the impression he always gave of his relationship with cycling. He did an interview in early 1992 – this is the year he won a gold medal in the individual pursuit at the Olympic Games, remember – in which he blithely stated that he didn't much enjoy riding his bike. He's spent the subsequent twenty years qualifying that statement, but the impression stuck with suspicious cycling fans: great talent, shame about the attitude.

I can remember my own first impressions of Chris Boardman, from when he was a rising star on the British time trial scene and I was a teenage fan of the sport. He seemed to get an inordinate amount of coverage in *Cycling Weekly*, because *Cycling Weekly* was obsessed with time trialling at the time. I was more interested in the colourful, cosmopolitan, sophisticated world of professional cycling. I thought time trialling was to proper cycling as non-league football was to the First Division.

Boardman, with his hangdog expression, both on and off the bike, his prematurely creased forehead and his flat-top buzz cut, seemed a different animal from the international pros. Boardman, as far as I could tell, rode and won time trials, and exuded laconic indifference to his superiority. He seemed to be obsessed with targets, progression and numbers, a control freak. I wanted emotional engagement and huge, preferably unrealistic, ambition from my sporting heroes, not a bullet-point list of realistic aims, each built on the foundation of the last. His middle name was Miles, for God's sake. Only Chris Boardman could share a middle name with the increment of distance for a road time trial.

Chris, I say as the motorbike buzzes past us on the track again, the coach blowing a whistle to indicate a sprint, the stereotype is that you were a scientist in a cyclist's body, that you didn't like cycling so much as treat it as an experiment. Here's your right of reply.

'Thanks. I appreciate it,' he says.

*

Christopher Miles Boardman was born in Hoylake, on the Wirral peninsula across the River Mersey from Liverpool, on 26 August 1968. Like many champion athletes, he chose his parents extremely carefully. His father, Keith, was a prolific time trial winner who once came fourth in the national 50-mile championship, and who was longlisted for the 1964 Tokyo Olympics team time trial squad. His mother, Carol, was also a keen cyclist. With two cycling parents, he was born with the genetics to be a good athlete. It's not known whether a pre-disposition to a sport or pastime is also inherited in the DNA, but certainly Keith and Carol stood back and let their son dis-cover cycling for himself, rather than force him into it.

In fact, his first sporting love was swimming, along with a bit of cross-country running. His childhood friend and future international team-mate Scott O'Brien, who would go on to come second in the national 25-mile championship in 1991 (Boardman won), recalls the young Boardman taking his watersports very seriously. O'Brien and Boardman used to knock around during the summer holidays: Scott's dad George had been an independent semi-professional cyclist in the late 1950s and early 1960s – he rode the Tour de France in 1961 – and he and Keith Boardman were friends. 'We met at the Harrogate Festival of Cycling one year, and Chris wasn't into cycling at all,' recalls Scott O'Brien. 'We stayed at the campsite and hung around the swimming pool. Chris was really into swimming, and I was dead impressed that he had this wetsuit to wear. I started going to his house and hanging out in Hoylake Baths with him.'

Tony Bell, who would go on to become a cycling journalist and write a book with Phil Liggett, *The Fastest Man on Two Wheels: In Pursuit of Chris Boardman*, which covered the rider's early career, used to see the Boardmans regularly in the local cyclists' café, the Eureka, which was in Two Mills, about 20 kilometres from Hoylake. 'He was quite a serious young man,' Bell remembers. 'So much so, we used to call him Uncle Chris, even when he was thirteen or fourteen. At that age he wore a fooking flat cap. He looked like an old man trapped in a young man's body.'

It was when he was thirteen that Boardman discovered cycling. Or rather, he discovered racing. In early 1982 he persuaded his reluctant parents to allow him to ride an evening 10-mile time trial just outside Chester. His mother and father were concerned that the challenge, difficulty and pain of racing would put their son off before he'd experienced the enjoyment of cycling. But they didn't see that that was the point. Boardman said of his first races, 'I wasn't interested in anything where I couldn't see a natural progression to go on to be a winner.' Enjoyment simply didn't come into it, or at least not in the traditional understanding of the word. Boardman derived his enjoyment from what other people found challenging.

He recorded 29.43 for that first time trial. 'It was only a little race,' says Boardman. 'People used to turn up in cut-off jeans or football shorts and have a go. I had chips on the way home.'

The next week, he had another try. Twenty-eight minutes. He was hooked.

By the end of the season, he had improved by over four minutes, with a best of 25.25.

In May 1982, Boardman's name appeared for the first time in the results pages of *Cycling* magazine (which didn't become *Cycling Weekly* until 1986) with third place in the juveniles category of the Rhyl Road Club 10-mile time trial. The following year, Boardman won an open 25-mile time trial, the Southport Road Cycling Club event, beating grown men at the age of fourteen. His 10-mile personal best by the end of 1983 was 21.04 – a phenomenal improvement.

'Chris had a proper, natural talent,' says O'Brien. 'I knew he was good as soon as he started riding a bike. You could tell. He was very dedicated. He cottoned on to the fact cycling could be a vehicle to take him where he wanted to go. And he liked to do things properly.'

It sounds like Boardman had an idyllic, happy childhood. But in the velodrome, he tells me that's not quite true. He drifted through his academic career at Hilbre High School in West Kirkby, where one of his classmates was actor Daniel Craig. He neither left much of an impression on the school nor let it make much of an impression on him. 'I had a very loving family, but I struggled through school and didn't enjoy it. I left school with quite low self-esteem. I can't say that I was bullied, but I didn't have a great time. I didn't leave with lots of friends, and I felt I was quite different. I never really had anything in common with people at school. When I left, I never looked back, and I never missed it. I didn't even go back and pick up my exam results. I just left. I didn't have a lot of self-esteem, so my self-esteem became wrapped up in winning.'

You don't need to be a professional psychologist to know that is probably not a very healthy thing to do in the long term. Boardman also suffers from dyslexia, which hadn't helped his academic career.

'When I found I could do things that other people couldn't do, it felt good, and I pursued that,' he continues. 'I was never winning on sports day. I was Mr In-the-Middle, just making up the numbers in the school photograph.'

There's a parallel to the way Boardman built his racing career in the vocation he chose for himself after leaving school. He trained as a cabinetmaker – a meticulous job which demands concentration and patience.

Boardman confesses that there was a small element of 'I told you so' in his becoming such a successful cyclist. In the end, the mediocre child who never stood out, the wallflower who nobody noticed, the boy who didn't make friends, compensated by driving himself to success in one of the hardest sports in the world. He assures me he's mostly over it. 'I'm not cured, but I'm a lot more balanced,' is the way he puts it.

Cycling fans fetishize the epic and romantic, but Boardman was a classicist. It took years for the cycling world to 'get' him, after he rode his final hour record in Manchester right at the end of his career and, for once, threw numbers, spreadsheets and pulse rates out of the window in a visceral display of willpower and fighting spirit. It was only when he retired that a lot of fans realized they'd liked him all along.

French fans loved Raymond Poulidor because he was one of them; he exhibited the humanity and vulnerability of normal people. Normal people's lives are full of highs and lows, so when a sports star experiences highs and lows, they can readily identify with him or her. Boardman's empirical and analytical approach to cycling, and his naturally unexcitable demeanour and character, smoothed out the highs and lows.

I tell Boardman that it used to drive me up the wall when he won world titles or yellow jerseys and would pronounce himself 'satisfied' to have got the job done. 'Satisfied' is what I feel when I've ironed a shirt and the creases are all straight. Where was the elation? The passion? The euphoria?

'My passion was in the understanding of the numbers and fascination with trying to improve,' he responds. 'We went out to see what I could do and we thought this could happen, and when it did, brilliant, it was great. I realize for the majority of people, being totally satisfied and content is not the big thing. But it was for me. Imagine, you have a tremendous meal, followed by smoking a cigar or cigarette – you get a feeling of contentment and satisfaction. That's what I got from a win.

When it all comes off and you get it right, it's like submitting a paper for marking and it comes back and you have ten out of ten. Great.

'A tremendous sense,' Boardman adds with a wistful expression on his face, 'of satisfaction.'

The problem Boardman has always had when it comes to his public persona is one of perception. During his racing years he inadvertently came across as arrogant, even though everyone who knew him swore blind that he was an individual of quiet charm, honesty and seriousness. Boardman treated training as a series of hypotheses to be tested, and he believed whole-heartedly in the conclusions he arrived at, which manifested itself as confidence, and in turn was interpreted as arrogance. 'You couldn't meet a less arrogant guy,' insists Tony Bell. 'At his core, there's a shyness and a level of uncertainty about things, and he hid that by doing the Uncle Chris thing – he put on the confidence.' In other words, it was a defence mechanism.

'But he was the ultimate sensible young man. One night one of the guys in the cycling club had organized a stag night with strippers and that kind of stuff. I was astounded to see Chris there.' Bell recounts that a stripper grabbed one of the lads out of the crowd and that things started to get a little raunchy. 'I glanced across at Chris and he was sitting there with his arms crossed, talking to somebody about cycling. He turned, saw all this stuff going on, and he didn't even bat an eyelid.'

Boardman, says Bell, just turned back round and carried on talking about cycling.

2

Saltcoats

From the train, the sky over the Firth of Clyde is virtually indistinguishable from the sea. Clouds the colour of gunmetal are dumping great quantities of rain, whipped into billowing sheets by the wind, on to fields that already look saturated, enlarging the muddy ponds of standing water. The tracks are right on the edge of the sea. On really windy days, the waves hit the rocks and great spumes of foam lash the trains.

From Glasgow Central station, the train to Saltcoats passes through the suburbs of the city, then out across dormitory towns in Renfrewshire and into North Ayrshire, en route to Largs. Even on a sunny day it's not the most scenic or inspiring journey. Today, it looks downright grim.

I'm the only person who alights at Saltcoats. It's a small coastal town on the firth which looks like it's taking the recession particularly personally. It might once have been non-descript, in better times, but it now seems to occupy the space between shabby and moribund. From the station I can see a deserted bookie's and a couple of shut-up shops, and everywhere the depressing drumbeat of rain.

Graeme Obree lives here. Over a crackly mobile phone

line he'd told me where to come. 'I live in Saltcoats – S-A-L-T-C-O-A-T-S. You can get a train from Glasgow. Call me from the station.'

Rather than wait in the station café, I stand outside to wait for Obree. Mindful of the fact that a Scottish journalist colleague told me he'd been mentally scarred when Obree jokingly accused him, a soft Edinburgh lad, of being 'wishy-washy', for some reason I expect Obree to think better of me if I appear not to be bothered by the rain. But when he appears, he's hurrying through the puddles under a large umbrella.

We talk over muddy coffees at the Café del Greco, a utilitarian canteen with metal teapots and mugs and saucers left over from the 1980s, before heading to Obree's flat – two rooms above a carpet shop on the edge of the town centre. Obree apologizes in advance for the mess.

In the front room, on an old sheet, there's a huge pile of bits of bikes – gears, chains, nuts, bolts, skewers, an old frame. A couple of bikes in various states of completion are propped up at the edge of the room. On the surface of the kitchen table I can see lines and angles drawn in pencil. His latest project, the 'Beastie', a bicycle-cum-deathtrap on which Obree intends to break the world speed record for two-wheeled human-powered vehicles, was sketched out and knocked together here. Obree's invented another new position with the Beastie: he'll lie prone on his front, with the front wheel – which Obree hopes will be turning at something close to 100 miles per hour – millimetres from his nose.

Also on the table: a vice, clamped to the edge; Obree's British Cycling life membership card; and reams of papers, letters and scrawled notes. It's more of a piling system than a filing system.

It's a spartan arrangement, which suits Obree. He likes the fact there are no neighbours, that the shop closes at five. There's nobody for him to disturb, and nobody to disturb him.

The first thing he says to me, before I've even asked a question, is: 'I never wanted to be a racing cyclist.'

Saltcoats is only 20 miles from Newmilns, where Obree spent an unhappy childhood. He was born in Nuneaton in Warwickshire on 11 September 1965, but his family moved to Scotland soon afterwards. The opening pages of Obree's 2003 autobiography *Flying Scotsman* are as unsparingly savage as misery memoirs get. By the time he reached his teens he'd been sexually assaulted at knifepoint, beaten up numerous times, bullied and ostracized at school, and had considered suicide. In Newmilns, minds were as narrow as the Irvine Valley in which the town sat. Obree memorably described the town as 'parochial enough to single you out, but large enough to be nasty with it'.

There were two things that the locals particularly didn't like: outsiders and police. Obree's father was both. Obree tells me that in *Flying Scotsman* he actually understated the violence he suffered as a child. He's forgiven the perpetrators, but not forgotten. 'These people were innocent kids until they were shown violence, and taught the attitude that, right, he's getting a kicking because he's police,' he says.

Schoolchildren can be notoriously unaccepting of people who are different. Some people have their difference beaten out of them as children. Obree had his beaten into him.

'I heard this analogy from somebody else,' he continues, 'but it applies to my life. There's a kid walking up the street and he sees a butterfly trying to get out of a chrysalis. He bends down and opens it all up, because it was struggling to get out. They go on to the shops, but when they come back past, the butterfly is dead. The mother said, "The butterfly needs to struggle to get out of the chrysalis to be able to fly." That is my story. The struggle made me strong enough to be world champion. If you overcome adversity, you have to be thankful for it. You'll be stronger for it.'

Obree almost didn't overcome the adversity. Suicide attempts punctuated his life for thirty-five years, both before and after the best years of his career. Obsessive training and ambition helped to ward off depressive thoughts, but Obree's formative experiences cast a long shadow over his life.

At the time, they fuelled an appetite for escapism. 'I spent my school days staring out of the window thinking about exploring the Amazon. I climbed trees. I hid in trees. And I was always wondering what was over the horizon. Cycling was the means of getting over the next horizon.'

Of course, the urge to explore wasn't just a case of a desire to see what was beyond the narrow boundaries of Newmilns. When you cross a horizon, you don't just enter a new land-scape, you leave the old one behind. Cycling enabled Obree to leave behind the misery that he associated with Newmilns.

Unlike Chris Boardman, Obree discovered cycling before he discovered racing. He rode for fun, then started riding with the Wallacehill Cycling Club in Kilmarnock, near Newmilns, from early 1981, when he was fifteen. At the Wallacehill CC, Obree experienced a process familiar to club cyclists the length of the country: the kicking. 'Inevitably, when I joined the club the feeling was, here's the newcomer,' Obree says. 'Let's stretch him and show him who's boss. They did, but I kept coming back for more.'

Obree's relationship with cycling developed in an entirely different way to his English rival's. Boardman raced that first evening 10, then saw a considerable improvement the next time he rode. His addiction in the sport was progress, and his evolution was deliberate and measured. Obree's came about by accident, a by-product of the fact that he just enjoyed going out on long touring rides. He was quite good – in local time trials he used to catch riders who'd set off ahead of him, chat for a short while, then zip on up the road – but not by design.

That was until the race that changed everything for him – the 1983 Ayr to Girvan time trial, an 18-mile event held in April. The big favourite for the race was Bob Addy, a former Tour de France rider. Obree, now seventeen, rode the race on a 1938 track frame bought for eight pounds, and wheels that were rescued from a friend's rubbish bin and painstakingly repaired and trued. He wore an old jersey that was so baggy he had to cinch it in using the pins on his race number. He beat Addy by 3 seconds. 'I think he was quite shocked, actually. Beaten by a junior from Ayrshire he'd never heard of, on this ancient bike! It was the first time I'd won something and the first time I'd achieved something in my life.'

Over tea, loaded with what Obree calls 'depth charges' – artificial sweeteners – he tells me that whatever it was inside him that pushed him to two world pursuit championships and two hour records, it was awakened on that day. The determination, he adds, was always there. 'I had straight Es in English at school, because I couldn't engage with it. My English teacher said there was no point in turning up to the exam because I had no hope.' Obree looks at me the way he looked at his English teacher. 'Watch me,' he snarls. 'So I got one poem, just the key aspects, and focused my mind. And I passed. It was the first English exam I ever passed. If somebody tells me I can't do something, I go, "Watch me." There was something waiting to come out, even when I was fifteen.'

Obree was handed three envelopes at the prize presentation after his beating of Bob Addy: first junior, first handicap rider and first overall. The effect of this win was to turn Obree from a leisure cyclist, albeit a committed one, into an obsessive. He tinkered with his bike, cutting out half the spokes in the wheels, figuring that he didn't need the extra weight and wind resistance. Then he drilled holes in the rims between the spokes, to save more weight, covering the holes with electrician's tape to maintain aerodynamic integrity. He gazed at trees and watched leaves to work out how air moved according to which direction the wind was coming from, and what the air temperature was, and whether or not all this could help him shave a few seconds off his personal best times.

By June that year he'd improved enough to come fourth in the Scottish 25-mile championship, although *Cycling* magazine was variously reporting his name as Graeme or George O'Brcc. He won the junior best all-rounder competition in Scotland, which aggregated times for riders' fastest 25- and 50-mile time trial results.

Boardman and Obree's obsessions with cycling were similar during this period in their lives. Two teenage boys with self-esteem issues, in two different places in Britain, had discovered they were good at something. In fact they were not just good at it, they both excelled. Both trained hard and took an unusually high level of interest in their bike set-up. But Obree seemed to deal with his obsession less well than Boardman, perhaps because the Englishman's highs and lows were far less magnified in general than the Scot's.

'Cycling's a great vehicle for obsessive behaviour,' Obree tells me. 'You can be obsessive about the equipment, the training and the result. But obsessional behaviour is like alcoholism or drug-taking. It's subjugating some other fear or emotion that you don't want to come to the surface – same as any other addictive behaviour.'

What were you subjugating?

'Multifaceted resentment,' he replies, enunciating the syllables clearly, with the practised facility of the habitual self-analyst. 'If I boil it away, I went on a journey of obsessional behaviour. It would be drinking alcohol to excess, or reading scientific journals to excess – I used to read big thick microbiology books. Building bikes to excess. Then cycling to excess, to the point of getting to the top of the ladder, which is the world hour record and the world championship. And there is nothing else in terms of ambition. You can do the same again, but you get to the point where there is no more obsessional behaviour left because you have reached the top of the ladder. Then, I have to actually deal with my personal issues.'

Dealing with his 'personal issues' happened during and after what Obree refers to as his 'gap decade'. They were years of mental illness and depression following his retirement as a cyclist, and featured several abortive comebacks on the bike.

'And then I came out as the person I am now,' he adds brightly.

The person he is now seems happy enough. A two-room flat above a carpet shop in Saltcoats isn't a typical retirement plan for a two-time world champion cyclist, but Obree isn't typical of the breed. He has accumulated little in the course of his life. Relationships, money and physical objects come and go without Obree managing to hold on to them.

In the course of my research for this book, I realized that most of my interviewees had three things in common with regard to Obree: estrangement, affection and concern. The majority had lost touch, but they'd ask after him and make me promise to give him their best wishes. They would also express regret that Graeme's life turned out the way it did, and that it was a shame he didn't have a more settled and contented retirement. But that's Obree: if he didn't have a slightly chaotic approach to life, he wouldn't be Graeme Obree. We can't have the genius innovator and world champion without the vulnerable individual.

'I didn't fit into society, I didn't fit into mainstream groups of people,' he told me at one point during our interview.

After we've finished talking, we walk back through Saltcoats to sit down for an eight-pounds-per-head fish supper at the

Salt Cot pub. As we walk down the main street, shopkeepers at their doors wave a greeting to Obree. Then we get to the closed-down Metro nightclub, where one of the local down-and-outs sitting on the steps calls out to Obree.

'Ye've got to come and meet Ronny,' Obree says.

Ronny looks about fifty, though he's probably ten years younger than that. He has with him for company a King Charles spaniel called Molly, which he recently bought for a fiver. Obree pets Molly's head and asks Ronny how on earth he's going to look after a dog. Obree then tells me that he recently went on holiday to Tenerife and sent a postcard addressed to 'Ronny, Metro steps, Saltcoats, Scotland' which got to its destination.

'Ronny, show him the postcard.'

Ronny pulls the postcard out of his pocket to show me, inadvertently dropping a small folded silver foil packet on the ground, which he picks up and carefully puts back in. I can clearly see the address, written in Obree's scruffy handwriting on the back, and the words 'Beer is only £1.10 a pint!'

Obree seems very comfortable chatting to Ronny and the others on the Metro steps. He's in his element among these people, whose transient lives will take them on to other places, unencumbered by material goods or human relationships.

3

The Time Trials of Life

Time trialling is to cycle sport as prog rock is to modern music. It's a dorky subsection of the form, populated by obsessives, outside the mainstream. It's not so much that the practitioners of each don't want to join the mainstream, more that they believe so passionately in the superiority of their own pursuit that they think the mainstream should move across and join them.

In most other cycling cultures, road racing is the dominant form of the sport. The bright, brash colour of a peloton, the nip and tuck of the tactics and the excitement of the sprint finish or the glory of a breakaway win have long attracted fans, sponsors and attention. In Europe, road racing is the sport of the people par excellence. Cycling in Great Britain, however, developed along different lines, and this being Britain, it started out as a bit of a class issue.

British bicycle racing in the late Victorian era was a swash-buckling, devil-may-care affair regarded with suspicion by the establishment. Rightly so, the establishment must have thought in 1894, when a woman who had been riding a horse as a bike race sped past complained to the local police force about her steed rearing in terror at the two-wheeled menace. It was the cyclists who ended up in a ditch, but it was too late: sensibilities had been offended.

The National Cyclists' Union, the sport's governing body, combined panic and deference in their response: they banned racing on the roads, before the authorities had a chance to do so.

In reaction to the NCU's pre-emptive and acquiescent capitulation, a rival racing body, the Road Racing Council, was set up by Frederick Thomas Bidlake, a man whose passion for bike racing was matched only by an officious fondness for measuring and recording time. It occurred to the RRC that if you tried to set records individually, from one point to another, it wasn't a race, it was a record. It also occurred to them that if lots of riders all cycled from one point to another point on the same morning, setting off one at a time, it still wasn't a race.

In order to prevent the authorities testing the hypothesis that a hundred or more cyclists competing with one another to get from one point to another as fast as possible *wasn't* a race, the RRC held their events under conditions of utmost secrecy. Riders wore black, events started at the crack of dawn and courses were given codes so that outsiders would not be able to find out where they took place. While the rules about all-black clothing were ditched after the Second World War, the course codes and unsociable hours continue to this day.

And so, while cycle sport in mainland Europe evolved through the twentieth century into a vibrant road racing scene, with the Tour de France and the Classics setting a model for the modern calendar, it became a parochial, inward-looking affair in Britain. The originators of British time trialling would well have recognized the sentiment expressed in the apocryphal newspaper headline 'Fog in Channel; Continent Cut Off'. Bidlake is quoted as describing bunched road racing as a 'superfluous excrescence'.

British time trialling, by its nature, has always attracted self-absorbed bureaucratic types, tech obsessives and eccentrics. Some of these individuals happen also to be among the finest athletes ever to have been born in Britain, men and women who prospered in the narrow confines of the sport domestically but suffered in terms of global recognition from the lack of international comparison.

The first post-war star of time trialling was Ray Booty, a genial giant of a man with a mop of unruly hair blown into a centre parting, a set of gleaming teeth that seemed just too big for his smiling mouth, and a pair of bottle-bottomed black-framed NHS specs. Booty might have looked like Clark Kent, but like Kent's alter ego he was extraordinarily strong. He won the British 100-mile and 12-hour championships five times each, and was the first man to beat four hours for 100 miles – a feat straight from the pages of *Boy's Own*. In a rare foray into international racing, he won the gold medal in the road race at the 1958 Empire Games, but he remained a committed and steadfast amateur, a part-timer who fitted cycling in around his job as an electronic engineer.

Booty wasn't the only British time triallist to win international medals. Beryl Burton was a two-time world road race champion so far ahead of her peers at home and blessed with such career longevity that she won a staggering twenty-six national 25-mile time trial titles between 1958 and 1986. In 1967 she set a national record for the 12-hour time trial of 277.25 miles, which didn't just break the women's record, but the men's too. Burton was so competitive that she wouldn't shake her own daughter Denise's hand when she outsprinted her mother for the national road race title in 1975. She was a competitive parent, but not in the normal way.

Through the 1960s and 1970s, times over the set distances of British time trials edged down, as riders sought the fastest courses, which were based on A roads and dual carriageways. The record for 25 miles was beaten six times between 1964 and 1966 before one of time trialling's most eccentric characters, Alf Engers, recorded 51 minutes dead in 1969.

Engers was a brash, cocky individual whose pinched features and hooked nose were as Dickensian as his name. He turned up to time trials wearing fur coats and paisley shirts and was the kind of divisive figure for whom the passion of his fans was only exceeded by the zeal of his detractors, who made their feelings clear on the letters page of *Cycling*. The dominant personality of 1970s time trialling, Engers won the blue riband event, the national 25-mile championship, five years in a row between 1972 and 1976, and, as we know, was the first man to break fifty minutes over the distance with that 49.24 in 1978.

The early to mid-1980s played host to a great rivalry between two more individuals whose nonconformity matched their physical prowess: Dave Lloyd and Darryl Webster. Lloyd was a heavy smoker before he took up bike racing at the end of 1969. Within two years he was participating in the world championship, and by 1973 he had turned professional. Lloyd rode in some of the world's biggest races, a rare Brit in Paris-Roubaix and the Tour of Switzerland. He was forced to take a three-year break in the late 1970s with a heart condition, but came back and dominated British time trialling, winning the 1981 and 1982 national 25-mile championships. He was eclipsed by Webster, a mercurial talent who won the next four titles before turning professional as a road racer. Then, an unhappy year at the Spanish Teka team in 1989 was followed by premature retirement at the age of twenty-seven. What should have been Webster's best years were spent ferrying around taxi passengers in his native Leicester.

So when Chris Boardman and Graeme Obree emerged as

time trialling's pre-eminent characters a few years after Webster and Lloyd, the sport was well used to dominant and quirky characters.

In fact riders such as Booty, Burton, Engers, Lloyd and Webster were and remain representative of time trialling in general. From national champions down to weekend warriors, the obsession with going as fast as possible underpins the whole sport. Although winning is important, every rider is essentially in competition with him or herself, which is why obsessive behaviour is usually rewarded: get things a bit more right than last time, and you could beat your personal best for the distance. Getting things right can encompass a whole range of variables: course and weather conditions, gearing, training, pacing, pulse, power, diet, level of focus, start time, traffic, clothing, bike, wheels, tyres, cadence, helmet . . . the list is endless. Every tiny gain counts, and Boardman and Obree were not unusual in their dedication to finding ways of going faster.

Breaking an hour for a 25-mile time trial is the cycling equivalent of the sub-three-hour marathon. It's a decent time for a strong amateur, but there are thousands of keen cyclists who invest large amounts of time, money and emotional well-being in trying and failing to do it.

Chris Boardman went under the hour in a 25 for the first time in 1983, aged fourteen, years before tri-bars and aerodynamic bikes made the feat more achievable. That he was a prodigy was not in doubt, so his father started casting about for a trainer for his son. Keith Boardman didn't have the temperament or willingness to jeopardize a close relationship. And he didn't have the naked ambition to play Peter Coe to his son's Sebastian, so he found a man who did: his own former coach, Eddie Soens.

Soens hadn't been the only candidate for the job. Keith also asked Doug Dailey, who would become the national cycling coach in 1986. Dailey had been involved in setting up the cycling North West Centre of Excellence at the Kirkby Sports Centre, where Boardman trained. Dailey, a former national road race champion, still raced as a veteran while coaching the younger riders. At the Centre of Excellence, Dailey was able to observe Boardman at close quarters.

'I remember spending a very uncomfortable Saturday morning off the front in a two-man break with Chris Boardman, during a training session,' he recalls. 'We used to ride out to the three-mile circuit at Bickerstaff, which had a very heavy back straight, for hard training. It was virtually a mini-race of an hour and a half or so. I remember getting off the front with Chris and was able to encourage him and watch him. He was very impressive for a young kid. We never had more than a hundred and fifty yards' lead for an hour – every time I looked back they were gutter to gutter behind us.

'Keith said, "Would you be prepared to coach him?" But I said no. I felt he was a special talent and needed real one-to-one coaching and lots of time. He went with Soens, which was better.'

Soens was a man whose training methods lay at the intersection between his experiences as a boxer, soldier and Scouser. He was a formidable motivator and disciplinarian who'd coached fellow Merseysider Norman Sheil to two world pursuit championship wins in the 1950s. He'd also turned Dave Lloyd from a man who smoked forty cigarettes a day into a cyclist who won twenty races a year. He took charge of Chris Boardman in early 1984.

Soens was the perfect mentor. He and Boardman formed a team that was exactly equal to the sum of its parts. Boardman, the quiet and diffident teenager, owned two extraordinary assets: a huge physical capacity for riding fast and efficiently, and the mental intensity and curiosity of a scientist, unable to have an idea without following it all the way to its ultimate conclusion. Soens was pugnacious and charismatic, the polar opposite to Boardman. He added competitive fire to his charge's talents.

Soens was an intense individual, by all accounts. Photographs show a compact man with a regulation short back and sides, and a face that frowned a little even when he was smiling. Boardman needed direction and an injection of confidence. Soens, a man possessing only a passing acquaintance with self-doubt, provided both.

'Soens had a talent for digging something out of somebody, finding what they had and bringing it out. He was a motivator,' recalls Tony Bell.

Bell was another older rider who got to observe Boardman at close quarters when he was young. 'He was sixteen, I was twenty-five, and me and him ended up off the front of a race. He coaxed me up the hill on the course every lap. I was knackered, and with a lap to go, he said, "Are you going to be all right now?" and then just took off. I didn't see him again until the finish.'

But winning didn't come naturally to Chris Boardman. The received wisdom is that he swept all before him in domestic time trials before going on to greater things in the Olympic velodrome and on the roads of the Tour de France. But it was never as easy as that. He spent most of his late teens not quite winning national championships, and trying to keep up with his own precocity.

Racing as a juvenile in 1984, several months into Soens's tutelage, Boardman was already attracting attention. At the English Schools Cycling Association Schoolboy International stage race based in the cosmopolitan environs of Butlin's at Skegness, he won the first two stages – a time trial and a hill climb – and his North team won the team time trial the next day. But he contrived not to win the overall title when an untimely puncture in one of the road race stages cost him time. Rival Andrew Perks won the last two stages, and the overall, with Boardman seventh. The puncture wasn't the only bit of bad luck to befall Boardman in the race. His bike had been written off after falling off a car roof and he'd had to borrow one. Road racing, and stage racing, is far less controllable than time trialling, and even at fifteen, Boardman was more at home in the latter. Road races involve luck, tactics and unpredictability, factors which didn't sit comfortably with his preference for order.

A month later, in July, Boardman set an extraordinary national 25-mile record for juniors, despite still being a juvenile, the next age group down. He rode 52.09 in the Drighlington Bicycle Club 25, 18 seconds faster than the previous record, and beat his dad in the process. At the age of fifteen, he'd ridden 25 miles faster than any rider aged eighteen and under in British history. With only a fortnight to go to the national junior 25 championship, he was the hot favourite.

He duly won the Nova CC 10-mile time trial the weekend before the nationals in 21.04, itself only a handful of seconds outside the junior record, and the time-trialling world waited for Boardman's confirmation.

Boardman's friend and team-mate Scott O'Brien recalled how seriously the rider was taking the championship, which was even being held in Merseyside. 'There was a lot of pressure on him because he was the hot favourite, even though he wasn't even a junior yet,' he says. 'I remember looking at his bike. He'd built it himself, and it was so extreme, to save weight and reduce wind resistance, like having no bar tape. If he could get an advantage by any means he would do it.'

Boardman may have applied sober attention to detail to his

bike, but he got carried away with his form. He rode two more races in the week leading up to the championship, so instead of tackling the 25 fresh, he started it tired and nervous.

Fifth. He'd blown it. Local rival Guy Silvester took the title.

People looking more deeply for cause and effect in Boardman's capitulation than mere inexperience recalled Keith Boardman's ride in the 1976 national 50-mile championship, also held in Merseyside. He too had let the pressure of being a local favourite get to him and regretted not doing himself justice and getting a medal at least. Maybe some obscure chromosome on the Boardman DNA made them choke on big occasions, speculated some observers. 'He has his father's dislike of the big occasion,' opined an editorial in *Cycling*.

A month after losing the national 25, Boardman won the English Schools 10-mile time trial championship. And at the following season's national junior track championship at Leicester's Saffron Lane cycling track, he had another chance for redemption. Eddie Soens was coaching him to be an individual and team pursuiter, the same disciplines as his world champion Sheil. Soens himself described Boardman as the best prospect he had seen since Sheil.

Cycling magazine reported, after the 1985 pursuit championship, 'Friday at Leicester was a night to savour, and those who saw [the winner of] the junior pursuit will be able to say in years to come that they knew him when he was just 16 years old and on his way to stardom.' The problem for Boardman was that the editorial wasn't referring to him. The prodigy had been soundly beaten by a rider four months younger than him.

Colin Sturgess, the son of two former national-level cyclists, had parachuted in from a childhood in South Africa and landed in Leicester almost fully formed as a world-class cyclist just a fortnight before the championship. He'd actually contacted Soens about the possibility of his coaching him on his arrival in the UK, but had been informed that Soens's books were already full.

In the qualifying round at Leicester, Sturgess rode the 3,000 metres in 3.44 – 9 seconds faster than Boardman. He was unaware of the magnitude of his achievement, asking if that time was considered fast; his rivals understood that the goalposts had been suddenly and dramatically moved. Sturgess rode a consistently fast series: 3.42 in the next round, and 3.43 in the quarters and semi. Boardman followed his 3.53 qualifying ride with 3.55, 3.47 and 3.47. He raised his speed again in the final, finishing in 3.40, but Sturgess was a couple of seconds faster and the comfortable winner.

Events outside Boardman's control had conspired to rob him of a national title, and he took it badly. If he'd had any ambitions to be the best junior in the world, it would have been a sobering thought that he wasn't even the best junior in the country. 'He was knocked a bit by it,' Scott O'Brien says. 'I remember him saying how bizarre it was when Sturgess turned up. Of all the times for two lads who were that good to come along at the same time. He'd been waiting to win for a long time.'

While Sturgess dominated the junior events, also winning the kilometre, Boardman won the senior team pursuit title with the Manchester Wheelers squad. A national senior title at sixteen was impressive, although Boardman had had trouble in the qualifying rounds. A team-mate, Darryl Webster, felt Boardman wasn't riding well enough, and told him so. 'He told Eddie afterwards that I was useless,' Boardman admits. 'I didn't want Eddie to agree, so I got my act together.'

But Boardman's satisfaction at winning a national title was short-lived. Eddie Soens suffered a heart attack during the championship, and died shortly afterwards at Leicester hospital. The death of his coach was bound to leave a deep imprint on Boardman. He named his first son Edward after him, and later spoke movingly of Soens in an interview with *Winning* magazine at the end of 1989. 'I miss him a lot. He was like another father, really. He said to me, "You'll be the best roadman this country's ever seen." He said it might take four, six years, but you'll do it. And I didn't really believe him, but I've seen the potential for that, and I would like to go on and win stages of the Tour de France.

'When he died, because I was young, I messed about that year. I was doing half an hour's training a day. That's what upset me the most, that I'd wasted his time.'

Keith Boardman identified Soens's death as the catalyst for his son to start taking cycling more seriously. 'The inner drive began to show,' he said. 'It was as if his race performances were a tribute to Eddie.' But Boardman is also quoted in *The Fastest Man on Two Wheels* – Tony Bell's account of his early career – saying that he'd been slacking off the training, albeit with the inference that he was going to knuckle down. Certainly when he met the man who would eventually replace Soens as his coach, Peter Keen, in January 1987 – a year and a half after Soens's death – he showed up for the first physical tests unfit, having more or less taken the winter off. In Richard Moore's book *Heroes, Villains and Velodromes*, Keen says Boardman's winter training had involved playing squash and riding his bike a bit. 'I dick around' was Boardman's description of his routine.

Boardman was still only eighteen when he met Keen, and it's unfair to present him as having turned instantly into a cycling monk when Soens died. Even individuals as congenitally serious as Boardman dick around in their late teens.

4

Senior Service

That Boardman and Sturgess were head and shoulders above their fellow juniors was clear in 1985. By 1986, their final year as juniors, both had already started to measure themselves against bigger targets. Their clash at the national junior championship in August was keenly anticipated, but their early head-to-heads came on the neutral territory of senior international competition.

Both were selected for the Edinburgh Commonwealth Games track squad in July 1986, for the individual pursuit, held over 4,000 metres. The British Cycling Federation (BCF) had already blooded Boardman at the senior world championship the year before in the Italian town of Bassano del Grappa, without any expectations other than that the excitement of participating in the worlds might be greater than the demoralization of taking a thrashing. He'd finished thirtieth out of thirty-one starters.

In Edinburgh, Australian Dean Woods was easily the strongest rider, qualifying 8 seconds clear and cantering to the gold medal. And Sturgess was still well ahead of Boardman – he took the silver medal, and had been a full 11 seconds faster than his compatriot in qualifying. Boardman qualified in eighth and last place for the quarter-finals. The seeding method for the quarters was to draw the fastest qualifier against the eighth fastest, second fastest against seventh fastest and so on, which meant that Boardman was up against Woods. The Australian made short work of him, catching him well before the end. At least the Englishman wasn't alone in his indignity: Woods caught Sturgess in the final too.

Boardman did win a medal, however. The team pursuit competition was contested between only four nations, and the England team of Boardman, Gary Coltman, Rob Muzio and Jon Walshaw beat Canada for the bronze medal after having been defeated by New Zealand in the semi-final.

While Sturgess was getting most of his success on the track, Boardman was still spreading himself thinly. Was he a time triallist, or trackie? By trying to be both he probably diluted his ability – no great problem in a young athlete. He rode a full season of time trials in 1986, recording fast times throughout the year. At the national senior 25 championship in June he was eighth, only 91 seconds behind his Manchester Wheelers teammate Darryl Webster – an excellent result for a junior. From there, he went to the Isle of Man for the annual cycling festival and won a road race (with the one tactic at his disposal – attack early and time-trial to the finish) and a 10-mile time trial. Then came the Commonwealth Games, followed by the British track championship and junior 25-mile championship, in the same week.

Unsurprisingly, Sturgess dominated the track championship at junior level – he won gold in the pursuit, kilometre time trial and points race. Perhaps Boardman was intimidated by the work needed to match Sturgess, because although he was training a lot on the track, his year looked more geared to time trialling than track racing. He was putting out consistently fast times in 25- and 10-mile time trials, and this year was his final chance to win the national junior 25-mile championship.

Having already beaten Boardman well on his favoured territory, the track, Sturgess now took him on at the 25. The two riders were very different in appearance and style. Sturgess was a great broad-shouldered bruiser of a cyclist, a bull on a bike. He thumped the pedals round, bending them to his will. Boardman was a thoroughbred, the owner of the indefinable holy grail of cycling style: class. He also had greater experience in the discipline, and for a good while that looked to be enough. With half the race covered, Boardman was over a minute clear of Sturgess, but two factors were about to come into play. First, Sturgess, whatever the event, was a fast finisher. 'He had this incredible ability to purge himself on the last lap of a pursuit,' recalls Doug Dailey. Second, Boardman's nerves hadn't yet settled. For such an unemotional individual, he suffered from that most human of characteristics: the jitters. He'd started too fast, and over the second half of the course, as Boardman's legs, then his head, buckled under the pressure, Sturgess gouged great chunks out of Boardman's lead. 'I blew up. I didn't ride many fast time trial courses because of track training,' Boardman said afterwards, although it's true that Sturgess was also lacking specific time trial preparation, so they were competing on a level playing field. But in the end, Boardman's time-trialling class prevailed, just. He held Sturgess off by 7 seconds to finally win the national junior 25 title.

That August the BCF sent Boardman to the world championship in Colorado, still more for experience than anything else. The trip to the States certainly broadened his horizons. He celebrated his eighteenth birthday there, in the lead-up to the competition, and was mortified when footage of a cowgirl kissogram hired to bring him a cake by his American hosts made it on to the CBS News evening bulletin.

On the track, even a 9-second personal best of 4.48 in the 4,000-metre pursuit was not enough to qualify him for the last sixteen: he was twenty-fourth in a field of forty-four. *Cycling Weekly* ran a photograph of Boardman leaving the track just after his ride in which the young man looked destroyed, his face contorted with the effort. He was still a couple of seconds off a medal chance. Maturity might gain him that time, but he needed more than that. Luckily, he found what he required.

While Sturgess and Boardman were developing into world-class talents, British cycling itself was changing. Doug Dailey was appointed as national coach by the BCF in October 1986, and one of his first acts was to introduce Boardman to Peter Keen. Race organizer Stuart Benstead had told Dailey about Keen, and urged Dailey to get in touch with him. Keen was a former national schools 10-mile time trial champion who was researching exercise physiology at University College Chichester. He was working with two-time world professional pursuit champion Tony Doyle, and was also heading up a funded research programme looking into nutritional products. If Boardman was a prodigy on the bike, Keen was a prodigy in the lab.

'Peter was already a senior lecturer at Chichester,' says Dailey. 'I was very impressed with what they were doing.' He started driving Boardman down to see Keen. 'I was getting up at some godforsaken hour on a Wednesday morning, picking Chris up and running him all the way to Chichester, then running him back. We'd leave at four a.m. and get back at eleven p.m., and we'd be belted for two days afterwards. We left in the dark and got back in the dark, but it was worth it.'

Simon Lillistone, one of Boardman's contemporaries in the British team, also used to visit Keen. 'It was a whole-day trip to Chichester in the old BCF Sierras. I'm not sure they were the best way to get us there but they were consistent. We were always knackered by the time we got there.'

At Keen and Boardman's first meeting, Keen wasn't impressed. 'I was certainly fitter than him at that point,' he remarked. Keen hadn't just been fooled by Boardman's lack of fitness. Boardman still has, to this day, a cutting of an interview in which Keen said Boardman's engine wasn't big enough. What he hadn't yet realized was that while Boardman's power was not unusually high, he presented a very small frontal area on a bike and could still ride efficiently while in that position. This factor, plus a remarkably efficient lung function, more than compensated for his relative lack of power.

If Eddie Soens derived his effectiveness from being Boardman's opposite – a fiery motivator driving him to improve – Keen's strength lay in his similarities to the rider. Keen needed a talented but malleable subject on whom to test his theories. Boardman was a perfect fit. First, he was hugely physically gifted, even if he had turned up unfit on that first visit to Chichester. Second, he was highly sensitive to his own body and could provide accurate feedback. It even turned out that being so unfit in early 1987 was an advantage: Keen sent him packing with a detailed three-month training programme, and when he returned in April he was in such good shape it convinced Keen that he'd found his ideal guinea pig. 'He'd made a staggering improvement,' Keen recalled. 'He was shocked into action by the January results, and shocked into listening by what happened in the subsequent three months when he made the improvement.'

For Boardman, Keen was very different from any other coach he'd encountered. 'Doug drove me down to Chichester, and Peter was there in his lab coat. He was very interested in understanding things. Even then, he'd give me a piece of paper with heart rate [levels], but also [information on] what they should feel like, which was unusual in those days. We looked at three things: power, pulse and perception of effort.'

The timing of their getting together was perfect. Keen was young, ambitious, full of ideas and was approaching coaching from a disinterested scientific angle, with almost a clean slate, rather than building on current and received wisdom. His position in the close-knit Doyle camp was very much one of an outsider, which meant he didn't have the authority to control the situation. There was also a hint that Doyle wasn't divulging all his training methods to Keen. While Boardman was a control freak by nature, Keen was one by necessity. In order to apply science effectively, he needed to control the variables, and Doyle had too many variables. Keen made it clear to Richard Moore in *Heroes, Villains and Velodromes* that working with Doyle was a frustrating experience. 'Most of what they were doing was bloody nonsense,' he explained. Plus, Doyle was the finished product. Keen needed to work with somebody from the ground floor.

Boardman was also young and ambitious, and receptive to Keen's ideas. Neither man was bound by a sense of loyalty to tradition. Theirs would become one of the most fertile and productive coaching relationships British sport had ever seen, but it wouldn't happen overnight.

Boardman turned senior in 1987, but his struggle to win a national championship continued. Nerves got the better of him yet again in the national 25 championship where he was only fourteenth, over two minutes behind gold medallist Darryl Webster. Then he received his third annual beating at the hands of Colin Sturgess at the national track championship. This time Sturgess caught Boardman in the semi-final of the individual pursuit, before going on to win the final. And at the end of the season Boardman was pipped for the gold medal in the national hill climb championship, by 0.2 seconds. 'I was a bit disappointed with this season,' he told *Cycling Weekly* at the end of the year. 'I didn't think I had improved by as much as I thought I should.'

Boardman trained consistently through the winter, for the first time, and during testing at Chichester Keen found that he was as fit in early 1988 as he had been in the summer of 1987. But once again he struggled to emerge from the shadow of Sturgess on the track, and prevail against more experienced riders in the time trials. He was only fifteenth in the national 25-mile championship, and runner-up to Sturgess in the national track championship individual pursuit for the fourth year running.

You get the impression it was starting to wear Boardman down. In the aftermath of the track championship he gave an interview in which he lugubriously talked down his potential in a way that would have shocked his old coach Eddie Soens. 'I'm as content as anyone can be with silver,' he said. 'I'm realistic. I know I hadn't got a chance of beating Colin. I was just hoping to get as close to him as I could. A lot of people said I would get caught, so as I don't consider myself a pursuiter, I'm pleased with myself.'

Boardman was clear from the start that it wasn't cycling that had attracted him to cycling, but winning. So the progression kept him interested. Still, as 1988 drew to a close, he looked like he was in a rut. Then three things happened that finally liberated him. First, Colin Sturgess turned professional, leaving the way clear for Boardman to attack the national track championship as the outright favourite. Second, he got married, to Sally Anne Edwards. And third, he won the national hill climb championship on Nick O'Pendle, a one-in-six stretch of Lancashire tarmac that twists north over Pendle Hill from the village of Sabden towards Clitheroe.

Just two weeks before the hill climb championship Boardman had given another interview in which all talk of not considering himself a pursuiter was forgotten. 'I'm looking forward to next year,' he said. 'I'd like to take eight national titles: the team pursuit, individual pursuit, both team time trial titles, the hill climb, the national 25 and the national 50.' Who cared that he could identify only seven of his eight targets when asked what they were? The point was this: Boardman's ambition had suddenly caught up with his potential.

Meanwhile, up in Scotland, Graeme Obree had worked out that he was more likely to gain success as a time triallist than a road racer. He was as attached as Boardman to the predictable nature of time trials, where sporting logic dictated the result rather than the impulsive tactical whims of ninety-nine other riders. The tribal nature of Scottish cycling complicated road racing there as well. 'I wasn't going to win road races in Scotland because there were so many guys who didn't want you to win,' Obree explains. 'It got to the stage in time trials in the late eighties that I could rattle up, have a puncture, change the tyre and still win the race. No hassle, no crashes, get your prize money. In the road races there was this whole East/West thing going on. If the race was in Edinburgh, the Glasgow and Ayrshire guys were all lumped in together, and they'd say, "Ach, ye Ayrshire testing bastard," so you knew you weren't going to win that race. Plus I couldn't sprint for toffee. Time trialling was where it was at.'

Obree was setting out on a less orthodox and even more gradual route to success than Boardman. With poor results from school, and not much in the way of job prospects, he'd embarked on an ill-fated business venture with his friend Gordon Stead. The Cosmos Cycles shop was a burgeoning business which surfed the first wave of the BMX craze but descended into farce when Obree and Stead concocted a preposterous insurance scam to fend off their lenders for a few weeks while their Christmas sales money was unlocked. He emerged with a suspended prison sentence, and a bleak outlook.

'Margaret Thatcher played a part in my success,' Obree says. 'There was no job and no hope. I was unemployed.'

With a large amount of free time on his hands, and no money, Obree was free to let his mind wander, and in late 1986 he idly speculated that by turning the handlebars up on his racing bike and crouching over them in a tuck position, he'd be more aerodynamic, and therefore go faster. 'I always questioned everything. I was destined to be an upstart.' When he was at school, his class did a project which involved making collage flowers to be put up on the windows and walls as decoration. 'All I remember thinking is, "You don't get flowers without bees, so I'm going to cut out bees."' While his classmates obediently churned out flowers, Obree busied himself making little bees, which buzzed among and around the petals. That's what Obree has been doing his whole life – cutting out bees while mainstream society makes flowers.

Obree tested out the new position at the end of 1986 and duly won his cycling club's Christmas 10-mile time trial, although the opposition was average enough that he'd have won it using a normal position. He refined it for the Scottish 25-mile championship the following summer and came second by 41 seconds to Dave Hannah, the dominant Scottish time triallist at that time. But he'd led at the halfway point. Then he won the Scottish 10-mile championship.

Ed Hood, a fellow Scottish time triallist, recalls a friend at a race telling him there was a guy out on the course riding 'a circus bike'. 'He'd started riding this daft bike,' says Hood. 'The first incarnation was pretty crude. I think it was painted bright orange. He was riding this thing he'd built himself and it had straight forks. The welding wasn't the best. He was producing spectacular rides, though. The position was ludicrous, of course, but we were all blown away with what he was doing.'

The position was exceptionally aerodynamic. Although Obree would refine it further by narrowing his bike and developing a custom frame and handlebars, he'd made his frontal area significantly smaller by effectively taking his arms out of the equation. Air resistance is the main slowing factor in cycling, so Obree was now able to go faster for the same amount of effort.

South of Hadrian's Wall, Obree's new position and fast improving times made little impact. *Cycling Weekly* carried a photograph of Obree at the 1987 Scottish championship, but it was buried towards the back of the magazine and wasn't picked up on by anybody. If Boardman or Keen did notice the ingenious aerodynamic position Obree had adopted, they certainly didn't appreciate its implications.

The following year, 1988, Obree won both the 25- and 10-mile championships in Scotland. He wasn't quite ready to challenge Chris Boardman yet, but both riders were on the cusp of their first big breakthroughs.

5

The Third Man

Whatever happened to Colin Sturgess?

More precocious and versatile than Chris Boardman and phenomenally gifted physically, he should really have been one of British cycling's greatest success stories. After turning professional at the end of 1988, he won the world pursuit championship the following year with an astonishing ride, then made a decent attempt at riding as a road professional before bad luck left him without a team.

If he'd fulfilled his potential, he could have been a multiple world pursuit champion, even a road Classics winner. Instead, his star burned brightly but briefly, and by the time Boardman was beginning to make his international name at the Barcelona Olympics in 1992, Sturgess was coming to the end of his cycling career.

He's kept in touch with the sport since. He's been an occasional, semi-anonymous and intelligent presence on internet cycling talkboards. He even made a comeback in the late 1990s, but then quit again, disillusioned with cycling. That career is another life now. He's too busy trying to keep his current life on course to worry about the past.

I tracked him down on Facebook, apologizing for the twenty-first-century method of getting in touch, and he immediately got back to me from Australia, his home for the last decade. We arranged to talk on the phone, and in the meantime I had a look back through old copies of *Cycling Weekly* and *Winning* magazine to remind myself of his achievements.

God, he'd been a force of nature. He was powerful and fearless, a thug on a bike, with a different body type and physical presence from the classic willowy cycling ectomorph. He looked like he'd ride through a brick wall to get to the finishing line first. He was an accessible champion, too, with an open interview manner, a ready smile and a laid-back attitude that made it seem like one of your mates was doing well at the world championship rather than an aloof, remote, focused figure. He was an ordinary guy, freakishly talented, rather than a freaky guy, freakishly talented.

He'd given an interview not long before I spoke to him in which he talked about recent troubles: a divorce, losing his job, suffering from bipolar disorder. It was hard to believe that this was the same person I'd seen pictures of in the magazines, atop the world championship podium in 1989 with his bright blue eyes, 1980s bleached quiff, rainbow jersey and gold medal, and huge I-love-you-world shit-eating grin.

On the phone, his voice crackles with nervous energy and enthusiasm. He's building from rock bottom, he tells me. The divorce is sorted, he's just got a few loose ends to tie up. He'll soon be back in the UK to start again.

Sturgess was born in Yorkshire and taken to South Africa by his parents Alan and Ann at the age of six. Ann Sturgess had raced with Beryl Burton, while Alan had been on the British team pursuit squad with Hugh Porter in the 1960s. He'd chosen his mother and father even more carefully than Boardman had, benefiting from both the nature and the nurture of cycling parents. There was nothing in South Africa for young riders so the Sturgesses set up a schools cycling association, and their son was racing by the age of eight. 'They didn't push me into the sport, but I was an impressionable kid and I got the bug,' he says.

Sturgess, then, had a head start in terms of genetics and knowledge. He also spent ten years growing up in Johannesburg at an altitude of 2,500 metres in an outdoors culture where everybody played sport. He got good at cycling without even realizing it, making the 15-kilometre journey to and from school every day before heading out on his BMX. He was given dispensation to miss rugby classes in order to train on his bike. 'Good job. I was one of the worst rugby players ever at my school.'

By the time he was a first-year junior, at sixteen, he was so much better than his peers that the South African Cycling Federation gave him special dispensation to ride in senior and open events. He won those too. But no amount of special dispensation would allow him to race internationally as a South African in the era of apartheid – the international ban on the country was still in force. The Sturgesses had a choice: their son could be a big fish in a small pond for the best years of his career, or they could move back to the UK.

'Being English, I was always a little bit of an outsider in South Africa,' he admits. 'You were definitely a foreigner. "Rooinecks" [rednecks], they called us, because we had pale skin that burned in the sun. I'd love to have competed for South Africa or Great Britain, but I was keener on doing it for Great Britain.'

Sturgess arrived back in the UK less than two weeks before the 1985 national track championship. By chance, Ann Sturgess's sister lived in Leicester, not far from the Saffron Lane velodrome, so the family slept in her spare room while Sturgess prepared for his slaughter of the innocents. 'Without blowing my own trumpet, yes, I beat some good opposition,' he says.

But Sturgess was still the outsider. He'd developed outside the BCF system, and continued to train outside it, with his father as his coach. 'I didn't want to train within the system and go down to Leicester for a three-day training camp and end up riding only fifty kilometres over three days. I would do a couple of hours easy in the morning, then we would be out every afternoon, sitting behind my dad's motorcycle for an hour or ninety minutes. That was five or six days a week. At the time it was bloody hard, but I realized it with hindsight because when I made my comeback I couldn't replicate those efforts.'

Sturgess's face never quite fitted in the same way as Boardman's. While Boardman went to the 1985 world championship, Sturgess turned down the opportunity, believing himself still too young to make an impact, and he thinks this almost cost him selection for the Commonwealth Games the following year. 'I wasn't originally considered. But I'd gone to a Centre of Excellence training day at the outdoor track at Halesowen. It was a massively blustery day and we were riding kilometre time trials. Everybody else was riding 1.11s and 1.12s, and I did a 1.09. It put a few noses out of joint, but on the strength of that they selected me for the Commonwealth Games. Unfortunately I was down for the kilo, which wasn't my best event. I rode the kilometre in Edinburgh and was absolutely useless, but I talked my way into riding in the individual pursuit as well.' He won the silver in that, with Boardman eighth, thus proving to himself that he could hold his own at world level. He was still only seventeen.

At the national junior championship later that year he was even more dominant than on his debut twelve months previously. He won everything – the kilometre, pursuit and points race – again beating Boardman in the pursuit. The situation was too raw for the two to be friends. 'We never really got along,' says Sturgess. 'It might have stemmed from me coming back from South Africa and beating him. I get on with most people – I'm very amiable. But I always found him a little stand-offish. In a rivalry, I can understand that, but I got on very well with all the other cyclists. On the other hand, I found Chris to be aloof and distant.'

Not that it mattered. Sturgess got the 1988 Olympics pursuit spot after coming fifth in the 1987 world amateur championship with a time of 4.30, which was world-class then. He was supposed to get a bike from his sponsors for the Olympics, but it was late arriving, and then he discovered it had been made in the wrong size. Sturgess had a 26-inch front wheel, and the forks were made for a 24-inch wheel. 'They said they'd just change the forks, but doing that pulls the entire geometry out,' Sturgess explains. 'It was only six weeks before the Games that Doug Dailey managed to get in touch with Harry Quinn, the framebuilder, and tell him it was panic stations, and we needed x, y and z, and could he do it.'

Sturgess didn't expect to win in Seoul, but he knew that he was capable of getting into the last four. He was beaten in the semi-final by eventual winner Gintautas Umaras of the Soviet Union, leaving him with a bronze medal ride-off with East German Bernd Dittert. His opponent led all the way, but Sturgess finished so fast that he was within touching distance when they both crossed the line on opposite sides of the track. 'I really thought I could have had him. I gave him a massive shock. Back then, they used to fire pistols as each rider finished, and I remember not being able to distinguish between my pistol and his, so I knew it was close. As I rolled up the banking, I looked around and saw my father drop to his knees, and I thought, nope, it's not happened. I went over to congratulate Dittert and he was in tears because he thought he'd lost it.'

Sturgess wanted to take his frustration and convert it into a points race medal, but the selectors wouldn't put him in the event. 'That took me a bit of time to get over,' he says. 'They didn't put anybody in.'

Rather than wait another four years for the Olympic Games to come round again, at the end of 1988 Sturgess signed a contract with the professional ADR team, before he'd even turned twenty. He'd lived with one of the team's mechanics when racing in Belgium as a junior, and this mechanic had tipped off the team's manager José De Cauwer about the rider's ability. Before the Olympics, Sturgess had gone over to Belgium with a composite team, representing the Wembley Road Club, to take part in the Tour of West Flanders. He won three stages, wearing the points jersey and catching the Belgian national champion, Danny Lippens, in the time trial stage. 'My friend went ballistic. He said I had to come and meet De Cauwer. About a month before Seoul, they drove over to Leicester where I was riding a track meeting and I signed a letter of intent to say that I would join their team after the Olympics.'

It should have been a dream. Sturgess's team-mates included Greg LeMond, who would win the Tour de France for ADR the following year, plus Classics specialists Johan Museeuw and Eddy Planckaert. 'On paper, it was marvellous,' Sturgess agrees ruefully. 'In practice . . .'

His first professional race was Paris-Nice, one of the world's hardest and most renowned stage races, which takes place in filthy early spring weather. It was no place for a young novice. Then he was thrown right into the hardened Belgian kermesse circuit – pro-am races where performance-enhancing drugs were rife and the racing was cut-throat. 'It was a very steep learning curve,' recalls Sturgess. 'There were no doping controls, and I think in my first race I lasted sixty kilometres before getting spat out the back.'

But within a few months, he'd won one. And better was to come in the 1989 world professional pursuit championship at the Tête d'Or velodrome in Lyon.

Sturgess had always been a fast finisher, able to produce a scintillating final kilometre in a pursuit match. 'I've always had a very good pain threshold,' he says. 'I was able to lift it even when I was on my beam end; I could find that little extra from somewhere. And my other strength was that I competed against other riders very well. I've done some good time trials in my life but I wasn't a classic time trial rider who could just ride against himself. But if you put me up against somebody, like in a pursuit, man against man, I was good. I always believed that if I could just suffer for five seconds more, I could get an extra five yards out.'

ADR were busy with LeMond winning the Tour that summer. In fact the management had been hands-off with Sturgess for most of the year, so Sturgess was free to train at home on the track, with his usual intense diet of motor-pacing. His form was excellent, boosted by the hard miles and high speeds of months of racing on the Belgian kermesse circuit. At the world championship, he felt in control. 'All the way through the series I felt comfortable. I felt I was riding within myself. If I needed to lift it by five seconds I could have done.'

Sturgess reached the final, where he came up against Dean Woods, who'd thrashed him at the Commonwealth Games three years previously. But back then Sturgess had been barely out of school; he had posters of the experienced Australian up on his bedroom wall. Now he was a hardened professional, and his moment had come.

Woods was a pure pursuiter, a diesel who started slow then built up to a steady fast pace which he held to the finish. Sturgess, on the other hand, was a fast starter and a fast finisher. Sure enough, the final provided a fascinating contrast in styles.

Sturgess led early in the race, but Woods was prepared for that, and he slowly pegged him back, then put pressure on in the middle section of the race, hoping to build a big enough lead to neutralize Sturgess's last-gasp acceleration. All Sturgess wanted was to be within a couple of seconds with a kilometre to go. Woods' lead at that point was only 0.33 seconds. Alan Sturgess yelled his son on from trackside, but as the bell rang Woods was still 0.22 seconds in front. Sturgess visibly kicked again, riding the last lap at an incredible speed and winning by over one and a half seconds. It had been one of the most dramatic pursuit matches in cycling history.

Sturgess experienced what he describes as 'pure elation' on the podium. And the effect on his status within the professional peloton was immediate. 'I was back in Belgium riding kermesses within a week, and the organizers were calling me out at the start to present me to the crowd. In races, I used to have to fight like crazy to keep my position, whereas now riders just let me in. It was instant respect.'

But there was a darker reaction to his success, too. 'Suddenly, at the age of twenty, I'd achieved my biggest dream. I had no idea where to go. Do I do it twice? Do I go over to the road?'

It took Chris Boardman three years after 1989 to win a world-level competition. Sturgess's rise was so fast there wasn't even time to digest it. 'I admire Chris no end for sticking with it. The easier thing might have been for him to go away quietly, but he stuck with it. He was married young and had children young. I was relatively free in that all I had was the bike, while Chris had all these other things.'

Things went bad soon after that world championship. ADR went broke, and the team that went on into 1990 was left with little money – so little that Sturgess ended the year 'thirty or forty thousand pounds' down. He did win the British professional road race championship, but it was a highlight in a tough year. He signed with the Tulip team in 1991, although there was background tension over his desire to take time out and ride the track world championship. The team wanted the points he was winning in road races, but he still saw himself as a track rider, with the potential to win another world title.

Unfortunately, this ambition also bumped up against the hard reality of professional cycling in the early 1990s, when competitors were starting to gain a huge advantage from erythropoietin, otherwise known as EPO, the performance-enhancing product that boosts the oxygen-carrying capacity of the blood. 'At one world championship I was told point blank by another team's helper that I had no chance of winning, and that his rider would win,' Sturgess states. The team helper hinted to Sturgess that his rider was using EPO, and sure enough, Sturgess was beaten at the world championship that year.

'That disillusioned me massively. I remember thinking, do I go against everything I've ever believed in and done, that my parents have told me? Or do I spend a third of my salary on the gear? I had a team-mate die in 1990 – Patrice Bar. Is it worth it? No.

'I thought, this sport is fucked. I was left with no contract at the end of the year, so I rode for a little South African team. Then that went pear-shaped as well, so I thought, give it up. Go to university and use your head for a bit. And get a girlfriend.'

Sturgess spent the next few years making up for the youth he'd spent on the saddle, although he was back racing again in 1998. He'd gained in wisdom, but his body didn't react the same way it did when he was a fearless youngster. 'I hadn't touched a bike in four years. I was smoking joints and on the booze. I'd lost that final kick. I was able to bring it up to a certain speed, like before, but I couldn't find that last seven-hundred-and-fifty-metre acceleration.'

He won a Commonwealth Games silver medal in the team

pursuit in 1998, and was victorious in races in Britain, but after finding a place on the British team he quit again in 2000, this time for good. He headed to Australia and got a job as a wine-maker in the Hunter Valley, where he fell victim to intermittent spells of depression and had a roller-coaster private life.

Sturgess's relationship with his cycling career is an un-resolved one. 'I used to be embarrassed about my career,' he tells me. 'I'd go out of my way not to bring up my sporting background. I worked in the Hunter Valley for five years and I don't think more than three people knew that I'd been a world champion. But I'm seeing things with more distance now. I'm able to talk about it and not feel too bad about it.'

When Chris Boardman won his Olympic pursuit gold, it stung Graeme Obree into raising his ambitions. He saw Boardman winning and thought, 'I've beaten him, that could be me.' When Sturgess watched Boardman winning, he must have thought, 'That *was* me.'

6

Big Fish, Small Pond

On the face of it, British cycling looked fairly healthy in the late 1980s. The nation had representation in the Tour de France. Scotsman Robert Millar had come fourth in the race in 1984, and won a few mountain stages over the course of the decade. The general public was barely aware that as well as the Tour de France there was also a Tour of Italy (Giro d'Italia) and a Tour of Spain (Vuelta a España), but Millar had also accumulated three second places over those two races. Sean Yates, a broad-shouldered time triallist from Sussex, who was even more diffident and laconic than Boardman but had more self-confidence about it, won a Tour de France stage in 1988. Malcolm Elliott won the points jersey in the Tour of Spain in 1989. On the track, Tony Doyle had won two world pursuit championships, in 1980 and 1986, before Sturgess did so in 1989. Cycling was a minor sport at the time in Britain, so it looked like the country was punching more or less at its weight.

However, all of these successes came at the professional level. The riders concerned had taken themselves out of the British Cycling Federation's system. Doyle was essentially a freelance pro who earned his money on the lucrative (for some) circuit of European Six-Day races. Millar and Yates, in order to succeed as European road professionals, had to *become* European in order to do so: both moved to France and started at the bottom of the cycling ladder, riding as amateurs before getting good enough results to attract the attention of a professional team. It was doable, but it involved considerable hardship, culture shock and penury.

On the amateur side, it's fair to say that Great Britain hadn't done so well. If there was a plan, it was that there wasn't really a plan, more a hope that things would turn out OK. There was no indoor track, which meant riders ran the risk of travelling miles to train at Leicester or one of the other outdoor tracks only to spend the day in the stands watching the rain pelting down. There was also the perception that Britain's amateurs weren't competing on a level playing field with the Eastern Bloc countries in terms of funding, organization and support, and of scientific preparation, both legal and banned.

There was one more problem. Paradoxically, the extraordinary strength in depth of the time-trialling scene exercised a chilling effect on the development of other disciplines; while the British did have a strong pursuiting tradition, fewer riders crossed over from time trialling to road racing or other forms of track racing. Boardman was a rarity in excelling at both.

During this period, Doug Dailey was the national coach. He's only recently retired from working with British Cycling. He saw out the London Olympics as the Great Britain team's logistics manager after almost a quarter of a century with the national squad in one capacity or another.

He's sixty-eight now and continues to radiate enthusiasm, energy, generosity and good humour. Our interview, in a comfortable front room warmed by a wood burner in the farmhouse he lives in on a hill high above Ruthin in North Wales, was punctuated by unprintable anecdotes and laughter.

Dailey, a former racer, grew up in Merseyside. He'd lived the dream through the 1960s, working flat out in the winter each year to fund a season of bike racing. 'I decided I would only race until I was thirty,' he tells me. 'I thought as long as I was in my twenties I'd get away with being a cycling bum. No one would criticize me.'

There was no support mechanism for cyclists to be full-time back then, which meant there was an insurmountable catch-22. To get good enough to race internationally, you had to be full-time; but with no funding unless you were professional, there was no way to be full-time. Dailey did the best he could, working through the winter as a contract painter for Tommy Soens (Eddie's brother), and he got good enough to win the amateur British road race championship in 1972, and to represent Great Britain at the Munich Olympics that year.

But when he hit thirty, in 1974, it was time to find a real job. The trouble was, he had no qualifications, had dropped out of a business HND course and had no other experience apart from working fourteen-hour days through the winter and training and racing through the summer.

Luckily, his retirement coincided with the opening of the new Kirkby sports centre. Dailey was well known in Kirkby for his cycling exploits and local cycling organizer Ken Matthews pulled a few strings to give him a job. 'I went straight in as assistant manager. I hadn't got a clue – I hadn't done a day's work in my life,' laughs Dailey.

The timing was perfect. There was a bike track at the sports centre, and Dailey was in his element. It was a bit fly-by-night, though. One individual ended up in prison for cooking the books, and it turned out the materials used for the dry ski slope were part of a dodgy building scam involving kickbacks and payments under the table. Some people ended up doing time for that one, too. But Dailey got on with organizing events and sport, building a BMX track, hosting cycling Centre of Excellence weekends and making sure that two rival boxing clubs who hated each other trained at the centre on different nights.

After thirteen years, however, he was ready for a change. He didn't want to go to a bigger centre or, worse, head office, where his wings would be clipped. 'Lo and behold, an advert came up for national cycling coach. I'd set up the Centre of Excellence, so I'd done a lot of coaching. I applied.'

Dailey was summoned to an interview at the Midland Hotel in Derby, where the BCF's Racing Committee, along with Arthur Pickburn, a member of the Finance and Marketing Committee, grilled him. 'I remember there were some bloody strange questions. I'd gone in there with my head full of coaching, and what I felt I could bring to it on a national level. But I remember Arthur Pickburn asking me, "Can you type?" I thought, bloody hell, what's that all about? It was only when I actually got the job that I realized that the job title may have been "national coach" but the reality was very different.'

It was easier for the BCF to get funding from the government for a national coach position than for an administrator or manager, so they'd advertised for a coach rather than the latter. What the BCF needed, on a day-to-day basis, was a gopher, a jack-of-all-trades who was willing to stick tyres on to wheels, do the admin, organize trips to races and manage the teams once there, all for thirteen grand and a company car. 'The amount of actual coaching was embarrassing, looking back,' Dailey admits. 'The job was a man-killer. The phone never stopped, day and night. Every communication with athletes had to be typed out. I'd wondered why the bloody hell they'd asked if I could type at the interview . . .'

Dailey had been hired during lean years for the British cycling team. The last Olympic medal had been a bronze for the team pursuiters in Montreal in 1976. There hadn't been a gold medal for a British cyclist since 1920. Dailey, however, had ambitions for the team. 'We always had strong pursuiters, and I think that was down to the time-trialling background,' he says. 'British time trialling was very strong and you didn't need a facility, or much money, to develop it. We had lots of outdoor tracks, so it was possible to ride around in a circle for four thousand metres.' He realized, first of all, that the team stood more chance of success at the Olympic Games than at a world championship. At the Olympics there was a limit of one rider per nation in the individual events, so strong nations, whose second-best rider might win a medal at the worlds, would only be able to win one medal at the Olympics.

Confidence wasn't high before the Seoul Games in 1988. One headline above a piece on Britain's cycling medal hopes read 'Lambs to the Slaughter'. And in most cases that turned out to be true, but two performances stood out: Colin Sturgess, of course, who came fourth in the pursuit, and Eddie Alexander, who came fourth in the sprint. Both had developed and trained outside the BCF structure, but their placings showed Dailey that success was possible. 'I felt 1988 was the start,' he recalls. 'I thought, bloody hell, this is doable. We can do something in the Olympic Games if we find the right athlete and concentrate our limited resources.'

Dailey knew that Boardman and Sturgess were likely candidates for support, although Sturgess was coached by his father. But when Sturgess turned professional, taking himself out of the running for the 1992 Olympics, Boardman became the focus. The teenage Boardman used to show up at the Wednesday night meets at Kirkby track. Having coached him at the Centre of Excellence, Dailey was well aware of his potential. 'He won everything he rode. They couldn't live with him. Chris was making normal, steady progress under the system that existed, with almost no funding, doing it the hard way. The next big step was when he and Peter Keen came together.'

A small series of events was unfolding which would lead to Boardman's gold medal in Barcelona. Dailey describes it as an exciting time. After years of mediocrity, British cycling was setting its sights higher, and the pursuit was going to be the target event.

'We were trying to bridge a performance gap across the board,' he says. 'There was a gap between our athletes and their level of performance, and international standards. Of course, there was the background fact that some of the international standards were artificially high, and we all know why. The cheating was a fact of life – you accepted it and got on with it. But Keen felt he could beat it, through correct training, recovery, feeding, position, monitoring and getting the peak right. No matter what was going on out there, we could win, especially in the shorter events. Pete had the athlete, he had the event, and it was a case of getting it right. It wasn't easy, though. If you look at Chris's career before 1992, he tried and failed a few times.'

If Chris Boardman had spent the years between 1985 and 1988 trying and failing to work out whether he was a trackie or a time triallist, he further complicated the matter in 1989 when he started winning road races too. He'd slimmed down from 71 to 67 kilograms, was maturing physically, and had had his confidence boosted by the national hill climb championship win at the end of the previous season.

Boardman wasn't a natural road racer. Dailey recalls trying to persuade him to do more road racing, but it was an uphill struggle. 'He was a control freak, and you can't control road racing. It kept getting out of control. When he did win, it was because he was out in the front on his own, and all of a sudden the situation was controlled again. You have to go beyond your comfort zone in a road race. You've got to get pretty uncomfortable to get off the front, and he didn't seem to have an appetite for it.'

Boardman didn't care for the tactics and occasional negativity of road racing, so he tended to deploy his primary weapon – his time-trialling ability – by attacking alone and hoping to hold off his rivals to the finish. By 1989 he'd developed enough strength for it to start to work in bigger events.

He'd already won six major time trials by mid-April, when he lined up in the GP of Delamere road race, which at 90 miles was considerably longer than any event Boardman had competed in before. It helped that his Manchester Wheelers team was the strongest in the race. In the group of seven riders that went away with 20 miles to go, three were from Boardman's team, and two of them – Ben Luckwell and Mark Gornall – were fast sprinters.

A quick reminder of the physics of bike racing: wind resistance is the biggest limiting factor when it comes to riding fast. A group of riders can go faster than an individual rider by taking turns to take the pace at the front while the others shelter behind him, thus resting. When everybody has the same interest in working together this is a harmonious arrangement, but in a road race, they rarely do. Craftier riders may sit back in the group, waiting for the finish and letting everybody else do the work, then outsprinting them at the end.

In the context of the GP of Delamere, this put the Manchester Wheelers in the best position. If they stayed together for a sprint, Luckwell or Gornall would be the probable winner. If Boardman could attack, and get away, the four members of the break who weren't in the Manchester Wheelers would be reluctant to chase him down, because all they would end up doing is bringing Luckwell and Gornall to the finish, with the same result. An alternative tactic would be for the three Manchester Wheelers riders to take turns in attacking, until the others were too tired to chase any more.

It was easy. Gornall attacked, and when he was brought back, Boardman went for it. Once he'd got a gap, the result was never in doubt. He'd won his first significant road race.

Two weeks later he competed in the pro-am Tour of Lancashire, a four-day stage race, where he would come up against the best professional road racers in Britain. Boardman's professed aim for the race was to 'get round'. But he must have harboured ambitions greater than that. It's unthinkable that a planner as assiduous as Boardman wouldn't have had a detailed look at the six stages, and seen that the third, a time trial with an uphill finish on Pendle Hill, scene of his national hill climb victory just eight months previously, suited him perfectly.

Boardman survived the city-centre circuit race on day one, then infiltrated a group of twelve riders who gained 19 seconds on the field the next day, putting him in the top ten. When he duly won the Pendle Hill time trial, he was leading the Tour of Lancashire, with only three stages to go. For an inexperienced amateur, this was impressive, although the reaction of the professional teams in the race was to make sure that his tenure with the race leader's jersey would be a short one. For the professionals, spread among a handful of strong teams, there was only one thing worse than a professional rider from a rival team winning, and that was a jumped-up amateur – a time triallist at that – winning. 'He won't keep it,' was the verdict of PMS-Falcon rider Keith Reynolds. Sure enough, Chris Lillywhite of the Raleigh-Banana team worked Boardman over, taking time bonuses in sprints and winning the race. But Boardman ended the race in third place.

He wasn't the only rider broadening his cycling horizons

that May. Graeme Obree won the Scottish pursuit title in only his second visit to a cycling track. Then, two weeks later, off the back of winning the Scottish 25-mile championship, he set a new British hour record on a warm evening at the Meadowbank velodrome in Edinburgh. Dave Lloyd's record had stood at 45.5 kilometres and Obree broke it comfortably, riding 46.289 kilometres. That was some distance off the world record, held by Francesco Moser, which stood at 51.151 kilometres, but that was already in his sights.

'I was fascinated by the hour record,' Obree admits. 'Moser rode fifty-one kilometres, and I thought, wow, that is a series of nineteen-minute ten-mile time trials. No cars. No traffic. Nothing. Just a man and a track. I thought it was amazing. Other cyclists were into the Tour de France, but I was a time triallist, and the hour record is the ultimate time trial.'

On the same day Obree won the Scottish 25-mile championship, Chris Boardman competed in the British version, and for the first time at the event he timed it right with his peak. He won by over a minute, with his younger team-mate and childhood friend Scott O'Brien in third.

Boardman typically played down his achievement afterwards. Interestingly, he said he considered his Tour of Lancashire time trial win had done more for his career than the national 25 championship would. Either this was true or it was Boardman's way of not getting particularly excited about a good result. It was perhaps a sign that he was beginning to realize that time trials alone were not going to support his family, which was up to three members with the birth of his son Edward earlier in the year. While the national 25 crown was impressive to time triallists, the Tour of Lancashire time trial had been in front of sponsors, in the context of a professional stage race. British professional cycling had always been a precarious existence, but there was more money to be made as a professional than as an amateur bowling up and down dual carriageways at the crack of dawn.

Boardman's win also showed how scientific training and measurement were starting to take prominence. In his post-race interview, he explained that his pulse had reached its maximum cruising level of 182 beats per minute 90 seconds into the race, and that he'd held it there for the rest of the ride. Boardman was never the most engaging post-race interviewee, but perhaps he betrayed more than the assorted journalists and readers of *Cycling Weekly* could have realized at the time. Numbers were the future of the sport.

There was another reason why Boardman rode to a pulse. He'd suffered terribly with his nerves as a young cyclist, which cost him one national junior 25 championship and almost cost him another when he set out too fast and Sturgess nearly beat him. By riding to a level dictated by his pulse, he let his body win races without his mind being allowed to interfere.

It hadn't yet occurred to anybody that Boardman and Obree were building up to a rivalry, mainly because Boardman was still so far ahead. With Sturgess, riding as a professional with ADR, now out of the equation, having won the 25 championship Boardman finally looked to be emerging as the dominant domestic racer. Obree's times over 25 miles were slower than Boardman's so he was not yet seen as his main opposition. And on the track, Obree was a relative novice, while Boardman was now favourite to win the national pursuit title that had eluded him since he was a junior.

It was serendipitous, therefore, when the draw was made for the semi-finals of the individual pursuit at Leicester in August 1989, that the first heat pitted Chris Boardman against Graeme Obree. It was the first head-to-head meeting of the two riders.

As first clashes go, it wasn't quite up there with Al Pacino helicoptering in to meet Robert De Niro in *Heat*, or even

Sebastian Coe racing Steve Ovett at the English Schools Intermediate cross-country race in 1972. But this first race between Boardman and Obree did hand the Englishman a primer on the Scot's unsettling tactical naivety. Obree started extremely fast, going 3 seconds up after a kilometre, but Boardman held his nerve, and his pace, while Obree slowed. The two were on level terms with three laps to go, then Boardman drew steadily clear. One-nil to the Englishman – although they wouldn't meet on a track again until the semi-final of the 1993 world championship in Norway.

Boardman went on to win the final, while Obree lost the third-place run-off against Glen Sword. Just to remind everybody who the best all-round track rider in the country was at that point, Colin Sturgess won the professional pursuit, easily, in a new British record time.

At the world championship in France, while Sturgess was stunning the cycling world by winning the professional pursuit, Boardman made it through the qualifying round of the amateur event for the first time. Eastern Bloc riders dominated, the Russian Viatcheslav Ekimov winning gold and East Germany's Jens Lehmann taking the silver. Boardman came tenth. The bumpy outdoor track hadn't been to his liking, but the result filled him with enthusiasm. The top six in the world was possible, and the Olympic Games, three years down the line, would be the target. With experience and improved fitness, he could imagine a trajectory from tenth place in 1989, to the top six in 1990, top three in 1991, and then Barcelona.

Boardman's confidence about his future in the sport was increased further when he competed in the Nissan Classic race in Ireland, and survived, against some of the world's strongest professional teams. An unfortunate puncture robbed him of a possible top five finish in the time trial stage.

He also won the GP de France, a 59-kilometre time trial held in Rouen. There had been significant British and Irish success at the event in the past, but interestingly, those previous winners were road racers rather than pure time triallists: Stephen Roche, who went on to win the Tour de France, Tour of Italy and world championship road race in 1987, had won it in 1980, and Sean Yates the following year. As an indicator of future stardom, the GP de France had form: Jacques Anquetil, a five-time Tour de France winner, won it as an amateur, as did Bernard Thévenet, who won two Tours in the 1970s.

A number of professional team managers were at the GP de France, but none appreciated what they had seen. 'Nobody said anything to me,' Boardman observed, but even he wasn't really looking at the possibility of becoming a professional road cyclist. His own assessment of the ride was parochial: rather than compare himself to the foreign riders he'd beaten, he estimated that the one and a quarter hours he'd taken to ride the course was about equal to a 'fifty-one-minute 25'.

Boardman won his third individual national title of the year at the hill climb championship to bring his domestic season to a close. In 1989 he had won national titles at 25 miles, the pursuit and hill climb – a broad range of disciplines. He'd also been part of the winning team at the national team pursuit and the two 100-kilometre team time trials.

Dailey was still encouraging Boardman to improve his road racing, and persuaded him to ride the Tour of Mexico at the end of the year, but it did not go well. 'Forty-eight hours after leaving, he rang me and said he couldn't handle it and was on his way home. My head dropped a bit,' Dailey says.

To be fair to Boardman, the Tour of Mexico was chaos. He was suspicious of road racing's infinite tactical variables any-way, but it was the poor organization in Mexico that dissuaded him from sticking it out. He'd been told it was a twelve-day race, but when he arrived it turned out to be sixteen days, and they'd mismeasured the longest stage: it was 150 miles long, rather than the advertised 112. At the back of the field there was a motley selection of amateur internationals, and at the front, riding his home race, was Raúl Alcalá, who'd come eighth in the Tour de France that summer and was driving the race along at 29 miles per hour. Boardman banged his knee in a crash, and pulled out, waiting two days at a hotel while the British Embassy sorted out a plane ticket home.

Early in 1990, the cycling division of the Athlétic Club de Boulogne-Billancourt, the Paris-based amateur feeder team for Peugeot's professional outfit, invited Boardman to join. ACBB's alumni included Stephen Roche, Robert Millar, Sean Yates and Australian Phil Anderson, as well as several major French stars. Boardman turned them down. At the time, the only route into the professional road ranks was rising slowly through the amateurs with a club like ACBB. It was a school of hard knocks, and for every successful professional, dozens of amateurs had been chewed up and spat out. From the outside, it looked like Boardman didn't have the appetite to develop into an international road professional, but it's an important distinction to make: it wasn't the racing he didn't have the appetite for, but going to live in a dingy Parisian bedsit, two or three to a room, when he had a family to support in Hoylake.

Still, when Boardman lasted only five stages in the Peace Race in May 1990, citing fatigue, the armchair critics nodded knowingly in unison.

Cycling is, at heart, a macho sport. The universal call of encouragement to the passing racing cyclist is 'Dig in!' The spectator doesn't wish for the rider to go faster, necessarily, just to try harder. Giving up is anathema. The sport's iconography is founded not just on glorious winners, but on the agonizingly slow zig-zagging of an exhausted domestique up a mountain pass, an hour behind the race leaders, or the shivering progress of a bunch of riders freezing in a spring hailstorm. Boardman didn't fit into this model of understanding. He'd already mystified traditionalists with his talk of pulse rates. Now he was committing the cardinal sin: the Englishman was, the armchair critics agreed, soft.

But he was still winning races and getting results. The England team won a bronze medal in the Commonwealth Games team pursuit early in the year, with Boardman one of the riders, although he had been advised not to participate in the individual event (surprisingly, since the winner, New Zealander Gary Anderson, was certainly not as fast as Boardman). In the Tour of Texas, Boardman won a road stage, and he also had the satisfaction of beating Sturgess in the Porthole Grand Prix time trial, held around Lake Windermere. The only setback came when Obree beat Boardman in that time trial 'Clash of Champions' in Newtownards, Northern Ireland. 'He spoilt my weekend,' said a shocked Boardman at the finish.

Thus, after one meeting on the road and one on the track, British cycling's greatest rivalry truly began.

'I'd had a comfy existence being the big fish in a small pond,' recalls Boardman. 'I was the national 25 champion and the hill climb champion. I was probably the only amateur at that time who could make a living just from racing, but I'd stalled. I was very arrogant. Then somebody else came along who, even when I was going well, could challenge me. Obree made me better – he showed me it was possible to go quicker, and that made us move forward.'

In the week after Obree's triumph in Newtownards, both riders stated their intention to go for the hour record. Boardman would go the week after the national 25-mile championship in June, adding, in a masterpiece of unwitting provocation, that 'all I have to do is book the track. There shouldn't be any problem.'

Obree, in turn, booked out Meadowbank stadium in mid-May, and broke the record again. He'd anticipated riding 47 kilometres, aiming to make Boardman think a little bit harder about his own attempt, but on a windy day, the conditions were so unfavourable that he added only 101 metres to his previous total. The new mark was 46.390 kilometres.

The Obree and Boardman bandwagon gathered pace, rolling up at the national 25-mile championship in Beverley, near Hull. Boardman was under pressure anyway, having been beaten by Obree in their previous meeting over the distance, but he was also suffering from excruciating stomach pains in the run-up to the race, pains which mysteriously came and went. He was driven to Humberside two days before the race doubled up on the back seat of the car with a bucket, in case he was sick. He suspected kidney stones or appendicitis.

The Scot took the risk of attaching a higher than usual gear on his bike, to give him the extra speed. Most racing bikes have gears, but Obree was fond of riding a single fixed gear on flatter courses, preferring to save the weight. On the rolling course around Beverley, however, he couldn't quite get on top of the gear, labouring the pedals round rather than cruising. A headwind on the middle section pushed his challenge back further. He ran Boardman close, but in the end the Englishman won by 30 seconds.

Obree was devastated. He'd come second in the national championship. The score in head-to-heads between him and Boardman in time trials was still one each, but he saw it as a desperate failure. 'I'd come last in a two-horse race,' he said.

Two days later, Boardman was in hospital undergoing a five-hour operation to sort out the twisted bowel that turned out to be the cause of the stomach pains. After that he had to take an enforced period of rest, during which time his team-mate Pete Longbottom beat Alf Engers's twelve-year-old 25-mile record, lowering it to 49.13. The length of Boardman's recuperation meant that he had only just got back on the bike by August, when the national pursuit championship came around. Simon Lillistone enjoyed the rare distinction of beating Obree in the quarter-final, then Boardman in the final.

Boardman, for his part, was relieved to be cycling pain-free and was looking forward to the world championship, which in 1990 was being held in Japan. Lillistone recalls that just before they flew to Japan, he and Boardman had been for a physiological test with Peter Keen in Chichester, and Boardman's numbers showed that he had moved forward after his enforced lay-off. His power output was comparable to Lillistone's, even though Lillistone was several kilograms heavier and five inches taller.

Boardman didn't travel to the Far East with the ambition of winning the individual pursuit. The main aim remained progression, so when he qualified seventh fastest in 4.36, with a 12-second beating of his previous best, he was encouraged. That result sat squarely on the line that aimed to connect tenth place in Lyon in 1989 with first place in Barcelona in 1992. Even more importantly than the improved position, his qualifying time was only 4 seconds slower than that of the eventual winner, Evgeni Berzin of the USSR. He could easily find 4 seconds in two years.

Boardman was knocked out by American Steve Hegg in the quarter-final, and he was concerned that he'd lost a couple of seconds in comparison to his qualifying ride, but it didn't matter. Boardman and Keen still had their eye on the bigger picture: a medal in 1991, and a gold in 1992.

Obree and Boardman were both enjoying good form, although Obree had been suffering from fatigue brought on by a brutal training schedule. In the run-up to the national track championship he had experimented with a system in which he would ride flat out, without a warm-up, his pulse rate rocketing to 200 beats per minute, for two minutes, then rest for an hour. And then repeat. 'I did that all day, maybe twelve or fourteen times a day, for a week,' he said. 'I thought that when I recovered I would really be on the ball, but I overdid it.'

Obree regrouped to win the Tour de Trossachs time trial in Scotland in October, which was when he really started attracting attention north of the border. The Tour de Trossachs is 28.5 miles long, with varied terrain and a long climb up from the start. 'Obree rode the race on a single chainring, over two whacking great climbs,' recalls Ed Hood. 'That was the first time I realized he was special. Graeme smashed the record for the race, devastated it. And that record was Robert Millar's. Millar set the record the same year he was fourth in the world amateur road race championship.'

The scene was now well set for the decider, the final best-of-three showdown of the year between Chris Boardman and Graeme Obree – the South West Road Club's Invitational 50-kilometre time trial, based at Cranleigh in Surrey, at the end of October.

By now the novelty of Obree's tuck position was beginning to wear off among time triallists – he'd been using it for three seasons, and the initial scepticism, and mockery, was beginning to die down. The position looked effective at speed, but with so much weight on the front wheel, the bike was less manoeuvrable. It wobbled a lot while he was getting up to speed, too. Keith Bingham, a reporter for *Cycling Weekly*, remembers attending the Cranleigh event to watch Obree in action. 'The start, wow. Getting it going, he was all over the place,' he remembers. 'He was very unstable on the bike. People were all talking about what fantastic times he was doing, but his bike looked awful. Some people couldn't take him seriously even though he was knocking out fast times.'

Boardman was one of the sceptics. 'It's aerodynamic, but not practical,' he sniffed. 'I think he could be a lot better if he changed a few things.'

After watching the start, Bingham went over to the approach to the finish, where the course ascended a series of drags between Ewhurst and Cranleigh. He wanted to watch Obree over the top of the final drag, before the descent to the finish. It wasn't a hard climb, just enough to really make the riders hurt. 'I watched all the riders coming up, and the top riders all looked impressive. But then *he* arrived, and it was a shock. He was going so fast, and he was absolutely rock steady – that's the point. He flew through and I was rooted to the spot. I realized that everything everybody had been saying about him was spot on.'

It wasn't enough, however. Boardman beat Obree and brought the 1990 season's score to two-one in his favour.

7

Shifting Goalposts

There was no doubt that Chris Boardman's star was waxing rapidly as 1991 got underway. Peter Keen felt that the abdominal problem Boardman had suffered in the first half of 1990 had been holding the rider back; now that it was sorted, he was recovering better from training.

He hit the early season time trials like an express train, shattering records as he went. Three minutes were ripped out of the North Road Hardriders 25 course best, from one hour to fifty-seven minutes in one go. Another record fell at the Porthole Grand Prix, an agonizing 3 seconds (for the Scot) separating him from second-placed Graeme Obree. One-nil for the season.

They came together again in the Weaver Valley Cycling Club 25-mile time trial. Boardman won again, this time by 20 seconds, with the next rider a full five minutes behind. Two-nil. At the Pro-Am time trial in April, Boardman put 32 seconds into Obree, and three minutes into a handful of road professionals. Three-nil. And the final blow: a decisive win for Boardman at the Lee Ards 25 race, scene of his defeat to Obree twelve months previously. This time, Obree was left a minute in the Englishman's wake. Four-nil. In each race, Boardman's confidence and form grew. Obree seemed to be standing still.

Boardman wasn't just dominating the time trials. He'd already served notice two years previously at the Tour of Lancashire that he had ambitions in road races. Now he set about fulfilling those ambitions.

In the 60-mile Circuit of Ashurst, against the best road riders in the country, Boardman employed his favourite tactic: attack from the gun, and turn the race into a time trial. He'd maintained a healthy lead, but just as he was beginning to tire, with fewer than 10 miles to go, the police halted the race, concerned about riders in the bunch crossing to the wrong side of the road. Boardman was granted the victory, although there was grumbling about the manner of the race's conclusion. He wasn't just soft, hinted his detractors, he was lucky.

What else was there to do except remove doubt by winning the next event decisively? In the Hope Valley Classic in Shropshire, Boardman found himself in the bunch, one and a half minutes down on a group of seven riders. On the 2-mile-long Drum and Monkey climb, he set about bridging the gap on his own. By the time he caught the leaders they had split up, so he just rode off the front and won the race by two minutes.

And then came the final confirmation that Boardman's critics were going to be in for a very long year: overall victory in the Tour of Lancashire.

The organizers had obligingly made the first stage an uphill time trial, on Harris End Fell, above Scorton. Boardman won, and in this one short test opened a chasm between himself and the rest of the field. The next rider was a full 26 seconds behind. Just like in 1989, the professional teams threw everything at the race leader, but this time he was equal to the task of defending the yellow jersey.

Obree also rode the Tour of Lancashire, but all the race did was reinforce the perception that he was a one-trick pony, a time triallist. He crashed on an uphill, attracting the derision of his rivals, then got dropped and lapped several times in the circuit race stage in Accrington. Obree's preparation had been insufficient. The Scottish team management had persuaded him to ride even though he hadn't raced over 30 miles that year. He pulled out of consideration for the Olympic squad and retreated home.

The uphill crash was bad enough, but Obree had already gained a reputation as a poor bike-handler. In *Flying Scotsman*, he recounts being mystified when Tony Doyle and Colin Sturgess combined against him in a bunched track race at the Cleveland Grand Prix at Middlesbrough's Clairville Stadium in 1989. Sturgess's memory of the incident is different: he recalls Doyle riding slowly in front of Obree so that he was effectively dropped from the bunch. 'Graeme's lack of bike-handling was legendary,' Sturgess explained. 'Tony took him out of the back simply because poor Graeme was a liability in a bunch.'

In 1990, Boardman and Obree had appeared very close in time trials, but in 1991, Boardman pulled away slightly. He maintained his superiority on the track, where Obree was still a relative novice. On the road, there was no comparison. Obree ploughed through road races like a racehorse with an unseated rider. The physical class was obviously present, but it was mis- directed and unfocused.

The way the pair tackled their respective careers was a function of their characters and psychological make-up. Boardman compensated for his dyslexia by being doggedly organized and analytical. He needed order, to keep the forces of entropy at bay. He's a list-maker, and ticking boxes reassures him of his place in the world. His career was planned on a macro and micro level – from year to year, and from race to race. This also fitted in with Peter Keen's coaching. Long-term targets were identified, and the process of achieving them involved working backwards, breaking training and racing down into phases all of which built towards that goal. The early season road races of 1991 were satisfying to win, but they were also building blocks for the 1992 Olympic gold medal. If Boardman's career were drawn as a graph, there would be a more or less straight line moving diagonally upwards, connecting that early-evening 10-mile time trial in 1982 to that gold in Barcelona, and on to the Tour's yellow jersey and to the world hour record he set in 1996. That meant that his early season successes in 1991, albeit fairly minor compared to some of the wins he'd already achieved, were at a level above what he was doing in 1990.

Obree, on the other hand, didn't have a long-term plan. He was capable of laser-like focus on a single goal, and working towards that to the exclusion of all else, but because he became obsessed about that goal he had no idea what to do with it once it was achieved. One of the symptoms of bipolar disorder is hypomania, a heightened mood of euphoria and optimism that isn't as destructive as the mania or depression sufferers also experience. Hypomaniacs exhibit desire for success, creative energy, and are host to floods of ideas; if this is harnessed, focused, it's a productive state of mind, albeit temporary and unsustainable. Obree wasn't interested in progression, in the process of building on successes to create a foundation for more success; instead, he concentrated on goals as an end in themselves.

That didn't mean he wasn't capable of extraordinary rides, of course. After the Tour of Lancashire he decided to put his international ambitions on hold until the next Commonwealth Games, in 1994, and devote his energies to building a business – a bike shop in Prestwick. During this time Obree was also experiencing one of his periodic downward mood swings. His father persuaded him to take part in the Scottish national 25-mile championship, and he proceeded to break his own record for the event with a 49.48 – almost three minutes quicker than he'd ever been before. It was only 24 seconds slower than Alf Engers's best, which had been a British record for twelve years, and on a significantly slower course. The next rider was over four minutes behind.

It would have been the time trial ride of the season, except that Boardman's run of form had continued through to the British championship, held on the same day in June in Thornbury, near Bristol. On a course where the previous record was 53.34, Boardman recorded 49.15 – just 2 seconds off Pete Longbottom's recent new record, on a course that wasn't ideal for fast times. Scott O'Brien was a distant second, over three minutes behind. If the finish hadn't been uphill, Boardman would have broken the 49-minute barrier; even so, he took 30 seconds out of O'Brien in the last half-mile.

A fortnight later he also won the national 50-mile time trial championship, in spite of being laid low the week before with a viral illness. Winning the 25 and 50 championships in the same season is a rare double: Boardman was only the sixth rider to achieve the feat in half a century.

For Doug Dailey, the 25-mile championship was confirmation that Boardman wasn't just the best in the country, he was world class. Dailey had a rough rule of thumb for judging athletes. 'The gap between a world-class athlete and a good national rider is about three minutes over a one-hour ride. Scott O'Brien was a very capable rider, and Chris put three and a half minutes into him in that one event.' That both Obree and Boardman had recorded similar dominant times on either side of the border proved to Dailey that there were two world-class cyclists in domestic time trialling.

But for Boardman, as ever, the national 25- and 50-mile titles were just staging posts along the way to the big one for 1991 – the world track championship, which would take place in Stuttgart. His aim was to get on to the podium.

The final lead-up to the worlds would involve a defence of his national pursuit title at Leicester, along with a crack at the Danish rider Hans-Henrik Ørsted's amateur sea-level hour record, which stood at 48.144 kilometres.

Everything initially went to plan. Boardman beat Colin Sturgess's track record in the semi-final of the pursuit and he duly beat Simon Lillistone by 10 seconds in the final. He bullishly predicted that he'd be capable of riding 4.32 in Stuttgart – the same time Evgeni Berzin had clocked to win the event in Japan a year previously.

Then Alan Sturgess, Colin's father, who was the BCF track coach for endurance riders, questioned Boardman's timing for the hour record attempt. Boardman was assertive in his response. 'Surprisingly, I know what I'm doing,' he said. Boardman and Keen had of course analysed the demands, and they felt the hour fitted in with their training schedule for the world championship. There was also the convenience of having officials, infrastructure and crowds already at the track – it was a lot cheaper to take advantage of that rather than try to stretch a meagre budget to buying them all in at a later date. Boardman added, witheringly, 'I've listened to advice before, which is why I only rode the team pursuit at the Commonwealth Games in Auckland.'

Boardman started carb-loading and laid off training, ready for his hour bid. Then it started raining.

After a day and a half of waiting and fretting and not wanting to let the spectators down, Keen and Boardman adjusted their plans. Keen looked at the record books, checked the training schedule, and realized that the world amateur 5-kilometre record would fit into it. Roared on by the Leicester crowd,

Boardman broke the record by two and a half seconds, recording 5.47. Perhaps it was the endorphins speaking, but Boardman even allowed himself to get a bit carried away after that performance. 'I never believed I would actually get to the point where I would be thinking about winning a world championship gold medal,' he enthused. 'It will be fantastic to pull that off.'

The cycling careers of Chris Boardman and Graeme Obree came before agents and PRs inserted themselves into conversations between riders and journalists, like pushy drunks at a party. There's a refreshing naivety about both riders' honesty in contemporary interviews. Both gave of themselves generously to the press, even if Boardman's congenital earnestness wasn't immediately compelling. These days, such outspoken confidence as Boardman displayed after that 5-kilometre record has been pureed out of the riders' repertoire by earnest individuals with polo shirts and smartphones. Media training has squeezed the interest and colour out of what athletes say, leaving us with a beige gruel of unsalted tedium.

It was Boardman's honesty with the press, and therefore the public, that tended to rub up his critics the most. If he rode to a certain pulse rate, rather than trying to guess how fast he could go on feel, he saw no problem in telling people that was the way he rode rather than inventing a more exciting alternative. If he'd felt good, and the win had been straightforward, there was no point in either being modest or overplaying it – he would say he'd felt good and that the win was straightforward. He never did shake off the reputation that he was arrogant, or that his approach was dry and empirical, but that's how he inadvertently came across. To him, it was just the truth.

The way Boardman saw it, winning the world championship individual pursuit would involve a series of predictable events, and some variables. The predictable events involved himself and his coach. He and Keen had the achievements of the year before as a guide, and based on Boardman's increased strength and fitness in 1991, the 5-kilometre record he'd just set, and the measurements they were making in training, they could identify to the nearest second or so how fast he was going to ride at the world championship. The variables involved his opponents, but the best evidence to hand – last year's results – supported the theory that Boardman had a very realistic chance of a medal, possibly even the gold.

Again, Boardman had no problem whatsoever with sharing that information, whether it sounded overweening or not. He had a chance to do well at the world championship, and the evidence he had in front of him was enough to make him feel confident.

In this case, however, that confidence was misplaced. Boardman did ride faster than he ever had before in Stuttgart, recording 4.31, but that made him only the fifth-fastest qualifier. The German team was in a different league. They had radical new carbon-fibre bikes, and Jens Lehmann and Michael Glöckner both rode 4.22 in qualifying – 4 seconds faster than any other rider, and a new world record. Evgeni Berzin, the reigning champion, was only marginally slower than his qualifying ride in Japan but didn't even make the last eight. In the end, Boardman finished ninth – two positions down on the previous year, and much further away from the gold medal in terms of time. It was disastrous.

The first inkling that the Germans were set to ambush everybody had come in qualifying. Boardman's team-mate Matt Illingworth was in the track centre with Boardman when the Germans did their qualifying rides. The Stuttgart track was an odd length at 286 metres, which meant that riders started in the back straight. 'Glöckner did his ride and did a 4.22,' Illingworth recalls. 'Peter Keen or Chris, I can't remember which, said they thought the guy had finished half a lap early. They were so far ahead we thought they'd finished in the wrong straight. Then Lehmann went straight afterwards and rode the same time.'

Boardman was devastated. 'I have scraped my way to where the goalposts were, only to find they have been moved,' he said. He described it as the most depressing event of his life so far – which is quite revealing of Boardman's competitive nature. For someone who always claimed to be interested primarily in his own improvement and performance, he didn't half take being beaten by other riders badly. Lehmann's improvement in particular had been phenomenal: he'd finished behind Boardman in the 1990 world championship, and had gained 14 seconds in a single year. The Brit found it all very difficult to cope with. 'I have improved seven per cent on last year,' he explained, 'which is a lot. I can't justify the sacrifices my family is making if I am not going to win.' He was seriously considering packing it in. A measure of how far behind he'd fallen was that Lehmann had ridden faster over 4,000 metres than the Great Britain team pursuit squad.

'Chris had a rough patch,' recalls Simon Lillistone. 'He was living in Birkenhead in a tiny terrace house, and by then he'd had his daughter [the Boardmans' second child]. It wasn't the nicest part of the Wirral, and he was working for Deeside Cycles delivering stuff, making a few quid. There wasn't much in it for him. He wasn't mercenary, he just wanted to earn a living and do the right thing. He wanted to be good at whatever he did. You can speculate as to why, but the goalposts had fundamentally moved. It was a massive kick in the teeth.'

Where had the startling improvement come from? The carbon-fibre bikes, made by German manufacturers FES, certainly contributed. Lehmann was a little older than Boardman, at a time of life when physical maturation can lead to big strides in terms of performance and he had the extra motivation from riding in front of a home crowd. Lehmann was never connected to doping, but this was, of course, the early 1990s, when rumours of EPO abuse by endurance athletes were gaining ground. Italian road racers especially were starting to achieve some extraordinary things in the Tour de France, Tour of Italy, Tour of Spain and the Classics, and there is little doubt that by the end of 1991 not all Grand Tour winners were clean. Colin Sturgess, as we have seen, also recounted that he'd been openly told a rival rider in a world championship had given himself such an advantage that he couldn't fail to win.

The worlds weren't a disaster just for Chris Boardman. The whole British team underperformed, with the exception of Shaun Wallace and Colin Sturgess, who achieved silver and bronze medals in the professional pursuit. And then the finger-pointing began. There were rumours of conflicts between coaches. Some riders were more used to working with Peter Keen than with Alan Sturgess, and vice versa. Sturgess pointed out that Boardman must have known Lehmann was on good form, since he had ridden 4.32 on an outdoor track for the recent German championship. He also made reference to that 5-kilometre record. 'It was brilliant, but if you were thinking in terms of a medal, he needed more speed,' he commented. Mick Bennett, a former double Olympic bronze medallist in the team pursuit, was blunter: 'Whoever advised him to do that needs a shotgun up his bottom.'

National coach Dailey appeared to be at odds with the BCF's Racing Committee, who made the selections for the team. They'd chosen several riders, in a team of fourteen, who hadn't reached the official qualifying standards. Dailey was diplomatic, and blamed the poor results on a lack of funding, but he was known to be a stickler for qualifying times, and also for spending money wisely on potential medals rather than using the same funds to bring a large team with little chance of success.

The whole thing looked like a shambles, and the professionalism and budget enjoyed by the German team rankled with the British riders. 'Our equipment was pretty average,' says Matt Illingworth. 'We were all riding different bikes, and wearing different helmets. You'd have one rider with a disc wheel on the front and another without. It was pretty Mickey Mouse.'

Even now, Boardman feels the disappointment of 1991. 'We were almost there in 1990,' he told me. 'We were so sure it was doable in Germany. We'd been just two seconds behind the winner, and from that moment we went into another gear. Everything, family, took a back seat to this one thing. And we overcooked it. We didn't do our homework properly on dates and travel and I was tired when we got there.'

After Stuttgart, Keen and Dailey went back to the drawing board. Boardman wondered if travelling to Barcelona was going to be worth it, but Dailey, who's an incurable optimist, knew that the Olympics would be more straightforward than a world championship. For a start, the one-rider rule meant that only one of Lehmann and Glöckner could compete. And with Lehmann the dominant rider, they knew their quarry.

Keen worked backwards over Boardman's year to find out if anything had limited him in Stuttgart. He noticed that Boardman seemed to have been just below top form in the second half of the year, ever since the national 50-mile championship. He'd been going well, but lacking the feeling of really being on top of his form that he'd previously enjoyed, especially when winning the national 25-mile championship. His subsequent ordinary form had to be a side-effect of the virus that laid him low between the two races.

Keen also got to work on Lehmann. He knew the rider's height and weight, and his time over 4,000 metres, and from an estimate of his frontal area, Keen extrapolated his power output. Then he worked out what wattage Boardman would have to produce in order to beat Lehmann's time. Before long they had a target, and twelve months to achieve it.

8

The Kook, the Geek, His Bike
and That Summer

The 'friends and family watching sporting success on TV' shot is beloved of television production crews – a piece of colour footage and human interest to back up the action in the highlights show. But one television news researcher should have known better than to phone Mike Burrows and ask if he could come round and film him watching the 1992 Olympic pursuit final.

Burrows was as closely related to the protagonists of the event as anybody except Chris Boardman's immediate family. The LotusSport bike Boardman was riding was his baby. It was a futuristic-looking one-piece carbon-fibre frame, the Lotus Engineering company's development of an original design by Burrows.

'Mike, can we come and film you at home watching the final?' asked the voice on the other end of the phone.

'No you fucking can't,' Burrows replied. And put the phone down.

To read the headlines after Boardman's gold medal in Barcelona, you'd think all the man had done was sit astride his bike and let it do the pedalling. There was barely room for a photo of the new Olympic champion on the front pages as the sleek, photogenic lines of the LotusSport hogged the attention. For success-starved British sports fans, the bike was *the* personality of the Games. It was the more popular member of the duo – it played Paul Simon to Boardman's Art Garfunkel, Paul McCartney to his Linda.

The LotusSport was beautiful. A polished one-piece frame with urbane lines, lacquered in the iconic black and yellow of the Lotus Formula One team, it flowed around Barcelona's Horta velodrome with liquid speed. To the general public, unaware of how fast bicycle design was moving in the early 1990s, it looked like sorcery. There was only one fork blade, and the back wheel attached on only one side, while the man on it was crouched low as he swept round the track, a long teardrop of a helmet resting on his back, his arms stretched out in front of him. It was the bike on which Boardman found all the time he needed to get back from Jens Lehmann, and won Britain's first cycling gold medal since Thomas Lance and Harry Ryan tasted victory in the tandem race in 1920. Seventy-two years of British Olympic cycling mediocrity had been ended in one fell swoop.

Mike Burrows, a visionary engineer with seventies hair and the obstinate confidence of the autodidact, had come into Boardman and Keen's world towards the end of 1991. A carbon-fibre frameset he'd been tinkering with and developing for years had been picked up by Lotus Engineering, who saw commercial possibilities for high-end racing bikes based on his design. They had the engineers to perfect the bike. All they needed was a guinea pig to test it out, and a showcase to present it to the world. In Boardman, they found both.

Burrows knocks about in an industrial unit on the outskirts of Norwich these days. His workshop is a cavernous Aladdin's cave of half-built bikes, lathes, metal shavings, carbon-fibre cloth, screws, tools, jars of unidentifiable liquids and odd-shaped recumbent bicycles. The smell is a mix of oil, rubber and metal. Over sausage, egg and chips at the local greasy spoon, in a stream-of-consciousness of engineering wisdom, cheerful profanity, creative energy and wild tangents, he told me about his latest experiments with short cranks, theorized about how Baron Karl Drais arrived at the invention of the hobby horse (the precursor to bicycles), and discussed everything from transport policy through mass-production cycles and the conservatism of the bike industry to split down tubes being a bad idea ('Why? Because you get shit all over your water bottle!').

Burrows is a genius – hugely intelligent, engaging, creative, nonconformist and wearied by the inability of 99 per cent of the population to see things the way he does. 'I've never been a natural rebel. I'm not a rebel, I'm right!' he declares, and I think he's only half joking. Or not joking at all. He reminds me a bit of Marvin the Paranoid Android from *The Hitchhiker's Guide to the Galaxy*, without the slightest trace of the self-loathing.

His father ran a model shop in St Albans, and to keep the young Burrows occupied he used to give him pieces of balsa wood and a knife to see what he could make out of them. Burrows developed an interest in model aircraft, which gave him a real-world appreciation of two things: aerodynamics, and seeing the whole when designing, not just constituent parts. 'If you work for Boeing, you work on this little bit here or that little bit there. You don't build aeroplanes, you build small bits of aeroplanes. But with model aircraft, you design the whole.' He got good enough at it that he represented Great Britain at the world gliding championship, building and flying model aeroplanes with a six-foot wingspan.

He started working behind the desk in his father's shop after school, where he professes to have learned nothing. He spent a lot of time chatting to the engineers who worked there, or who visited the shop, and found himself absorbing their knowledge.

Relations at home got a little strained after Burrows turned over the company minivan – his father's minivan, in other words – at an autocross race, so he left to work at Crew and Saunders engineers in St Albans, turning the lathes on huge blocks of steel, while he looked for another office job. Two and a half years later he'd learned a lot about engineering and satisfying customer requirements, and moved to Norfolk to be an engineer – not that he'd ever aspired to be one, and without ever having served an apprenticeship. 'Life took me in a weird direction,' he tells me. 'I didn't plan to turn the minivan over and start working in engineering. I didn't plan to come to Norfolk. And I didn't plan for the car to blow up and start riding a bicycle.'

Burrows drove a Mark One Ford GT Cortina, but he'd had problems with it when he'd had the engine rebored. While it was being stripped down and sorted out, he borrowed his wife's bike to commute to work. But by the time the car was fixed there had been an oil crisis, and petrol had doubled in price. He left the car in the garage and carried on cycling. 'I bought a bike for forty-two pounds – load of shit, obviously – and became a cyclist.'

A friend in the local Cyclists' Touring Club chapter suggested Burrows try racing in an evening 10-mile time trial. In spite of the fact that he'd hated sport at school, he rode the 10 and put in a 27.05 on a touring bike. He became fascinated with the modifications another friend had made to his time trial bike to make it faster – drilling out holes to save weight – and he realized that tinkering and engineering could improve his times, and that that was more up his street than dieting and training.

Specifically, Burrows realized that working on aerodynamics would improve his times. In an effort to reduce air resistance he designed and built a bike with a small frame – just 16 inches,

RIGHT: The photograph in *Cycling Weekly* of a teenage Chris Boardman with Mike Burrows' prototype Windcheetah.

MIDDLE: Graeme Obree, Boardman and Pete Longbottom on the podium after the 1992 national 25-mile championship.

BOTTOM: It was hard to say who was the bigger star at the Barcelona Olympics – Boardman or the LotusSport bike.

A youthful Chris Boardman, a few days short of his 17th birthday, with an early Windcheetah at the 1985 World Championships at Bassano, Italy.

ABOVE: Obree was adept at playing it up for the cameras, whether reading Francesco Moser's book or eating jam sandwiches.

ABOVE: Deciding which bike to use before the first world hour record attempt at the Hamar velodrome north of Oslo.

RIGHT: After falling short of Moser's record, Obree wanted to go again that same afternoon, but Vic Haines persuaded him otherwise.

ABOVE: 17 July 1993: Starting the second attempt on Old Faithful; in Obree's words, his eyes 'went kind of numb round the edges'.

BELOW: Celebrating the new world hour record of 51.596 kilometres in a deserted velodrome. Boardman would break it six days later with rather more fanfare.

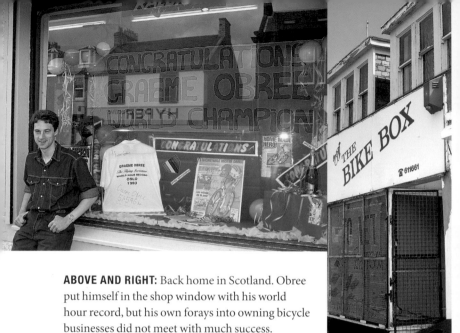

ABOVE AND RIGHT: Back home in Scotland. Obree put himself in the shop window with his world hour record, but his own forays into owning bicycle businesses did not meet with much success.

BELOW: The master bike builder at work. Obree was, and remains, a pioneer of ingenious design.

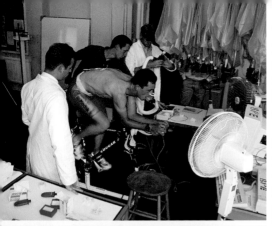

TOP: Boardman testing at Eastbourne in July 1993 ahead of his world hour record bid; Peter Keen left nothing to chance, controlling the variables.

MIDDLE: Keen sprayed Boardman's skinsuit with ethyl alcohol to keep him as cool as possible in a baking Bordeaux velodrome on 23 July.

BOTTOM: On the way to a new world hour record of 52.270 kilometres and indulging in a rare moment of pure, emotional celebration.

Overall, Boardman had the upper hand over Obree in head-to-head contests, but the Scot won a notable victory in August 1993 at the world individual pursuit championship in Norway. Photographer Phil O'Connor captured the two men in rare moments of conversation and kinship three months later at the Bordeaux Six-Day race.

TOP: Bordeaux, 27 April 1994: Obree preparing for a new tilt at the world hour record.

MIDDLE: He raised the mark to a phenomenal 52.713 kilometres, but the UCI were on the point of banning his tuck position.

BOTTOM: Compared to a year earlier, Obree was confidence personified for this bid: 'I'd learned to draw the energy out without thinking I needed to die,' he said.

TOP AND MIDDLE: Obree in his tuck position, racing in an invitation time trial on the roads of Scotland and on the Herne Hill track in 1994. Even when he tried to play within the UCI's rules, however, they found a new way to disqualify him from the world championship, which Boardman won that year.

BOTTOM: Superman. By experimenting with tri-bars, and building the stem up, Obree found an even better position, which would lead to a second world pursuit title in 1995.

compared to the 23-inch frame he'd been riding before – with a long seatpost to compensate for the smaller frame. He'd be riding in the same position, only there would be a lot less bike to catch the air. The seatpost, of course, was narrow, the better to reduce wind resistance.

Then in the early 1980s, a friend got his hands on some carbon-fibre. 'We were going, "Shit! Ooh! Stuff!"' Burrows recalls enthusiastically. 'What could we make with this?'

He shows me a clump of dry carbon fibre that he's got lying around in his workshop, a dark, fibrous cloth that looks like a roll of ordinary material. Combine it with epoxy resin, however, and you can mould it into any shape you want, and once it has dried it's extremely light and very strong in the direction of the fibres. Manna from heaven for engineers. 'I realized I could make my small frame in one piece, and it would be much faster,' he says. The important factor was the shape: the streamlined frame was much more aerodynamic than traditional round bike frame tubing. And with the centre filled in, airflow was less turbulent.

Burrows registered his design for the monocoque frame with the Patent Office in 1982, and by 1984 he had made his first rideable model, complete with a small front wheel. He took it to a few bike manufacturers, but their reaction was one of incomprehension. '"Why did you cover the frame up?" "I didn't cover the frame! This *is* the frame!" I got nowhere. They were as thick as shit, the lot of them.'

Burrows focused on developing and refining the bike, which he called the Windcheetah. Mark One was built with carbon-fibre laid around a solid polyurethane core, with normal bike forks. It made its first competitive appearance on May Day 1985 at the VC Baracchi 10-mile time trial. Later that year, Jim Hendry, chief executive at the BCF, took the bike to the world championship in Italy, where the Union Cycliste International,

cycling's governing body, promptly banned it from international competition (the Road Time Trials Council, the
governing body for time trials in the UK, were fine with it).
The Great Britain team did get a chance to try the bike out
on the velodrome, however, sending one of their younger squad
members out for a few laps – sixteen-year-old Chris Boardman.
There's an old photograph, printed by *Cycling Weekly* in 1992,
showing a teenage Boardman posing uncomfortably with the
bike, wearing cycling shorts, a baggy T-shirt and a pudding-
bowl cycling helmet.

Burrows' next innovation was inspired by a nineteenth-
century bike called the Invincible, made by the Surrey
Machinist Company, which he saw at the Transport Museum in
Coventry. Instead of two forks, either side of the front wheel,
the Invincible only had one. Burrows imitated the design on
the next version of the Windcheetah, realizing that there was
nothing more aerodynamic than a non-existent fork blade on
one side. Then, for version three, he replaced the small front
wheel with a regular-sized one, having learned that there was
no significant difference in drag between the two. The final version Burrows made, number four, had the monoblade fork
made of carbon fibre, and its completion in 1990 coincided
with the UCI quietly changing its technical rules, and making
one-piece frames race-legal.

It still might have ended there, except for a chance encounter
with Rudy Thomann, a retired Formula Two racing driver from
France who was working for Norfolk-based Lotus as a test
driver. He spotted the bike hanging up in Burrows' office,
thought the Lotus engineers might like to have a look at it,
borrowed it and took it to work with him. Burrows knew Lotus
Engineering well. They'd outsourced a bit of machining work
to him for the Lotus 72 Formula One car.

Thomann called Burrows and invited him to meet the Lotus

board of directors. They thought it might be possible to make and sell a limited number of the bikes as exclusive, hand-made Lotus bicycles. There wasn't a fortune to be made, they said, but if Lotus were ever to get into bicycles, this was going to be the moment. The car-making part of Lotus Group had hit hard times, with production running at single figures per week, but the name still had cachet. Burrows was a happy man. 'Lotus understood composites, they understood aerodynamics and they understood innovation, which the bike industry was completely oblivious to,' he says.

And this is where Chris Boardman came in.

'It was as simple as, what are we going to do for marketing? We thought, well, the Olympics are coming up and Chris got thrashed last time. We weren't even talking about winning the Olympics at this point, just making and selling bicycles.'

Burrows got a number for Boardman and rang him.

Doug Dailey recalls that Boardman was very keen to work with the new bike. 'Chris was fascinated by aerodynamics and technology, and this thing was carbon fibre. This was a real step forward. And Chris needed their help. He could file, chisel and drill steel, and work on his own bikes, but with carbon fibre he needed help. Chris was very good at recruiting the best people to work with. He was prepared to work with Peter Keen and he was prepared to work with Lotus. He realized he couldn't possibly do it on his own. He put a lot of time in with Lotus.'

Boardman made regular trips down to the MIRA wind tunnel near Birmingham, where Lotus tested their cars. 'Because of the Lotus connection, we could use the wind tunnel cheap, but getting it cheap means things like using it at eleven o'clock at night in February,' says Burrows. 'It's fucking awful. It's a thirty mile-per-hour gale in there, and you're sitting on a bike, not pedalling. You get very cold. You could see Chris shivering on the drag profile.' They tested Boardman on his own bike in the tunnel. Then they put him on the Windcheetah. The results weren't good. 'Chris wasn't as good on my bike as he was on his bike. Shit! What have I fucking got wrong here?'

The problem was that Boardman was in the wrong position. The bike was still set up for Burrows, and he was taller and, importantly, a lot less flexible than Boardman. 'He's very bendy, a real India rubber man,' Burrows observes. They gaffer-taped Boardman's arms to the underside of the handlebars so that he would be in a position very similar to that which he adopted on his time trial bike, and the results were better.

The Lotus aerodynamicist Richard Hill pushed further. Could Boardman lower himself even more? He was now in a more extreme position than he'd ever ridden before, but the results were so good that Boardman made the adjustments. He now had a significant advantage: for the same power, he was travelling faster through the air, and in one go the gap to Lehmann had been decreased, without even starting to work on his physical strength. 'Chris was very open-minded – the perfect person to ride the bike,' Burrows tells me.

Both parties were satisfied with the results of the wind tunnel tests. LotusSport had their marketing strategy in place, while Boardman could see the advantage in riding their bike rather than a normal track bike. You get the impression that Boardman was testing out Burrows and Lotus as much as they were testing out him.

Burrows had let the design registration of the Windcheetah lapse at the end of 1987, having been disappointed with the lack of response from the cycling industry. He still held copyright over the appearance of the bike, but he signed over his rights to Lotus in 1992 and they took the project on, using him as a consultant. The first LotusSport model was a replica of the Windcheetah Mark Four, but the Lotus engineers saw room for improvement and adaptation. They tried making the frame in two halves, each side formed and dried separately before being glued together. This meant that the polyurethane core could be eliminated, saving weight. By the time Boardman was doing tests on the second and third versions, using tri-bars and his new lower body position, he was showing huge improvements. The tri-bars alone would have made a big difference.

The BCF were also involved, because they were concerned about the bike's legality. The UCI rules stipulated that new equipment couldn't be used in the Olympic Games without having been used before in international competition. They had been caught out in 1987 when the Italian team attached restraining cords to their waists at the last minute before the team time trial at the world championship, which allowed them to anchor their bodies and generate more power. Subsequently a new regulation about brand-new equipment in major championships was introduced.

'Lotus produced a prototype, which was a bit on the heavy side – very bloody heavy, in fact,' Doug Dailey recalls. 'We got Bryan Steel to ride it in a couple of World Cup events.' Steel was a talented rider, one of the best and most consistent pursuiters in the country. He rode at international level but wasn't the same world-class athlete as Boardman. The inference is that if Boardman had ridden the Lotus in international competition in the run-up to the Olympics, it would have attracted swarms of blazered UCI officials with tape measures, looking for an excuse to ban it. Steel wouldn't draw as much attention.

'Bit naughty of us,' adds Dailey.

The bike debuted before those World Cup events, in May at the televised pre-Olympics track meet in Leicester, where there were so few spectators that the BBC producer there told Burrows they'd never film another cycling event again. The Lotus design started to draw the attention of the cycling world only when Steel appeared on the cover of *Cycling Weekly* riding the bike, and the magazine published a follow-up story in the next edition with the headline 'The Lotus Burrows Bike, Explained'.

At the World Cup events at Cottbus in Germany and Hyères in the south of France, UCI officials and rival team managers started sniffing around. Steel was riding an early prototype, one of the models which still had a foam core, so it wasn't light. 'The UCI commissaire came over and started checking the weight,' Dailey remembers. 'He felt it was heavy, so he didn't bat an eyelid.'

And with that, the precedent was set. It had been ridden in major competition and scrutinized by shrugging commissaires. The LotusSport bike was legal for the Olympics.

At Hyères, the Germans were still dominant, although there was amusement in the British camp at their reaction to the new bike. They certainly seemed to be more interested in it than the UCI officials. 'They were very upset when we turned up with the Lotus,' said Bryan Steel. 'We watched their equipment man take two rolls of film while I was riding round the track.' In return, Burrows carried out a quick assessment of the FES bikes the Germans were using. He felt the aerodynamics were vastly inferior to those of the Lotus. 'They've got normal forks and a round seatpin,' he remarked in disgust.

There was a small complication back home, however. Boardman had unwittingly entered into a dispute with his bike sponsors, Ribble Cycles, who were unsurprisingly miffed that Boardman wasn't going to be riding one of their bikes to an Olympic gold medal. Ribble insisted that Boardman was contracted to ride their bikes and were threatening legal action; the BCF remained adamant that they could dictate what equipment British riders used in international competition. The LotusSport bike story was beginning to build momentum.

The dispute between Ribble and Lotus would rumble on, but

meanwhile Boardman and Keen continued honing form for the Olympics. Unusually, Doug Dailey had managed to squeeze some more money out of the BCF for 1992. In previous years, the coaching budget was Dailey's salary plus about £20,000, but with a realistic chance of a medal in Barcelona he'd managed to persuade the authorities to part with enough money to fund two foreign training camps, one at the indoor velodrome in Ghent, Belgium, the other at Hyères. Too many Leicester training days had been spent under shelter, waiting for the track to dry and fretting about yet another missed session.

Simon Lillistone was struck by two things at the Hyères camp, which was held in July, in the final run-up to the Games – Boardman's form, which was rapidly building to its best ever level, and the arrival of an up-to-date prototype of the LotusSport bike. Rudy Thomann, the ex-racing driver, was in his element as the British team got a brief insight into the glamorous world of motorsport. Thomann needed to get the bike down to the south of France, so he took it apart, put it in the front seat of a pre-production Lotus S4 which needed to get some miles on the clock, and drove it all the way down the Autoroute du Soleil through France, much to the envy of the racing cyclists who saw him pull up in the car park.

The bike was now almost the finished product. Only one more LotusSport would be made: Prototype Four, which was the bike Boardman would use in Barcelona. The trouble was that in the week before the Olympics began southern and eastern England sweltered in a heatwave and the Lotus engineers were having trouble getting the epoxy resin that was fixing the carbon fibre to set – it was just too warm. They were forced to switch production to night-time, in order that the frame could harden and be bonded together.

On Friday, 24 July, Richard Hill flew to Barcelona with the frame, carrying it as hand luggage, and the next day Rudy

Thomann and the Lotus engineers assembled the bike. Boardman had his first and last practice ride on the final prototype on the Sunday, the day before the competition started. Initially, the weight had been a worry, but they'd got it down to just under 8 kilograms – still on the bulky side, but on a flat track, not a problem.

Dailey remembers clearly how much attention the Lotus engineers gave the bike. 'In true motor racing fashion, they stripped the whole damn bike down and rebuilt it after every ride. They couldn't leave it alone. That's what F1 mechanics do – you strip everything down and rebuild for the next Grand Prix.'

That's not to say that they were infallible. Dailey also recalls Sandy Gilchrist, the British cycling team's mechanic, calling him over to the bike after one stripping-down and rebuilding session. 'The bike was under lock and key. It was real cloak-and-dagger stuff. We used to cover it with blankets to keep everybody away from it. Sandy said, "Come and have a look at this." The Lotus guys had been working one on either side of the bike. They'd put the bloody cranks on at ninety degrees to each other!'

Chris Boardman's first competitive outing in 1992 had been a New Year's fancy dress 25-mile time trial which he rode on a tandem with his wife, both of them dressed as bumblebees. There's a photograph of them in *Cycling Weekly*, enjoying the fun of it, tapping round the course in a little less than an hour and a half.

On Boardman's wrist there is a pulse monitor. Even when he was having fun, he was being serious.

Boardman had thrown himself into preparations for the Olympic Games. Initially he'd felt overwhelmed by the prospect of having to replicate the experience of the twelve months leading up to the 1991 world championship, when he thought he'd identified where the goalposts stood and dragged himself to them, only to find that they had been moved. But if he'd done it once, he could do it again. He was a year more physically mature and experienced, and he and Keen were a year older and wiser. Training theories that hadn't worked could be jettisoned, while those that had could be refined and improved. He'd reduced his training hours significantly, but raised the quality of his sessions. Keen was pushing at the cutting edge of sports science, risking going against the traditional, time-honoured training method of riding many miles.

Boardman had also joined a new team, the GS Strada outfit, along with a few other Olympic hopefuls.

But while in 1991 he'd swept all before him in the early season time trials, beating Graeme Obree four times in a row, in 1992 he experienced a run of bad luck which he must have hoped wasn't going to follow him all the way to Spain. He punctured in his first serious race of the season, the North Road Hardriders time trial. It's worth noting that his biggest disappointment about it was not so much missing the win as the £300 first prize. He mentioned it in an interview at the race headquarters, and then again in a separate interview with *Cycling Weekly* two weeks later. 'That could have been a new bed for Edward,' he commented.

Boardman often talked about money in interviews during his early career – another reflection of the directness with which he views the world. He's not a particularly materialistic individual. He certainly retired a wealthy man, and has made a lot more money since then through his work with British Cycling, his bike company and his media work, but he hasn't spent it ostentatiously. He wasn't obsessed with having a lot of money as a young man so much as obsessed with having so little of it.

Making money from being the best time triallist in the country in the late 1980s and early 1990s simply wasn't easy. Even on the track and the road only a handful of individuals were making a comfortable existence from racing bikes. As late as 1989, a typical payday from winning a time trial was meagre compared to the time spent training and the expense of equipment. When he won the Weaver Valley 25 in 1989, Boardman's haul included an engraved tankard, a meal for two at a local hotel, a bottle of fizz and £35 in 'vouchers and cash'. Later that year, Boardman rode the Manchester and District Time Trialling Association's Christmas 25, in atrocious weather. He'd been in two minds whether to ride, but his dad persuaded him to do it. 'I rang him at ten o'clock last night and when he told me there was a thirty quid first prize, I decided to get my bike out of its bike bag,' he said after winning the race.

In 1990, at the end of the season, he described the wrestling he did with his own ambition when he was close to a course record in the Merseyside Wheelers Invitational time trial. He could have gone for the record, but it might have jeopardized his win, and going into the red might have cost him. 'I was going to go for it because it would have bumped up the prize money to £230, but I thought I would play safe,' he said at the finish. Better a safe £150 than a risky £230.

At least by 1991 the paydays were getting a little better. When Boardman won the North Road Hardriders time trial early that year, he took home £200 for the win, and £250 for becoming the first rider ever to finish it in under an hour. After the trial he'd talked about taking risks on the damp roads but had justified it to himself. 'Money is an amazing motivator,' he remarked.

As he went into the Olympic year, times were still hard. His experience at the 1991 world championship had made him question two things: whether he would ever be good enough to win a world title, and whether the whole effort was worth it or not. Every week, month and year spent training, resting and living the life of an athlete for a place on the periphery of the top ten cyclists in the world was a week, month and year spent not earning a living wage. He vented his frustrations again in an interview at the end of 1991 and denied rumours that he was earning a good wage from the Manchester Wheelers riding time trials. 'It's a myth,' he insisted. 'I wish it wasn't, but it is. I'm not living in a mansion. I can't claim the dole because I'm not available for work because I'm away, so I get help from my wife. The club pays my racing expenses and I get clothing and equipment. The sport pays for itself but I'm sick of it. We haven't had a holiday for six years, since before we married.'

After Boardman's puncture in the North Road event, he suffered the same fate in his next race. He just loaded his bike into the car and drove home. Then he developed chest pains in his next time trial, after having pulled a muscle doing stomach exercises. The pain cleared up in time for his next race, the Porthole Grand Prix, but his whole family came down with a bout of sickness the day before the race. He rode anyway, but took a 40-second beating. Bad luck had come in threes.

The Girvan Three Day race in Scotland was next on Boardman's schedule, but another mechanical problem cost him the race. After three of four stages he was in the race leader's jersey, but during the final stage one of the cranks fell off his bike and he lost five minutes. It appeared that bad luck was dogging him in 1992.

Boardman won the prologue time trial of the Circuit des Mines in eastern France in early May, but crashed out the very next day. His experience of racing in a bunch was well behind his physical capacity. While the prologue win demonstrated that he was one of the fastest riders in the race, he hadn't learned the dark arts or the feel of manoeuvring in a peloton, especially an experienced international one. About 50 miles into the second stage, when the peloton was strung out in a single line at the edge of the road, he'd missed the shouts, not sensed the minute changes of direction ahead of him. The line suddenly flicked towards the middle of the road as riders swerved to avoid a traffic-calming measure, a three-foot-high post at the edge of the road. Boardman just got his bike around it, but the loss of control sent him over the handlebars and crashing to the road. He had a miserable 60-mile ride to the finish after that, then spent a night in the local hospital before being discharged and spending the rest of the week sitting in the team car.

Boardman may not have been getting much satisfaction out of the racing, but his training had come on in leaps and bounds. About six weeks before the Olympics, Keen ran his final set of tests on Boardman, on a Kingcycle which Doug Dailey had installed at his house to test local riders. 'The dining room used to be my office, and in the corner I had an eight-by-four sheet of Formica with a Kingcycle on it, in front of an Amstrad computer,' Dailey explains. 'Pete ran Chris through the test protocol, while my job was making the tea in the kitchen. Then Pete came into the kitchen and said, "The gold medal is on!" Chris had hit the power values they had worked out they needed to beat Lehmann.'

It was in June that results finally caught up with Boardman's physical condition. A week before the national 25-mile time trial championship he finally broke the 25-mile competition record, near High Wycombe. It had been held since the previous June by Gary Dighton, and Boardman smashed his mark by 48 seconds, crossing the line in 47.19. He'd been expecting to ride even faster – times for 25-mile time trials were tumbling with the advent of tri-bars – but he'd been unable to engage his top gear. If he'd had it, he estimated he would have been in the mid-46s.

It felt almost inevitable that the following week Boardman would take his fourth consecutive national championship at the distance, and he did, beating Graeme Obree by well over a minute. Obree had mainly kept his racing north of the border through 1992, concentrating on trying to build up business at his bike shop, and he'd shown up on a radical new bike whose frame he'd built himself. Boardman's excellent form continued with victory in the national 50-mile championship a week after that.

The physical and psychological demands of racing a four-minute pursuit and a 50-mile time trial (which for Boardman that year took one hour and forty-three minutes) are very different, and Boardman came in for some criticism for racing in the latter event with so little time left before the Olympics. There were only four weeks between the two, and it was assumed that during that period Boardman's training would be tapering towards shorter and shorter efforts. Worried observers thought it was the equivalent of a 1,500-metre runner going out to compete in a marathon.

But Keen and Boardman not only saw that 50-miler as another race (though it was a prestigious title to win), they also saw it as a perfectly timed training session. Keen was the pioneer of a system of training involving riding to certain levels, based on pulse rates and perception of effort, for certain amounts of time. In very basic terms, level one involved riding steadily and easily; level two involved riding at a pace at which conversation was possible, but punctuated by pauses to catch breath; level three was fast cruising, at a rate at which the body could only just sustain – uncomfortable, and requiring concentration; and level four was the sort of riding the human body can't sustain for long, like a sprint, or a two-minute interval up a hill. 'That was audacious,' reckons Doug Dailey. 'They treated the national championship as a one-hour-and-forty-five-minute level three ride. All he had to do was ride at a fixed power, and it was good enough to win. He could have dug in more, but he didn't need to. He was miles ahead.'

When, in July, Boardman joined the pre-Olympics training camp in Hyères, he concentrated on doing training rides and timed efforts on the earlier prototype of the LotusSport. When he knocked out a 4.28 4,000 metres on the outdoor track, they knew he was ready for Barcelona.

Four years before Barcelona, Simon Lillistone had been a wide-eyed young athlete in Seoul, one of the lambs to the slaughter that the British media had predicted would have a hard time in the competition. For Lillistone, who'd grown up watching the glamorous LA Games on television, and was now representing his country, the 1988 Olympics combined the excitement of competition with the holiday of a lifetime.

He went to the opening ceremony, and hung around the athletes' village, star-spotting. One day he was standing in the queue for dinner behind a guy with a plaster stuck to his head, then suddenly realized it was the American diver Greg Louganis, who earlier that day had cut his head on the springboard during competition in front of tens of millions of television viewers. Lillistone celebrated with the British team when Adrian Moorhouse came back to the village with his swimming gold medal, and gawped at the tiny Eastern European gymnasts and the seven-foot basketball players.

He recalls that in Barcelona the mindset had completely changed. 'It was different to 1988. Pete Keen was there with us, we had doctors and psychologists. We had a good time, but we were there to do a job. The team was more organized and more ambitious, and in Boardman they knew there was a real prospect of a gold medal.'

At the empty Horta velodrome, the British team went through their final training sessions, and the feeling that

Boardman was about to do something special grew. He rode a 3,000-metre effort – three-quarters of the length of the pursuit event – and stopped the watch at 3.18. If he'd maintained that pace for another kilometre, he'd have clocked 4.22 – the same as Lehmann had in an indoor velodrome at the Stuttgart world championship. Just four rides – a qualifying round, the quarter-final, the semi-final and the final – lay between Boardman and a gold medal.

But it was won on the first ride. In qualifying, the world got its first glimpse of Chris Boardman and the LotusSport bike: the Brit recorded a new Olympic record of 4.27. Boardman was slower than he and Keen had anticipated, but so was everybody else. The temperatures in the cauldron-like velodrome soared through the day. The hot, airless, oppressive conditions weren't conducive to fast times, but he was still 3 seconds faster than Lehmann, and the Australian Mark Kingsland, which meant two things: first, he would have a favourable draw for the quarters, and second, nobody was at the same level as him. At the speeds these men were riding at, 3 seconds wasn't far off 50 metres' difference.

The British press, still wondering where Britain's first gold medal was going to come from, immediately sensed that one of the stories of the Games was unfolding in the velodrome. The national newspapers, not having touched a cycling story for years, descended on the cycling team. They also descended on Boardman's family in Hoylake, and on Mike Burrows and Lotus Engineering in Norwich. The royal family started taking an interest. Doug Dailey was trying to keep on top of managing the squad and the increased media attention, and now Princess Anne wanted to come to watch Boardman. 'She came and saw the qualification, and then she changed her itinerary so she could come and watch again the next day,' Dailey says. 'We weren't used to royalty.'

Boardman began to feel the pressure. He suffered what he described as a series of panic attacks after the qualifying round, and had several sessions with the BCF psychologist. 'Nerves' can be an irrational reaction, and Boardman preferred to deal in rational processes, but the actual process of rationalizing these sorts of situations continued to be a problem for him. The only time he seemed to function normally was when he was riding, when he could forget about thinking, just for four and a half minutes – or less.

After the qualifying round, two more people realized that they needed to be in Spain. That Monday of qualifying, Sally Anne Boardman decided at the very last minute to go and watch her husband win a gold medal; she flew out the next day, and managed to get a ticket for the semi-final and final from a tout outside the velodrome. She paid 3,000 pesetas (£16) – double the face value. The editor of *Cycling Weekly*, Andy Sutcliffe, left it even later. He'd got himself an Olympic press pass, just in case, but hadn't flown to Barcelona. As the momentum built behind Boardman's effort, he phoned the chief executive of IPC Media, the owners of the magazine, to sign off on a plane ticket so that he could go out and watch the final the next day. 'It's going to cost a fortune,' he warned. He got the green light, flew out to Spain, and slept on the floor at the place where one of the British photographers at the Games was staying.

The quarter-finals, on the Tuesday, were faster than the qualifying round, with a breeze cooling the velodrome. Boardman's nerves can't have been helped by a faulty starting gate, which didn't release his bike, but he beat his opponent, the Dane Jan Bo Petersen, easily on the restart, overtaking him en route to recording a 4.24 – another 3 seconds faster than his qualifying ride, and still 3 seconds faster than Jens Lehmann in his quarter-final. Boardman sat up for the last half lap – he wanted his opponents to see that he could go faster. He said later that it was after this round that he knew he could win.

Boardman's fast quarter-final ride once again gave him a favourable draw, against the fourth-fastest qualifier Mark Kingsland. This time he rode his pursuit against the man, not the clock. It didn't matter if he took five minutes over it, as long as he finished ahead of the Australian he would be in the final. He eased into the lead after a kilometre and just stayed a couple of seconds clear of his rival all the way to the finish, recording his slowest time of the series, 4.29. Lehmann rode a couple of seconds faster in winning his semi-final, aiming to gain the psychological advantage over his rival.

The final was run just an hour later, on a sultry evening in front of an expectant crowd. The sky was turning a dusky dark blue above the bright floodlights. 'The velodrome was up on the Montjuic hill, overlooking Barcelona,' recalls Andy Sutcliffe. 'It was a stunning setting; you could see the lights of the city below. It was hot, even at night. And there was a feeling that something electric was going to happen. It wasn't just the Brits. There was a buzz about the Lotus bike. Everybody at the Olympics knew they had to be there. I didn't think for one millisecond about being a journalist or writing about it. I just watched it. It was the most exciting thing I have ever seen. I felt for those four minutes we were at the centre of the universe.'

In the home straight: Jens Lehmann. The world champion, a tall, muscular man with a shadow of stubble on his face, riding a low-profile carbon-fibre bike with a tri-spoke front wheel. His machine looks technologically advanced, but it's still recognizably a bicycle as most people would understand it. Apart from his unusual physical ability, he has the reputation of being able to turn himself inside out in a race. 'He used to put himself in a terrible state in a pursuit,' says Doug Dailey.

In the back straight: Chris Boardman. Unemployed cabinet-maker, occasional world championship top ten pursuiter.

Slighter than Lehmann, and much lower over his bike. He can't match Lehmann's power, but he punches a much smaller hole in the air than the German, and he's hoping that will compensate. Also in the back straight: the LotusSport bike. The star of the show. The bike is the central character in the building media coverage of the event.

Boardman had spent the day feeling nauseous at the prospect of competing in an Olympic final, and on the start line he felt the pressure of the occasion. He looked down at the track, trying to ignore the knowledge that the attention of the crowd, and the watching world, was on him. He and Keen had set a schedule of 4.26 for the final. Lehmann had ridden a fast semi-final, but they'd seen him repeatedly rubbing his legs during his warm-up for the final, indicating that they were fatigued. If Lehmann was still in touch after 3 kilometres, Boardman had room in the schedule to lift the pace for a fast finish if necessary.

From the gun, Boardman's lead grew. He covered the opening kilometre a second faster than Lehmann. After another kilometre he was 3 seconds clear. His lead was already insurmountable. Keen said later that after one lap he knew the gold medal was safe.

Simon Lillistone watched the final from the track centre, where he was warming up waiting for his own event, the points race, along with Curt Harnett, a Canadian sprinter. As Boardman circled the track, the pair realized that he was already in the same straight as his opponent. Off every bend, Boardman was catapulting himself out faster than Lehmann, and was fast closing him down. Harnett summed up the disbelief in the stadium: 'Holy shit, that doesn't happen in the fucking Olympic final!'

It looked like Boardman was hunting down his prey, but he was just riding to his pre-planned schedule, while Lehmann had cracked. By half distance he was already saving himself for the team pursuit, which would start the next day. Boardman then did the unthinkable: he caught his opponent in an Olympic pursuit final. As he sped past the beaten German, he punched the air. The gold medal was his.

As the British press pack filed their stories and went off to explore Barcelona's nightlife, Boardman went to bed, his gold medal under his pillow. He'd planned the previous twelve months meticulously, but his schedules had only taken him up to 9.05 p.m. on Wednesday, 29 July. Unable to sleep, he went out and sat on the beach with Peter Keen until three in the morning, discussing the race and thinking out loud about the future.

Initially, that future looked a little bit like the past. Sometimes life-changing moments don't immediately change lives.

Andy Sutcliffe spent two days chasing the British Olympic Association for an interview with Boardman. He had to wait while Boardman competed in the team pursuit with Great Britain – they came fifth – and then for Boardman to manage the now endless demands from other media.

They eventually sat down together in the athletes' village. 'He was scared shitless,' recalls Sutcliffe. 'He'd won a gold medal, but there was nobody supporting him, no minder or agent. I was trying to say, "Things are going to change now, you're going to be fine," but he was saying, "When? When I get back, do I have to sign on?" We sat there, me, Chris Boardman and a gold medal between us on the table with a couple of bottles of Coke. The guy who ran Ribble Cycles was trying to take legal action about the bike. Everyone was telling him how much money he was going to earn, but he was saying, "I haven't got any fucking money. My wife needs some money for the electricity bill."'

Dailey had known that Boardman was under pressure from the mundane grind of trying to make ends meet. He'd driven the rider from Hoylake to the airport on the way to Barcelona, and Boardman had shared his worries. 'His house was only a little two-up-two-down terrace. It was hardly palatial living, and he told me he'd had some threatening letters from the bank. Going into the Olympic Games with that kind of problem – I thought, that's not good enough. When he got back from the Games, the bank manager invited him out for lunch.'

The BCF, and even the BOA, were also having trouble dealing with the attention Boardman was attracting. But it could have been worse; he was protected to an extent by the extraordinary interest that had sprung up around his bike. Boardman and the LotusSport were the most famous British Olympic sporting pair since Jayne Torvill and Christopher Dean. It had caught the imagination of the British public, and that swung some of the spotlights away from a grateful Boardman.

The bike was in fact emerging with quite a lot of the credit. 'Their F1 Beats Our Trabant' was the headline on one German newspaper the day after the final. The PR behind the bike, after all, had a firm grounding in the world of Formula One, where it is in the manufacturers' interests to assert the prominence of the car in a Grand Prix victory. Mike Burrows had also said that the final LotusSport model was worth 'ten to twelve seconds' over 4 kilometres. The question was, then, where would Boardman have come if he'd not been riding it? 'If he'd done it on his own bike, he'd have probably got a bronze,' Burrows reckons now. 'Maybe silver, but more likely bronze. Over the Germans' bikes, it was around three and a half seconds. Mentally it was worth more because it was the fastest bike in the world.'

Even Boardman got a bit carried away at the time. 'The bike

was obviously a significant advantage or I wouldn't have been using it,' he said. 'It's certainly an advantage if you can ride in that position. It could have made the difference between a gold and a bronze, I think.' But notice that Boardman mentioned the position, rather than the bike itself. It's significant that the bike made a big advance in wind tunnel testing compared to early versions when they simply put tri-bars on it. And the 'ten to twelve seconds' that Burrows mentions would have been in comparison to a normal bike, while Lehmann was riding an aerodynamic carbon-fibre bike of his own. Boardman estimated that the LotusSport would have been about 3 seconds faster than Lehmann's FES, and considering he caught his rival inside the distance, it's possible to conclude that the best rider won after all.

Later in the year, British professional pursuiter Shaun Wallace used a LotusSport in the world championship, in Valencia. He'd won a silver medal in 1991, and he did the same again in 1992. So much for the bike being the winner of the gold medal.

Rudy Thomann recognized that the combination of rider and bike was the important thing. 'Chris is a fantastic rider, and he's the only man who could make the dream come true,' he said.

Boardman on his own bike would probably still have won. Perhaps a different rider, bronze medallist Gary Anderson of New Zealand for example, could have won had he ridden the LotusSport. As it was, Boardman plus the LotusSport seemed an invincible combination. And as Doug Dailey pointed out, they don't give the medal to the bike.

Like any successful double act, there was tension between Boardman and his bike, or rather the makers of it. To the general public, Boardman and the LotusSport were synonymous, but it wasn't clear what the future of their relationship was going to be. Ribble Cycles rebuilt bridges with Boardman after the final, not wanting to sour the relationship, but they continued to carry a grievance against Lotus. Lotus Engineering, for their part, were starting to talk about continuing to support Boardman, and producing the bike for the cycling market. Hints of bad feeling came out when an attack on the world hour record was mooted. Asked whether Lotus would sponsor Boardman for such an attempt, their spokesman said, 'If he rides our bike it will be a form of sponsorship. He certainly can't afford to buy one.'

At this point, Burrows' relationship with Lotus appears to have been definitively severed – just after he'd been invited to their factory to pose for pictures with the engineering workforce. 'It went quiet,' he says. 'They didn't want to talk to me any more. I'd signed over my copyright to them. I got paid for the specific work I did, and it was agreed that I'd get paid a royalty of twenty-five pounds per bike that they made and sold.'

Initially, Lotus were preparing to build a limited number of replicas of Boardman's Olympic bike, at a cost that was put at 'a considerable amount of money', and they also had plans to put a model on the market for racing cyclists costing £3,500 – expensive for a bike in the early 1990s. They were the first to admit that they had limited experience of the bicycle market. It was a difficult one to break into.

The Lotus company was undergoing a period of turmoil, too. With car production extremely low, owners General Motors were trying to sell the company, which consisted of two entities: Lotus Cars and Lotus Engineering.

By the end of the year, Boardman had been allowed to borrow the bike for a couple of races and public appearances, but there was still no deal. For their part, Lotus insisted they couldn't talk about future involvement until 31 December, when Boardman's contract with Ribble expired. In January

1993, the *Mail on Sunday* carried a story claiming there was a 'rift' between the two parties, and that Lotus were finding it difficult to get the bikes mass-produced, although they'd sold five Olympic replicas, at an estimated cost of £15,000 each.

In February, Lotus entered an agreement with British Eagle Cycles to distribute a time trial model of the bike starting in the summer, but it was a further two years – during which time Boardman occasionally rode a Lotus bike for his professional team, Gan – before the road model of the Lotus bike was finally available to the public. British Eagle, in turn, had passed production of the frames to a company in South Africa.

It is not known how many Lotus bikes were sold in the end. The UCI banned the frame again in 2000, putting a dent in ambitions to sell large quantities. Burrows got a few cheques for £25 after the replica Olympic models were sold, but he got headhunted by the Giant bicycle company soon after, and in order for Lotus to release him from his contractual obligations he agreed to forgo his royalties.

For Burrows, the 1992 Lotus bike was a missed opportunity, not because of the money but because he'd hoped it would be a genuine revolution in bicycle manufacture, inspiring people to ride. 'You had this wonderful, clean, healthy athlete with a family, a high-tech company and a mad professor,' he reflects. 'You couldn't want a better story. But it all collapsed in a heap.'

9

The Hour

The day after Chris Boardman rode to the greatest triumph of his career so far, Graeme Obree walked past a newsagent's and, seeing the headline and photograph of the gold medallist on the front page of a newspaper, stopped in his tracks. He was skint, and attempts to get sponsorship for an assault on the world amateur hour record had come to nothing. What's more, business had been slow at his new shop, and he'd offloaded it after only a few months, leaving himself with a pile of debts. 'I was trying to get back on benefits. There were no jobs and I had no money. I'd gone out to buy a nineteen-pence Saver loaf, and I saw on the newspaper "Boardman Wins on Super Bike".'

Obree didn't ride for three months after that. His initial reaction was that obsessive training and racing had put him into poverty, that he'd failed. He enrolled on a secretarial course when the unemployment office threatened to cut his benefits if he didn't, figuring that typing skills might come in useful for a training manual he was thinking of writing.

But he couldn't quite shake the thought out of his head: Chris Boardman won a gold medal. I beat him once.

The hour record wouldn't go away either. Both his British

records had been 5 kilometres shorter than Francesco Moser's, but Moser had set his distance at altitude. They said that was worth a kilometre. Since Obree set the last mark, he'd taken three minutes off his best time over 25 miles. That was worth another 2 kilometres. If he went to an indoor track, which was also reputed to be worth around 2 kilometres compared to outdoors, he'd be close.

'You know what?' he said to his wife and a couple of friends as they took a walk on the beach on New Year's Day 1993. 'I'm going to break the hour record.'

The hour is one of cycling's most simple and brutal challenges: pedal for sixty minutes around a track and see how far you can get. The record has been broken by some of cycling's most legendary figures. To hold it, in the twentieth century at least, was on a par with having won the Tour de France, a Classic or the world championship. And unlike the Tour de France, it doesn't suffice for a rider merely to be the best that year. The hour record holder must, by definition, be the best ever. It's a comparison across the ages. There's no runner-up place or silver medal in the hour record. There is only success or failure, with a strict demarcation between the two.

Its history has been one of revolutionary new benchmarks, often followed by a flurry of attempts as new possibilities are realized, then long periods where the record was seen as insurmountable – even to try would be futile.

The first hour record was set by Henri Desgrange, who was more famous for inventing the Tour de France than winning bike races, but in riding 35.325 kilometres in Paris in 1893 he set the first officially recognized mark. Today, a half-fit amateur cyclist could match that. A few riders took it on over the next five years, gradually increasing the distance, then in 1898 things started getting more serious when Willie Hamilton took the record above 40 kilometres in Colorado Springs. The beneficial effects of riding at altitude weren't known about in the 1890s, but the record was impressive enough that nobody beat it for seven years. A future Tour de France winner, Lucien Petit-Breton, took the laurels in 1905, and then the best possible thing happened: two riders, talented in different ways, who despised each other started to take an interest.

Marcel Berthet was a track rider. Oscar Egg was a Swiss cyclist who would go on to win Tour de France stages and whose high opinion of himself was exceeded only by the level of his contempt for others. Berthet set a mark of 41.520 kilometres in 1907, then Egg had a go. Between 1912 and 1914, the pair took it in turns to break the record. They exchanged put-downs in the press and their attempts became huge events, drawing massive crowds. Egg had notched up 44.247 kilometres when the Great War finally put an end to the rivalry. It was another nineteen years before that distance was bettered.

Egg's ego wouldn't allow him to countenance anybody surpassing his achievement, and he became an hour-record rent-a-quote, telling the press and anybody who would listen that the hour was 'a dreadful thing', adding that he had 'terrible memories of it'. At the same time he needed riders to try to break it in order to validate the quality of his own record, so he put up a prize of 10,000 francs for the first rider to exceed 45 kilometres.

Another burst of pre-war activity, this time in the 1930s, finally saw Egg's record broken, by a Dutchman, Jan Van Hout. Then a French rider, Maurice Archambaud, raised it to 45.767 kilometres.

It is from this point that the hour record increasingly became the property of cycling's greatest riders. The next holder of the record was none other than Fausto Coppi, whose 1942 attempt finished just 31 metres ahead of Archambaud and stood for fourteen years. Coppi was known to cycling fans as *il campionissimo* – the champion of champions. He was a cultivated, aristocratic cyclist of elegant charisma and human frailty, but capable of extraordinary achievements on the bike, including winning the Tour de France twice and the Tour of Italy five times.

The man who beat Coppi's record was as contrasting a character to the Italian as Obree was to Boardman. Jacques Anquetil, a five-times Tour de France winner with a ruthless streak and a deadeningly conservative tactical approach, nudged the record over 46 kilometres in 1956. This inspired a renewed period of interest, and the record was raised four times in quick succession before a Dane, Ole Ritter, re-discovered the advantages of record bids at altitude, riding 48.653 kilometres in Mexico City in 1968, just two days before the opening ceremony of the Olympic Games.

The next rider to hold the record was Eddy Merckx, owner of the untouchable status of greatest ever racing cyclist. Merckx was peerlessly strong, a malevolently intransigent competitor who won the Tour de France and Tour of Italy five times each, and the Tour of Spain, to complete the set. His 1972 mark, 49.431 kilometres, was regarded as one of his finest per-formances, an effort of terrifying and reckless self-immolation after which he needed to be helped from his bike. After he'd started too fast, his hour had spiralled down into a chaotic act of dogged willpower. The distance he set was widely seen as unbeatable.

And on equal terms, it was. But twelve years after Merckx, Francesco Moser flew out to Mexico City and pulverized the record, by well over a kilometre. Incredibly, while Merckx had been barely able to walk after his ordeal, Moser went again four days after this first attempt and added another 300 metres. The record now stood at 51.151 kilometres.

Moser was a prickly, standoffish one-day race and time trial specialist. He won a very soft edition of the Tour of Italy the same year as he broke the hour record, on a course which was more or less specially designed for him by the race organizers, but he wasn't in the class of Merckx. What's more, by 1984 he was coming to the end of his career. Man against man, he wouldn't have stood a chance. But Moser had scientific ingenuity on his side. He rode a revolutionary aerodynamic bike – different-sized disc wheels, with a low-profile frame and cowhorn handlebars. After nearly three more decades of aerodynamic research, his position doesn't look that good, but at the time it was a significant advantage. There were rumours that the rear wheel for the attempt was weighted in order to create a flywheel effect. One method suggested to me was that there were radial tubes inside the disc wheels filled with oil, with ball bearings at the hub end. As he accelerated, the centrifugal force moved the ball bearings to the rim, building his momentum as he rode. As my source said, it sounds too bizarre not to be true. Reports also stated that an advance party had gone to the velodrome in Mexico City and painted a smooth, two-foot-wide layer of varnish around the inside of the track, to reduce Moser's rolling resistance.

There was also scientific back-up in the form of the methods employed by Moser's sports doctor, Professor Francesco Conconi, of the University of Ferrara in Italy. Conconi was revolutionary in his field, working with heart rates and the anaerobic threshold, and he imposed a regime of interval train-ing on Moser comprising long timed efforts up a steady climb, when previous training wisdom had involved nothing more scientific than riders battering themselves over long periods of time and racing themselves into shape.

Conconi was also a pioneer of blood doping, which involves transfusing previously withdrawn blood back into the body in order to increase its oxygen-carrying capacity. It is a matter of record that Moser blood-doped when he broke the hour record. That alone would have made a huge difference, probably enough to overtake Merckx. Blood doping was not banned at the time. The International Olympic Committee didn't make it illegal in sport until 1985, although this didn't put an end to the practice, which still continues to this day in some of the murkier corners of the peloton.

After 1984, nobody touched the hour, until Graeme Obree and Chris Boardman started looking at it in the early 1990s. Moser had set a formidable target, and the hour is a relentlessly gruelling effort, an endurance test in the purest sense of the word. Agony must be endured for a full hour – one minute, one second at a time. That was one of the things that gave Obree the confidence to ride the hour. His greatest asset was neither his bellows-like chest cavity nor his intuitive ingenuity. He was physically gifted as a cyclist, and his invention of the tuck position on a bike meant that he had already put himself among the best cyclists in the country, but it was his ability to tolerate pain, to a frightening degree, that made him such a formidable time triallist and pursuiter.

Of course, that shouldn't be surprising. For an individual who had experienced the emotional anguish of vicious childhood bullying and periodic attacks of bleak depression, the prospect of an hour's suffering on a bike would have been fairly straightforward in comparison. The pain he put up with on a bike was not the worst pain he'd felt in his life.

Pain is a given in racing cycling. American Tour de France winner Greg LeMond's memorable maxim, that cycling never gets easier but as you get fitter you just ride faster, indicates that from the Tour winner down to the unfittest fourth-category cyclist, the suffering involved in making a bike move fast is a shared experience. But with Obree, it seemed different. It seemed like there was some hidden compulsion to put his body through excruciating experiences. There's a certain macho enjoyment of pain among most cyclists, but Obree's attitude to physical pain was more unusual than that. His descriptions of being beaten up as a child are horrific, but there's an almost transcendent ecstasy in them, too. It's not that he enjoyed it, but he certainly had a complex relationship with the violence inflicted on him.

Ed Hood once watched Obree in a Scottish 25-mile championship held on the Dundee road. 'I've never seen anybody hurt themselves so much on a bike,' he recalls. 'It was like someone was placing burning coals on his skin. He was in agony, torturing himself along this dual carriageway.'

Obree knew to what lengths he was prepared to drive himself in order to break Moser's hour record. He knew, therefore, standing on that beach on New Year's Day 1993, that he could do it. 'As soon as I said it I knew I wasn't good enough,' he clarifies, 'but it was certain, in my mind. I was doing it. I would make myself good enough.'

On 2 January, Obree went out on his regular training circuit. He knew it like the back of his hand, and he knew exactly what he was capable of on it – on some hills, he would ride in a certain gear if his form was good. But he realized he'd settled into a comfort zone. That is the point of comfort zones – they're comfortable. From now on, riding at levels he knew he was capable of was not acceptable any more. 'It's Newton's law of physics,' he says. 'An object will carry on in a certain direction until some other force changes it. The world didn't change. I didn't change. But my perspective of what was acceptable changed. I can train harder. I can suffer more.'

While he began the process of beating his body back into shape, he also started working on his bike. He wanted to design a new version of the tuck position models he'd been riding since the mid-1980s, but to do that he had to change his perspective on that, too. He wanted to go back to the beginning, with no assumptions about the way it should be designed, so he rode his current bike, trying to imagine it was the first time he had ever ridden it. 'I started from the point that all I can do with this bike is balance it. I immediately thought, "Those pedals are too wide apart." How could I not have noticed that?'

The problem, however, was that if you narrowed the bottom bracket, your knees would knock against the top tube of the frame. That, concluded Obree, would have to go too. With some old frame tubes that were knocking around his friend's bike shop, he pieced together the bike that would come to be known as Old Faithful. In the narrow bottom bracket that he constructed, he fitted the infamous washing machine bearings for which, more than any other thing, even more than the successes and the depression, he would be remembered. That's the difference between Graeme Obree and most people. To most people, putting washing machine bearings in a bike, then using some of the side panel metal as struts for the frame, is an act of eccentricity. To Obree, it was obvious. The entire bike had cost him about £70.

But though Obree worked hard on his bike and his form, he needed more. Organization and direction did not come naturally to him, as they did to Chris Boardman. This is where Vic Haines, businessman, barrow boy, former cycle speedway champion and tandem record-setter, came in. They had ridden together on a short-lived mountain bike venture a few years previously.

Haines has a succinct and direct manner, and he recalls Obree's mountain bike skills vividly. 'He was crap,' he states.

Vic Haines is collateral damage in the Obree story, although the first thing you have to know about him is that he can look after himself. Everybody I spoke to while researching this book asked, 'Have you spoken to Vic yet?' Obree mentioned him in passing, then caught himself and skipped forward, glossing over the story. Haines was the man who managed Obree through to his hour record bid in Norway and fronted the cash for it, but Obree split from him almost immediately afterwards. I'd been warned: he's still a bit pissed off.

He invites me over to his house in Suffolk. He wants to show me the bike that he still owns, the Mike Burrows-built replica of Old Faithful that Obree rode in his first attempt. Haines kept the bike in his company's boardroom for years. Now it's kicking around his house, and he wants to get shot of it. 'Old Faithful was a piece of shit, so I had this made, not just because it was a piece of shit and I didn't want us to go all the way there and it let us down, but you also have to have two bikes exactly the same for an hour record.'

Everything that Haines says, there is a reason for. His opinion is that Obree wouldn't even have got to Norway, let alone on to a cycling track there, if he hadn't been there to sort everything out and save Obree from himself. In this case, the subtext is not only that he didn't think very highly of Obree's bike, but that if he hadn't had the replica made, Obree would have been in contravention of the UCI rules dictating that two bikes had to be brought to an attempt. Without Haines taking care of details like this, he hints, Obree would not have been able to break the hour record.

It's a beautiful bike. There are no tyres on the wheels, and no pedals, but it's otherwise in excellent nick, hardly having been ridden. Something that is easily forgotten about Obree's innovative bike designs is just how narrow Old Faithful and the Burrows replica are. Looked at from the front, the bike's hardly there. It sports a Burrows monoblade fork, just like Boardman's Lotus.

'Look in there,' Haines tells me.

On the end of each handlebar there's a piece of curved glass, and if you peer in you can see the words 'Kiss this!' written behind, magnified by the lens.

He points out a flower transfer on the frame. 'That's Mike Burrows. He's into flower power and all that shit.'

Haines has also got the helmet Obree wore for his hour records, a model called the Aerovic, which Haines designed himself. He sold hundreds of them at £20 each in the early 1990s. Inside Obree's helmet there's a St Christopher taped to the lining. Obree's wife stuck it in there before the record bids.

Haines then demonstrates just how aerodynamic Obree's position was. He crouches over the bike, his arms tucked in. 'Your arms are in the way. Your head's in the way. You've got two legs. So what Graeme did is take the arms out of the equation.' He moves his legs together in the tuck position pedalling style. As his leg comes up, it moves inwards, rubbing up against the other leg, replicating Obree's knock-kneed pedalling style. 'Move the top tube out of the way, and have a bottom bracket that's only an inch and a quarter, and don't pedal like you do on a normal bike, but pedal like this, and you've got one slightly fatter leg, rather than two,' he continues.

Obree used to drive Haines up the wall. When they shared hotel rooms, Haines recalls Obree starting conversations at four in the morning, his mind racing with ideas. 'He'd start talking to me. I had to tell him, "Just go to sleep!" He always wanted to save money, so I'd organize for him to go to a race and he'd take the train. I said, "It ain't your money, don't worry about it." But he'd take the bike on the train. And then puncture on the way to the start. So he'd phone up, asking how to get to the track.

'Before his hour record, I said to him, "Are you going to have a drink? Have you thought about hydration?" "Good point," he said. And he got a big bottle of water and he drunk the whole fucking lot. He's got one-point-something litres of water inside him. And off he went.

'That gets you folklore status and all that,' Haines concludes, 'but in my book, it makes you a prat.'

Even now, in his sixties, Haines, the former champion cycle speedway racer, is compact and wiry. He grew up in the East End, failed his eleven-plus, and ducked out of school, starting a car cleaning round instead. He began pulling his mates out of school to do the round for him so he could go out training for cycle speedway. He was national junior champion at sixteen, with his father managing and training him. One day he got home to see that his father had put up a poster of one of his keenest rivals. 'It stays there until you've beaten him,' he said. Haines sat in the living room watching the television, doing bicep curls with a dumb-bell. He wouldn't stop until he'd done a thousand. Then he did 1,500 with his left arm because it was weaker. 'So I beat the geezer on the poster. Came back the next day, and there was another poster there, the next bloke above me in the averages. I worked until I had an unbeaten average. I was obsessive.'

At inter-club competitions, riders would introduce them-selves to Haines and he'd turn his back. No socializing, no talking, no acknowledging rivals, until after he'd beaten them. Then he'd buy them a drink in the clubhouse.

Haines talked a local carpet shop into sponsoring him for £2,800 a year. Meanwhile, he started up his own industrial cleaning company. By the time he sold it he had 250 employees and was turning over five million pounds a year. Among many others, his company cleaned for Richard Branson and Alan Sugar. He shows me Sugar's number on speed dial on his mobile phone.

As cycle speedway dwindled in popularity in the 1980s, Haines discovered road cycling, specifically tandem time trialling. He set five competition records for 10 miles between 1979 and 1989, plus one more in 1998, the 30-mile record, with

Sean Yates. Haines liked the camaraderie of cycling, but he didn't fit in with any of the local teams, so he sponsored a club, the Leo Road Club, called it Fresh Start-Team Clean (after his cleaning company), and pulled in riders he liked the look of, and his mates. Sean Yates was there, and Haines started backing Obree in 1993.

They made an odd couple, but Obree had the cycling ability and the ambition to break the hour record, and Haines had the money and contacts to organize it. Haines also had the instinctive understanding of the showman and the gift of the gab. So they needed each other, but their characters were incompatible. Obree was obsessive and flaky, given to day-dreaming, while Haines was a straight-talking wheeler-dealer. Everything Obree did seems to have got Haines's back up. They would have made a good sitcom.

Obree was so short of cash when they were discussing arrangements that he had to tell Haines to call the payphone at the end of his street at a certain time, so he could go and answer it. 'He was poverty-stricken,' Haines recalls. 'I paid off the arrears on his mortgage, and got him some windows, because his house had no windows. He said it was "spartan".' Obree also used to go and stay in Haines's old house in Leigh-on-Sea, Essex. Three times a week he'd get on the turbo trainer on the patio in the garden, and do one hour on it – 30 miles. He was training for the hour record, so his training sessions lasted an hour.

Obree was under no illusions: going for Moser's hour record on an indoor track would be expensive. Britain had no indoor velodromes at that time, so it would necessitate a trip abroad. Obree realized that to attract backing for a world record attempt he would first have to break his own British record, to show that he was serious. He'd looked at the Good Friday track meeting at London's Herne Hill as a possibility, but it was held in April and his form wasn't yet at the point where he could be confident of setting a significantly better mark. He was lucky, however. The meeting was rained off, and postponed to the end of May, which was enough time to get into good shape.

In the huge, shallow bowl of Herne Hill, the venue for the 1948 Olympic cycling track events, Obree made his attempt on a cool, breezy Saturday afternoon. For many of the spectators it was their first encounter with Obree's tuck position, and they were a hard crowd: as he rolled away from the start, the reaction was muted. The track at Herne Hill is 457 metres long, much bigger than the tighter circuits at Leicester and the European indoor velodromes, and the atmosphere, fittingly for its location in gentrified south London, remained more polite than raucous, any applause and cheers quickly dissipating into the afternoon air.

Haines told the few members of the press at the meeting that Obree's target was not just his 46-kilometre British record, but ultimately the 51.151 kilometres of Moser himself, the reaction to which was one of affronted scepticism. 'The cheek of the man,' wrote *Cycling Weekly*, half in jest.

But as Obree built momentum and settled into his rhythm, the crowd and the press started to realize that they were watching something special. He beat his 10-kilometre record by 46 seconds, and his 20-kilometre record by over a minute and a half. The pitch of the race announcer's voice began to rise. At halfway, Obree was behind Moser's world record, but he was maintaining an average similar to Eddy Merckx's distance. A rising breeze pushed against him every time he entered the back straight, but he visibly accelerated round into the home straight as the wind got behind him. Even spitting rain couldn't put him off, and in spite of the fact that Obree slowed in the third quarter, a strong finish gave him a new British record of 49.383 kilometres – almost 3 kilometres further than his previous best, and only 50 metres short of Merckx's record, which had been set at altitude.

*

The same weekend, Chris Boardman set a new national 25-mile record, recording 45.57 at an event organized by the Oxford University Cycling Club. With the national 25-mile championship being held in Cornwall the following weekend, and both riders participating, interest in the rivalry suddenly became sky-high again. Boardman even said in an interview that he felt Obree's hour record ride was a more impressive exploit than his extraordinary 25.

The records show that Chris Boardman won the 1993 national 25-mile title by 10 seconds. A tight head-to-head battle resulted in a winning time of 48.45 for Boardman and 48.55 for Obree. Third-placed Paul Jennings, an international cyclist, was over three minutes behind.

Contemporary reports describe a mechanical problem Obree experienced before the halfway mark. At that point he was 24 seconds up on Boardman according to Haines, in which case the unscheduled stop cost him a minute, because at the halfway mark Boardman led by 34 seconds. Obree could only claw back 24 of those in the 12.5 miles back to the finish.

The front wheel had been touching the forks, Obree explained at the finish. He was using customized wheels which would normally have twenty-four spokes, but he'd done his trick of taking out half of them and filling in the holes in the rims with tape. 'You could see his wheels distorting when he pedalled,' says Ed Hood, of Obree's bike. 'As he rode past, you could hear the tyre just swishing against the frame, every pedal stroke.'

The explanation Obree offered was a plausible one, but what he had actually suffered from was an irrational crisis of confidence. Believing himself to be going badly, he'd pulled up and invented the problem in order to give himself an excuse. By the time he realized he'd actually been well ahead of Boardman when he stopped, it was too late.

He was also riding the wrong bike. On the rolling Cornish roads, he should have had gears; instead, he was riding a fixed-wheel model with only one gear, and he'd been having to work too hard up the hills, then pedalling too fast down the other side.

There had been a problem with the geared bike when Haines and his mechanic Alan Rochford gave it a once-over on the morning of the race. 'We got up double early, five o'clock,' Haines recalls. 'The gears didn't work on Graeme's bike, so we needed to adjust them. Alan put his allen key into the rear changer, and it just came off in his hand.' A welding job previously done by Obree had come unstuck. Haines thought it was the Scot's fault, and told him so. 'He came down and said, "What's happened here?" I said, "It's come off because of the way you welded it, you dopey prat." He just went, "Oh dear. Fixed gear it is, then."

'I was amazed he rode a forty-nine on that course with one gear. But this is why he endears himself to people. If Boardman had lost because of a mechanical, he'd be looking for a gun. Obree just came downstairs for breakfast the next morning, and said, "I think I've had a nightmare. Tell me it's wrong. I dreamt I lost the national 25 by ten seconds to Chris Boardman. It's not true, is it?" I said, "Nah, it was twelve seconds." He said, "Ah, thank God. What's for breakfast?"'

No story better illustrates the gulf between the way Obree portrayed himself to the world, and the way he really felt. He took the blow of having his bike broken on the morning of the event with equanimity, even indifference, then made light of the fact he'd lost the race by 10 seconds, after bad luck, or bad judgement, had cost him a significantly larger amount of time. Inside, he was consumed with self-loathing and low self-esteem, first about having felt that he wasn't riding well, and second for having faked the mechanical that cost him the race.

It's hard to believe that nobody saw the mask slip, but Obree was so good at disguising his true feelings that everybody thought he was a harmless, ingenious eccentric. Universally, of all the people I asked, including many who'd spent many months, even years, working closely with Obree, not a single one had the slightest inkling of the mental illness that was blighting his life.

It was at this time that Obree started threatening to park his tanks on Boardman's lawn. Boardman had announced some months previously that he would be making an attempt on Moser's hour record. Now Obree, emboldened by his British record, and by his physical superiority over Boardman in the national 25-mile championship, wanted in. He made an appeal for a backer for his bid, then set off warning bells in the Boardman camp, themselves highly advanced into their own hour bid, by telling the press that he was aiming to go for the record the week before Boardman. Haines even thought out loud that Obree could join the Boardman bid – have a go at the record directly after the Englishman.

Boardman was understandably peeved at this announcement. 'Go and make something up for yourself,' he comments, looking back. Chris Boardman had controlled the controllables, done the planning and executed his training. Then Graeme Obree lobbed a huge, unpredictable variable into the calm order of Boardman's attempt. And it was the biggest variable of all: if Obree was successful, Boardman and Keen wouldn't know what they were aiming for until it was too late to do anything about it. Suggesting doing it in Bordeaux, where Boardman had booked his attempt weeks before, was even more provocative.

Furthermore, hour record bids need the support of the national governing body. The BCF had been wholeheartedly behind Boardman's bid, but when Obree achieved his British hour record it was impossible for them to ignore him, and in the spirit of fairness, they put their weight behind his bid too. Boardman felt they should wait until his attempt was over before supporting a rival's. 'The BCF discussed Obree's bid at a meeting of the Racing Committee and had seen enough evidence to know it was a serious attempt,' Doug Dailey said. It was decided the president of the federation, Ian Emmerson, and Dailey would go to support and witness the ride.

The relationship between Boardman and Obree had been civil, because neither was particularly confrontational, and with a few exceptions Obree hadn't been a consistent rival to Boardman. But the British hour record and 25-mile time trial championship negatively affected Boardman. He let it all out in his regular column in *Cycle Sport* magazine, the new publication that had just hit the shelves the month before the official hour bids. 'I can see the mistakes he is making and it makes me cringe,' wrote Boardman. 'I don't think he can get the record. He's trying hard to get it right but he hasn't really got his feet on the ground. He's a better rider than before, but he desperately needs to make some money – the problem is, who's going to give money when he insists on riding that hobby horse?' Obree's best bet, Boardman continued, would be to carry on time trialling and get a good job.

The pair retreated from the national 25-mile championship, and went off to finish their preparations for the hour rides.

Meanwhile, Mike Burrows, having been frozen out by Lotus, approached Haines to see if he could help Obree. He offered to make the replica of Obree's bike that was necessary for the bid. A colleague would build the frame while Burrows added a layer of carbon fibre to make it aerodynamic. By Burrows' calculations, it was more aerodynamic than Old Faithful, although he didn't manage to replicate the narrowness of Obree's bottom bracket. Obree's was 68 millimetres; the best Burrows could do was 70.

While Burrows was designing the bike, Haines called Richard Hemington, the managing director of Specialized, who had agreed to provide wheels for the bid, and promised a good bonus if he broke the record. Burrows would need to fit the wheels to the monoblade fork he was attaching to the bike, which would necessitate changing the bearings and fittings in the wheel. Haines recalls how Burrows went about refitting them. 'Richard turned up in his BMW, with a nice suit on. Mike asked him, "Have you got the wheels?"' Burrows took one wheel from Hemington and proceeded to saw it in half, to the managing director's horror. 'That's twelve hundred pounds,' he gasped, while Burrows looked inside to examine the structure. 'I needed to look for myself,' Burrows said, before working on the second wheel so that it attached to the monoblade.

The second bike was soon ready for the bid.

On 17 June 1993, Kelvin Trott, the manager of a recruitment consultancy that specialized in placing accountants, picked up his copy of *Cycling Weekly* as usual. Trott was a former junior time triallist with the Hounslow and District Wheelers who'd long since given up ambitions of racing but who had grown fascinated with following the times recorded by the country's best time triallists. His own name had once appeared in the time trial results at the back of the magazine, in 1973 when he'd come in the top thirty of the junior Best All-Rounder competition – a fact his wife had recently become aware of after he found the entire year's worth of *Cycling* magazines on eBay and bought the lot, in order to show her. 'You never forget your best time as a time triallist,' he says. '23.36 was mine [for 10 miles]. That was before aero bars!'

He went straight to *Cycling Weekly*'s report of the national 25-mile championship. He was excited to read about the close race between Boardman and Obree – he'd followed their results for years. Then he read the appeal by Obree and Haines for backing for his hour record bid. On a whim, he picked up the phone.

Kelvin Trott is still in the recruitment business. We meet in a plush office in St James's Square on a dark and chilly London evening. Our conversation is interrupted occasionally by the ringing of his mobile phone; by the time we are done, one more of his clients has been placed with a firm, starting in January, and the voice on the other end of the phone sounds happy as Trott congratulates him. He's a garrulous and enthusiastic man with laughter lines tracing narrow parabolas away from his eyes. 'Never heard of him,' he'd joked when the receptionist indicated to me that this was the man I'd come to talk to.

Kelvin's got something to show me. He brings out a piece of triangular metal tubing which has been crudely mounted on a wooden base. It's screwed in from the bottom with a bolt sunk in a hole that looks like it's been hacked out with a blunt chisel. These are Graeme Obree's handlebars. Not from Old Faithful, but an earlier version, one of the rough and ready black bikes he'd beaten into shape and ridden in the late 1980s and early 1990s. They're more developed than the simple upturned drop handlebars he started out on, but really they just look like a set of dark-coloured welded metal tubes. Obree knocked it together with the base and presented it to Trott as a trophy after he took the hour record.

Trott is that rarest of beasts, a sponsor who demands nothing in return except the satisfaction of having contributed. His firm's name, Choice Accountancy, was associated with the bid, but there was no marketing strategy, no calculation of how much exposure had been achieved, and no return on investment. He just saw that Obree needed money for his hour record, and had a bit of spare cash to put into it.

He'd never expected actually to sponsor Obree. When he

contacted Haines, he assumed that major sponsors would already have put in the big money, and that all he would be doing was helping out a bit more. But Choice Accountancy turned out to be the main backers. Haines put money behind the bid as well. He had attracted offers of equipment, but what the bid lacked was the money to fly UCI officials, BCF officials, medical staff and helpers to wherever the bid was going to take place and put them up in hotels. Trott ended up putting about £10,000 in – the deal was done on a handshake after a short conversation at his office in Surrey.

Meanwhile, in a piece of timing that must have left Boardman feeling like Julius Caesar at the Theatre of Pompey, it emerged that he had been left short of backers for his bid and that he would have to bear some of the costs himself. At this point, Obree was still angling for a slot at the Bordeaux velodrome Boardman had booked too, after Vienna, Haines's and his first choice, told them they were full.

Obree's confidence was sky-high. Haines had entered him for the national 50-mile championship on the Sunday three weeks before the hour bid, and also a 10-mile time trial the day before, near Gravesend. Trott came along to watch, and in an act of seigneurial benevolence put up a prize of £1,000 for anybody who could beat the national record in the event, which stood at 18.34. 'It was stupid, really,' he says now. 'We had an idea Graeme could do it, but if six people had broken the record, we'd have been stuffed.'

Luckily for Trott, it was blowing a gale at the race – not ideal conditions for record-breaking. Haines asked Obree if he was going to go for the record, but the Scot wasn't optimistic. 'I'll roll round and do a nineteen,' he said.

'See that guy there?' Haines responded, pointing at Trott. 'If you break the record, he'll give you a thousand pounds.'

Eighteen minutes and 27 seconds later, Obree was £1,000

richer. Trott remembers being in the car behind Obree as he rode down a drag with the wind behind him, and estimating that the Scot was riding at somewhere between 50 and 60 miles per hour.

The next day, Obree took part in the national 50-mile time trial championship and pulverized the opposition, also breaking the national record for the event, one that had stood for ten years. It took him 1.39.01 to cover the 50 miles – an average speed of 30.3 miles per hour. He'd only have to average 31.8 miles per hour on an indoor track, for less time, and the hour record would be his. Obree had broken two national records in two days – his form was rapidly approaching its zenith.

The record attempt was to take place on Friday, 16 July. Two and a half weeks before that, Bordeaux finally rejected Obree's request for track time, but a location was found when the Norwegian Cycling Federation offered the temporary velodrome in Hamar, 130 kilometres north of Oslo. It was the venue chosen for that year's world championship, in August; they hadn't finished building it yet, but the track was rideable. The velodrome was a temporary structure: after hosting the world championship, the spectacular arched building based on the underside of a Viking ship would be converted to its planned use – a speed-skating rink. It wasn't the best choice. It had tighter banking than most modern tracks, and longer straights. Doug Dailey felt that on tracks with longer banking sections, the slingshot effect through the bends would be better. But it would have to do.

Obree's form may have been at an all-time high, but two things hadn't changed: his financial situation, and his capacity to wind up Vic Haines. A fortnight before the hour record bid, Obree accepted an invitation to go and ride in a penny farthing exhibition race in Market Harborough, near Leicester. 'I did it for a couple of hundred quid because I was broke. I almost went right over the bars, spent all that time travelling, and missed the training.' It wasn't ideal preparation for an attempt to break a long-standing world record. Haines flew off the handle when he found out. 'I'd put all my money behind him to break Moser's hour record, and he was sitting up, as high as the ceiling, on a penny farthing bike. It drove me nuts.'

Ten days before the bid, Obree went on a short visit to Hamar with Haines and a *Cycling Weekly* journalist, David Taylor, for a reconnaissance of the track. The plan was to train on the track, get used to the conditions and the banking of the velodrome, and fine-tune Obree's form. With the builders still in there finishing it off, Obree and his entourage were permitted to use the track only for an hour a day. Obree did laps while builders dropped nails which rolled on to the track and down the banking. The work was almost finished though, so each day they were there they spent more and more time on the track.

On the Thursday he did a dress rehearsal – an unofficial record attempt. Obree would ride the full hour, with David Taylor counting off the laps and recording them on a sheet of paper while Haines did the timing. In front of two Norwegian journalists, two members of Norway's female cycling team, Haines and Taylor, Obree tapped out the laps – 16, 17 seconds each.

After one hour, to a polite round of applause, Obree's distance was calculated: 51.525 kilometres – 374 metres further than Moser had ridden in Mexico City nine years earlier. All Obree had to do now was go home and keep his form on the boil for a week, then come back to Hamar. He was ready.

10

Scousers Abroad

'Please, no more Boardman stories,' wrote a correspondent to *Cycling Weekly*'s letters page in the spring of 1993.

In the absence of any other significant international success by British cyclists, the magazine had focused quite heavily on Chris Boardman since the run-up to Barcelona. In fact even before that he had been a regular cover star, and all of his time trial and road race successes were featured in the news pages. As early as 1991 irritated correspondents were complaining: '*Cycling Weekly* has its favourites who receive more than their fair share of attention. However, nothing compares with the current Chris Boardman phenomena [sic] with your periodical becoming something of a fan club magazine.'

Boardman wasn't the first cyclist to win races and appear in *Cycling Weekly*, but there was something different, both in the coverage and the perception of him. He was unusual in that he was multi-talented, winning time trials, road races and track races, all at a national or international level, yet there seemed to be a curious lack of ambition. The last rider to be able to do what Boardman did was Sean Yates, but as soon as Yates got to the level of the best riders in Britain he went to France to start on the bottom rung of international amateur road cycling. Boardman hadn't taken that step, so he continued to hang around the British scene, thrashing everybody at will and providing column inches for the cycling press. The effect of this, combined with a personality that occasionally came across as robotic, was to divide opinion.

British cycling at this time was deeply parochial, even after Boardman's Olympic success. The domestic professional road-racing scene was more or less cut off from the European professional circuit, and, it was acknowledged, was at a much lower level. Time trialling was a law unto itself – no other country had such an extensive calendar of individual racing, and the majority of club cyclists were obsessed with times and set distances. Change, if it came at all, was glacial, and the sport was run by a hierarchy of committees. *Cycling Weekly* was the only magazine covering the domestic sport.

It was into this world, in 1991, that Andy Sutcliffe arrived when he became editor of the magazine. 'Cycling was a drab, grey sport run by drab, grey people,' he says. *Cycling Weekly*'s pages had been dominated by time trialling for years, but the new editor's heroes weren't Alf Engers, Dave Lloyd and Darryl Webster but Eddy Merckx, Bernard Hinault and Freddy Maertens – the stars of the Tour de France and the Classics. International cycling was becoming more popular thanks to Greg LeMond's Tour de France wins in the late 1980s, which coincided with Channel Four showing the race in a daily evening highlights programme. Sutcliffe sensed that for the sport to grow in popularity in the United Kingdom it needed to look outwards, not inwards.

With his growing international profile, Boardman was the vehicle Sutcliffe attached the magazine to in an effort to pull the sport away from its conservative roots. 'Chris appeared, and he was obviously intelligent, as was Peter Keen. His ambitions were interesting, his approach was interesting, and he was very easy to deal with. You didn't have to be Einstein to work out that if Chris Boardman or Graeme Obree did something successful, we would sell more magazines, and more people would get into cycling. With Chris and Obree, you had two people with the same sort of talent going for the same things. It gave us something to report on.'

When Boardman announced at the end of 1992 that he was preparing for an attack on the hour record the following summer, Sutcliffe was sceptical but supportive. 'I could see a career path that involved winning pursuit titles, being the biggest fish in domestic British cycling and maybe turning professional, even becoming an international pro. I didn't see the hour record as an option at that point because Moser's record was still untouchable. It was like Bob Beamon's world long jump record. Selfishly, I'd have wanted him just to turn pro, ride abroad and win prologues, so I could put a yellow jersey on the front of the magazine. The hour record seemed crazy, but I knew him and Keen well enough by then, and I had learned not to underestimate them. The cycling establishment was saying, "Don't go for the hour record." But Boardman and Keen were saying, "Our testing has shown it's possible, and that is what we're going to do." Then I realized the hour record is actually incredibly exciting. Iconic. It's beyond cycling, like the Tour de France.'

For Boardman, the hour record was one of a few options that had presented themselves after Barcelona, and the most logical. He was offered a professional contract for 1993 by one of the domestic British teams, but it looked too much like a dead end. There were around thirty registered professional road racers in the country in 1992. 'It doesn't mean anything to say you are the best pro in Britain,' he said. If he'd put himself on the market he would probably have been able to find a contract with an international team, but he would have been employed as a domestique, a team rider, rather than a team leader, with a correspondingly low salary.

Boardman's first instinct was to focus on the world amateur pursuit championship. He'd beaten the reigning world champion in Barcelona, so there was no reason why he couldn't go and win the title the next year. He also had one eye on the next Olympic Games. But his new manager Harry Middleton, a long-time acquaintance of Boardman's parents, was keener on the hour. He pointed out to Boardman that very few people would be able to name the last five world pursuit champions, but everybody in cycling knew who held the hour record.

The hour record had been on Peter Keen's radar for a few years. He'd done some rough back-of-a-beer-mat calculations in 1990 and thought that while it wasn't currently possible, it was an achievable target in the future. Keen, more as an academic exercise than a realistic one, worked out a graph which plotted Boardman's speed over a certain distance against what would be needed for him to break Moser's record. He was close enough at that point that they didn't immediately bin the idea, but far enough off that they filed the graph away and focused on achievable targets, such as winning an Olympic gold medal.

Towards the end of 1992, the idea came up again. 'We'd focused on the Olympic Games because it was the biggest thing for an amateur, and when it was done, we asked ourselves, "What are we going to do next?"' Boardman says. 'Pete, being Pete, did some quick calculations and said, "You know, we're not a million miles away."'

Boardman travelled down to Brighton to meet with Keen, and they sat in a lecture room while Keen wrote equations and figures on the blackboard that showed how Boardman was going to beat Moser's record. The magic figure, Keen reckoned, was 430 watts. If Boardman averaged that power output for sixty minutes then the record would be his. The problem was, up to that point, he hadn't even been able to hold 400 watts for ten minutes.

Immediately following his gold medal in the Olympics, Boardman had enjoyed a lap of honour at the 1992 national track championship, then duly won the amateur individual pursuit at a canter in front of large crowds. He also broke the world 5-kilometre record with a time of 5.38 – 9 seconds faster than the previous mark. As a comparison, the professional pursuit event, also held over 5 kilometres, had been won in a time of 6.05. There was no doubt at all who the best track rider in the country was.

The interesting thing about these two rides was that Boardman used the LotusSport bike for the 5-kilometre record, but his Ribble track bike for the pursuit. The tension between him, Lotus and Ribble was still not resolved. He got away with riding the Olympic bike for the record by wearing his Great Britain strip rather than his club colours.

And that was more or less it for Boardman's racing schedule in 1992. He launched a half-hearted and belated PR campaign for the BBC Sports Personality of the Year award, but the British public showed themselves not yet ready to give the award to a cyclist for the first time since Tom Simpson in 1965 and he didn't make the top three. A survey commissioned by Raleigh Cycles after the Olympics had shown that four out of five people remembered the LotusSport bike winning the individual pursuit, while only one out of five remembered the man riding it. Perhaps the bike would have had a better chance against the eventual winner, F1 driver Nigel Mansell.

One of the reasons why Boardman turned down the

opportunity to race with a domestic professional team for 1993 was that he wanted to form his own team, bringing in his closest cycling friends to ride for and manage it, so he diverted one of his sponsorship endorsements into the first team he'd ridden for as a thirteen-year-old, the North Wirral Velo Club. He was joined by Great Britain team-mates Simon Lillistone and Matt Illingworth and a handful of others, coached by Peter Keen and managed by Harry Middleton.

Through early 1993, Boardman and his North Wirral Velo team-mates were dominant, winning time trials and road races and hogging the news pages of *Cycling Weekly*. A measure of how far Boardman had progressed came in the Tour of Lancashire, the race he'd led in 1990 before the professionals outrode him, then narrowly won in 1991, just holding off the professional challenge. In both these rides Boardman had gone into the race lead after the uphill time trial – his territory. In the 1993 event, Boardman invaded the territory of his road-racing rivals, going clear with Banana-Falcon rider Brian Smith on the hilly second stage to Blackburn. Smith was a hardened professional, but Boardman simply rode him off his wheel in the final 4 miles. A ten-man chase group managed to limit their losses to 90 seconds, but the bunch was six minutes behind. Boardman duly won the uphill time trial, then successfully defended his lead, even in the face of the whole race trying to gang up on him on the final stage.

Matt Illingworth's recollection of the last day is that while the rest of the team were tired, the race leader was more than capable of matching his rivals. 'Chris rode eighty miles on the front on a really hard day,' he says. In fact, the only setback in the entire week was when thieves put a brick through the window of Boardman's car overnight and took 120 cans of Thwaites beer which he'd won from one of the race sponsors.

However, the priority was the hour record. Two weeks after

the Tour of Lancashire, Boardman and his closest advisers piled bikes and luggage into an old Nissan Patrol van and drove from Merseyside to the car ferry terminal at Portsmouth, crossed the channel to Ouistreham, then continued on to the Bordeaux velodrome to do some testing for the bid.

As well as setting up North Wirral Velo, through late 1992 and into 1993 Boardman had been building his inner circle, the small, tight-knit, loyal group of helpers who guided his career. Keen had been there since the late 1980s, Boardman's wife Sally was involved in a lot of his career discussions and was an honorary member, and there was also Harry Middleton. Boardman also brought Pete Woodworth, an old North Wirral Velo clubmate, into the fold.

Woodworth was variously described as Boardman's agent, his logistics officer and his computer expert. In truth, he played all three roles. He was a quiet, efficient fixer who did Boardman's contract negotiations, logged the rider's training efforts into a computer programme he'd written himself, and generally solved problems so that Boardman didn't have to. It was Woodworth who put forward the idea of going for the hour record in Bordeaux the day the Tour de France had a stage finish within a stone's throw of the velodrome. Without that suggestion, Boardman's subsequent career might have turned out entirely differently.

Woodworth is still living in Hoylake, where we meet for a coffee in a smart but sparsely patronized café on the main street, amid a modest and tatty parade of shops. He's affable, genial and polite, in a slightly formal way, and I can see why Boardman liked having him around: he exudes avuncular calmness. Boardman may have been outwardly an unexcitable individual, but he could get quietly very stressed out and anxious. In those situations he didn't need or want someone to tell him to pull himself together, he needed someone who would see solutions, not problems, and sort them out without panicking.

In the 1970s, Woodworth worked at Asda. It was a time of expansion for the company, and he was part of the team that opened up new stores, at the rate of almost one a week. He became adept at what he describes as 'getting stuff done' – overcoming the logistical and practical issues associated with getting new operations up and running. In his early thirties he took a sabbatical to go and study computer science, just as the early 1980s computer boom was starting. He never went back to Asda, starting his own business consultancy instead. He'd tried to help Boardman get sponsorship before the Olympic Games, putting together a marketing package to send to local companies, but the early 1990s recession had really kicked in and nobody was interested. That was when Boardman introduced him to Peter Keen, and he wrote some software for monitoring training. It was pretty basic, Woodworth tells me, but he started getting asked along to training trips to help assess equipment and run the software, and before long he was indispensable, although he still insists that 'anybody could have done it'.

Woodworth accompanied Boardman, Keen and Middleton to Bordeaux. The journey was a nightmare – they had a tyre blow-out on the way – but when they arrived they were impressed with the facility. While Boardman and Keen tried out five different bikes, Woodworth kept his ear to the ground, picking up information and talking to people he met in the velodrome. That's when one of them told him that the Tour de France was going to have a stage finish in Bordeaux that year. At that point, no venue had been decided for the hour record bid. Stuttgart had been mentioned as a possibility, as well as Colorado Springs, to take advantage of the altitude. Colorado might even have been the first choice, except that the expense of getting there, acclimatizing and doing the ride was beyond Boardman's budget. Woodworth understood fully that Boardman was doing the hour record to broaden his own marketability in the cycling world, even if he was still talking down the prospects of a professional career. What could inflate his value more than a successful attempt in front of the journalists and teams of the most important bike race in the world? 'After the first session, we went and had a meal,' Woodworth recalls. 'I asked Pete and Chris why they were doing this. If the reason was to be a showcase for Chris, why not do it properly?'

Woodworth knew that Bordeaux was unlikely to be an important stage of the Tour. It was flat country, which usually ended in a sprint, and in 1993 it was only a couple of days before the end of the race in Paris, so unlikely to affect the general classification. The journalists would have little to write about at the Tour, which would give Boardman a good chance to steal the headlines. The risk was that Boardman would get only the one opportunity, on Friday, 23 July, to get it right, and he'd have to do so in the full glare of the international sporting media. For someone who suffered badly from nerves and pressure, this was a big challenge.

On the track, Boardman and Keen continued to test the bikes. Lotus had pointedly not supplied them with a model. Boardman described the atmosphere at discussions between him and the Lotus management team about using one of their bikes for the hour as 'hostile', although he was at pains to praise the Lotus engineers with whom he had worked. 'One of them asked me if I really believed I could get the hour record without the bike.' Middleton knew that Halfords had bought one of the handful of Lotus bikes that had been put up for sale so he approached them to borrow one instead. Two days after they had given the go-ahead, they changed their mind.

Boardman rode laps at certain speeds on each bike while

Keen and Woodworth logged his pulse, monitored his fatigue, and tried to work out which one was the best. They settled on a Corima, a French model.

Confidence was high. They had a venue and a bike, and Boardman was coming into some excellent form. His new British record of 45.57 over 25 miles, set at an average speed of 52.5 kilometres per hour on the same weekend as Obree's British hour record at Herne Hill velodrome, would not be beaten for another sixteen years. For the hour, he'd have to hold that speed longer, but riding in a velodrome is generally faster than riding outside on an out-and-back course, especially since it had been raining and Boardman had had to ease off on some of the corners. Boardman's team-mate Simon Lillistone was riding up the finishing straight in Oxfordshire, wondering why the crowd were giving him so much applause and encouragement, before realizing that they were actually cheering for Boardman, who'd started five minutes behind him.

Form is the holy grail of competitive cycling. It's not quite the same thing as physical fitness, although that is a significant part of it. It's a unique confluence of perfect physical and mental health, plus some variables that can be so unpredictable that getting them right is more a matter of luck than design. A rider could follow identical training schedules over a period of months, a year apart, yet enjoy great form one year and poor form the next. For Boardman and Keen, the search for top form, and the challenge of keeping it, was the most important and interesting aspect of their careers. They approached the conundrum with the meticulousness of scientists, measuring everything that could be quantified, with the sole aim of getting Boardman to a particular race in peak condition.

At the Oxford University Cycling Club 25, Boardman probably hit top form. But by the time of the national championship one week later, it had slipped. For his record ride,

Boardman's pulse had stayed above 180 for the whole distance, but he couldn't hold that effort just eight days later. 'I couldn't get my pulse above 174,' he reflected at the end of the race. 'I don't know what is wrong.' He'd still beaten Obree, but only just.

Then, at the end of June, on the eve of a second trip to Bordeaux, Boardman's financial backing fell through. With only a month to go until the record attempt, and announcements having been made, it was too late to postpone, so he had to front the costs himself. With the Bordeaux track costing £1,000 per day for training, it was becoming less a shop window for himself than a spin of the roulette wheel. And with Obree having now announced his own bid, a week ahead of Boardman, the pressure was mounting on all sides. 'It could be seen as quite bad sportsmanship,' said Boardman of Obree's decision. 'It's a bit of a bummer to put in so much effort and preparation and then have someone come along and flick you. It's irritating that he could rain on my parade by stealing the record before me.' The cracks were beginning to show.

During the June trip to Bordeaux, just three weeks before the attempt, Boardman held things together on the track, recording an unofficial beating of Francesco Moser's 10-kilometre world record, by 22 seconds. But off the track, the Boardman camp got a triple whammy of bad news. 'It was a disastrous trip,' Woodworth recalls. 'On the third day we were there, we were effectively told that the French Cycling Federation [FFC] weren't going to allow the bid, that the owners of the velodrome weren't going to allow us in there again, and the Tour de France were really annoyed that he was going to do it on that day.'

Woodworth and Middleton were summoned to a meeting while they sent Boardman home on a plane. They sat on one side of a table, and eighteen people, including representatives of the velodrome management company, their lawyers, and people from the Société du Tour de France and the FFC, sat on the other. The Société were objecting because it was going to clash with the Tour. This didn't chime with something Boardman had said a couple of weeks previously, that they had been in touch with the organizers of the Tour and that the race's director Jean-Marie Leblanc was 'over the moon, and all for it'.

Woodworth had found out that while the velodrome was owned and built by Bordeaux council, it was run by the same umbrella company that managed the Bercy velodrome in Paris, and owned the Tour de France. Bercy was a thriving, busy venue, but Bordeaux was marginalized, and Woodworth inferred that the company preferred events to happen in Bercy rather than elsewhere. But he'd also heard from a local journalist that there was an ongoing conflict between Bordeaux council and the velodrome managers because the venue was being under-used. The council was getting criticism from the local media because it had built a white elephant, and then signed over the running of it to a company that wasn't putting on events there. Woodworth says that in three visits to the velodrome, they never saw anybody else using it.

He managed to persuade all the parties present in the meeting that the bid would be in everybody's best interests, using his knowledge of the tension between Bordeaux council and the venue managers as leverage.

At least the velodrome had also rejected Obree's bid to break the record at the track the week before Boardman. The national track championship was taking place there, and the clash meant Obree had to look elsewhere for a venue.

In mid-July, Boardman did his final big test before the actual record – an hour-long ride on a static bike at Keen's lab in Eastbourne, during which he averaged 410 watts. It was less power than they needed according to their original calculations, but their opinion now was that it was enough.

Boardman flew with Woodworth to Bordeaux, while Keen drove down with Boardman's North Wirral Velo team-mate Paul Jennings in a truck belonging to, of all people, Mick Jagger. The Rolling Stones' manager, Alan Dunn, was a keen cyclist and cycling fan who'd spent a season racing in France with Boardman's manager Harry Middleton, and he'd agreed to loan them the transport to get the bikes and equipment to Bordeaux. There was a moment of levity when Keen was stopped at customs at Dover and asked who the van belonged to.

At this point, the bid looked less organized and was operating on a shoestring far tighter than Graeme Obree's. 'We stayed in university accommodation, crappy student halls in Bordeaux,' says Andy Sutcliffe, who'd joined the bid to cover it for *Cycling Weekly*. 'They had Jagger's credit card and truck, and I realized they had no money. They were basically Scousers abroad. They couldn't speak French, so they were only eating in places where there were pictures of the food – because they could point at it – and eating the *plat du jour* for eight francs. I realized that for all my talk after he won the gold medal about his life changing, well, it hadn't, had it?'

The only saving grace was that Boardman's form was starting to come round again. As Obree launched his bid for stardom, Boardman had one week until the biggest test of his career.

11

Three Hours

French sports writers who cover cycling have a sentimental, nostalgic, romantic outlook on the sport. This is partly a function of the history of the Tour de France: when newspapers were the sole chroniclers of the race, before the 1950s, the sheer scale of the challenge lent itself to Homeric prose and mythology. The Tour takes place in magnificent surroundings and features supreme efforts of endurance and willpower, so the reports were part epic poetry, part travelogue and part philosophy (and, probably, part fiction). Even when radio, then television, then the internet in turn supplanted the newspapers in prominence, the florid style was passed down generations of writers.

It was Pierre Ballester, a journalist from French sports daily *L'Equipe*, who gave the name 'Old Faithful' to Graeme Obree's bike. Ballester had been sent by his newspaper to search out a story in Norway after Adam Glasser, a British cycling journalist who got on well with Obree, had sent them a short piece giving them the scoop on the location of the Scot's hour record bid. The name seemed so apposite that Obree started using it as well.

The irony was that Old Faithful wasn't particularly old, having been completed only two months previously. And neither was Obree particularly faithful at first. Egged on by Vic Haines, he'd decided to use the Burrows bike for his attempt. Even Obree had been captivated by this new bike, saying that it made Old Faithful look like 'ironmongery'.

Haines had been busy putting together an entourage of journalists, photographers, mechanics, helpers and hangers-on for the hour bid, as well as the UCI officials, and for the BCF Doug Dailey and the president Ian Emmerson. The entire party was booked into the Best Western Hotel in Hamar. Ballester would be there for *L'Equipe*, and David Taylor for *Cycling Weekly*, along with the magazine's photographer Phil O'Connor.

O'Connor was in the tricky position of having done quite a lot of work chronicling the Boardman bid. He'd missed Obree's Herne Hill British hour record at the end of May because he'd been watching Boardman set his 25-mile record at the Oxford University event. 'I spent a lot of time with Chris and we got on quite well,' O'Connor says. 'I liked him and I used to go down to Eastbourne to do pictures of him training in the lab with Peter Keen. I heard Obree had done forty-nine kilometres at Herne Hill, and I thought, "Where did that come from?" I missed it because my heart was in following Chris, but I wanted to see both. It all happened really fast. I got a phone call from David Taylor, saying, "We've got a plane leaving, and you're on it."'

Before leaving for Hamar, O'Connor had been in Bordeaux where Boardman and his team were putting the finishing touches to their own preparations. 'Corima's bike got delivered and I got a few pictures of that. Then I said, "Right, bye, I'm off now, I've got to get a flight." They were probably thinking, "Yeah, you're going to fucking Norway, aren't you?" They weren't saying it, but I could see it.'

Confidence in the Obree camp was high, but Dailey was concerned, having had a look at the lap times and performance in the unofficial hour record that Obree had set the week before. 'Graeme had done the trial, and they gave me a printout with all the split times. I was looking to see how steady he was. It's very important – you have to lock on to the right pace, and then hold it. You didn't see fluctuations in speed in the hour record – that's the method you needed. I was looking at the kilometre times, and it all looked good. But right in the middle there was one kilometre which was seventeen or eighteen seconds faster than all the rest. They'd missed a bloody lap. All of a sudden I was worried, because they hadn't gone as far in the trial as they thought they had.'

Obree had beaten Moser's mark by 374 metres in the test. If they had missed a lap, the safety cushion would become only 124 metres, or half a lap. Less than 10 seconds, over an hour – a tiny margin.

In Hamar, the Burrows replica bike was put together on the eve of the bid. Late in the afternoon, the UCI officials approached Haines and informed them they wanted to look at the bikes. Haines was worried whether Old Faithful would pass muster – the UCI had a reputation for unyielding strictness regarding adherence to technical rules. He bluffed the officials into waiting an hour while he set things up. 'You're fine to look at the bikes, but we can't go up now,' he said to them. Lowering his voice conspiratorially, he explained, 'Graeme's resting. Come up in an hour.'

Haines went up to Obree's room, and gave him his instructions. 'Just lie on the bed,' he told him. 'Just say hello when they come in. I don't want you having a conversation with these people.' In another room, he got the Burrows bike out and put it up on the table.

When the UCI bike inspectors arrived they couldn't help but be impressed. Haines showed them the monoblade fork, and explained how it worked, then told them about the £200 tyres which had been glued on specially for the attempt. The lacquerwork looked beautiful. 'Would you like to meet Graeme?' Haines then asked. 'He's still resting, but I'm sure it will be fine.' The inspectors each put their heads round the door of Obree's room, and the Scot asked them how they were doing, from his position on the bed. Then Haines asked if they would like a glass of champagne. 'I got the champagne down them, and then they fucked off. Done.' They hadn't even seen Old Faithful.

Obree slept badly the night before the attempt. A noisy disco downstairs kept him awake until 3.30. Then Haines woke him up for media duties at seven, which meant he was occupied and unfocused through the morning. Haines spent the lead-up to the bid trying to psyche him up, not understanding that Obree didn't respond to external motivation. Obree's attitude to the ride was that if he succeeded, he would avoid what he described as emotional annihilation. Terror of failure had got him to the start line of his hour record bid, not a desire for self-improvement.

On the track, with Obree ready to go, in front of a coachload of cheering local schoolchildren who'd been bussed in to provide atmosphere, the starter inadvertently ratcheted up the pressure on him by reminding him of the magnitude of the record. 'Remember, this is Moser's hour record,' he said. Obree recalled that his thoughts on the start line were that he was committing sacrilege.

As Obree set off, Phil O'Connor remembers being disappointed that he wasn't going to be riding Old Faithful. 'Introducing that new bike was odd. When they got to the track and built it, that was the first I knew about that. It changed my perception of what it was going to be.' O'Connor had already sold Obree pictures to the national press. The dailies had cottoned on to the fact that there was a rider racing on a bike made from an old washing machine, and O'Connor was feeding them images. 'I thought he was going to ride the washing machine bike, and break the hour record on it. Suddenly he was riding this other bike and it took the shine off it. It's like he sold out.'

He needn't have worried. It soon became clear that Obree wasn't up to speed. The bike was wrong.

Obree and Haines had had a conversation shortly before going to Hamar in which Obree had stated his desire to push the record out of reach for any rivals. Haines thought this an extremely bad idea. He told Obree about the modus operandi of Sergei Bubka, the Ukrainian pole vaulter.

In 1993, Bubka was a three-time world champion (he'd win a fourth title later that year) and had won the gold medal at the Seoul Olympics in 1988. But he was well on his way to a rich retirement not because of the titles, but because he had made a career out of breaking the world record since first setting a new mark in 1984. Each time he broke it, athletics meet organizers and sponsors paid him generous bonuses, so rather than break the record once or twice and get one or two payments, he eventually set seventeen outdoor and eighteen indoor world records, generally by increments of a centimetre, pocketing a large cheque on every occasion. Haines envisaged Obree following a similar path. He wasn't good enough at road racing to make a career out of that, so the best option for him was to turn himself into an hour record specialist and track racer.

'If you put the record out of reach, you're going to break it once, we're going to get paid for it, and then you're finished,' Haines told him.

Despite this advice, Obree had persisted in his ambition to beat the record by as great a distance as possible. To this end, he had asked Burrows to put a bigger gear on the replica bike, a fifty-four-tooth chainring instead of a fifty-two, and to lower the handlebars so he could get a more aerodynamic position. The problem was not that the position wasn't comfortable, but that the handlebars weren't adjustable. (If Burrows had been there, he could have told them that all they needed to do was put the handlebars in a vice and bend them up.) Haines wanted Obree to ride the gear he was used to, not the new one.

With Obree in a slightly new position, one that he hadn't spent any time getting used to, his body was now failing to produce the power it was capable of in its usual posture. As he settled in to his attempt he lost ground incrementally on the schedule he'd set to beat Moser. 'I've never seen him struggle,' said Haines. 'He is bloody strong, and has got a big engine. All his power is there in his lungs, and he's very determined. But I could tell from the colour of his face that he wasn't going to do it.'

The numbers confirmed it. Obree was aiming for 52 kilometres – a healthy beating of the record. After 10 kilometres he was 2 seconds up on Moser's time, but as 15 and 20 kilometres came round he started to drop back. At the halfway point, Haines wrote 'More now' on the blackboard. Obree tried but failed to pick up the pace. At 40 kilometres he was a minute down on his schedule, and 26 seconds down on Moser – an impossible distance to close. He fought on, though, and when the UCI official Martin Bruin fired the pistol to signal the end of the hour, Obree had reached 50.690 kilometres – 461 metres short.

'It was obvious quite quickly that he wasn't going to get it,' says O'Connor. 'One thing I've learned from watching hour records is that an hour is a hell of a long time. Once you're off, you never get it back.'

Dailey felt Haines should have pulled him out. 'If you fall behind in an hour, you may as well stop. He wasn't on the pace, and you can't do a seated acceleration on those gears. If that had been Chris Boardman and Peter Keen, they'd have aborted it. Waste of time. But Graeme is Graeme, and Vic is Vic, and they had to do the full hour. Bloody hell, it was embarrassing. An hour record is an amazing thing when you get it, but such an anticlimax if you don't.'

Obree was devastated. The crushing sense of failure wasn't helped when a worker at the track, dressed as Mickey Mouse, misinterpreted the result as a success and marched over to give Obree a bunch of flowers in an excruciating presentation ceremony. Obree had broken the sea-level record, but the brutal logic of the hour record doesn't deal in degrees of success or failure. Obree had blown it.

From his position on the outside of the crowd, O'Connor noticed that intense conversations were taking place between Obree, Haines and Ken Farnes, another of the UCI commissaires. Obree was asking them if he could go again, that afternoon. He was convinced he could find an extra lap and a half. 'I told him, "You ain't doing nothing now. We'll go tomorrow,"' says Haines.

The realization had hit Obree: it had all been wrong. The bike was wrong, of course, but he'd been in the wrong frame of mind all day. From the media engagements in the morning, when he'd had to do photo shoots with jam sandwiches and interviews, to allowing himself to become overawed as the starter readied him – he'd done it all wrong, and it had resulted in a failure. 'It happened in the thirty seconds it took me to get from the track's edge to where the guy was trying to hand me the flowers. I said, "I'm going again later, and I'm going on Old Faithful, and I'm doing it my way." I think everybody there thought, "Ach, he needs to get it out of his system and show face."'

Back at the hotel, Obree disappeared to his bedroom while Haines got to work. Ballester was going to leave, but although Haines persuaded him to give it one more day, *L'Equipe*'s photographer gave up the ghost and flew back to France. Phil O'Connor headed to Oslo and managed to persuade the picture desk of one of the national newspapers to process his film and send it to *The Times*, who ran a picture on their back page on the Saturday morning. Haines also got on the phone to Kelvin Trott, to ask for more money: the UCI officials and Obree's entourage needed to stay an extra day at the Best Western and reschedule their flights.

Trott not only released the funds, but on a whim went to the airport and got himself on a flight to Oslo that evening. 'We arrived in Norway, and got a train to Hamar,' he says. 'We had a few drinks on the train and got off at the station, but we didn't know where the hotel was. We popped into a bar for another drink and started playing pool with the locals, and all of a sudden it was three a.m. We thought we'd better find the hotel, so we walked out of the bar and discovered where we'd been drinking was actually the hotel.

'When I saw Graeme the next morning, he assured me he was ready and going for it, but the only problem was the noise from the disco downstairs kept him awake half the night again.

'That was us,' he laughs, slightly uncomfortably.

Obree had been well aware the night before that the effort of having already made one attempt on the hour was going to cost him physically. He could be as determined as he wanted, but if his legs were stiff, the second attempt would have no more chance of success than the first. He would need to get up and stretch several times during the night. But setting his alarm would have woken him suddenly from deep sleep and left him feeling tired, so he'd come up with the ingenious solution of drinking quantities of water so that a full bladder would wake him up more naturally than the sudden ringing of an alarm clock. Every time he woke up he did a series of stretching exercises on his legs to loosen them up, then repeated the process. He'd done this overnight routine once before, after breaking the national 10-mile record, in preparation for the national 50-mile championship the next day.

The second record bid was set to start at nine a.m. Obree woke late, went straight to the velodrome, and arrived with only a few minutes to spare. No schoolchildren had been bussed in this time, and there were fewer journalists. In fact the only spectators were Obree's entourage and a bemused group of tourists being shown around on a guided tour. 'He just walked in, clip-clop clip-clop, cycling shoes already on,' Dailey recalls. 'He got on the bike. No real warm-up, he just started. That was the old Graeme. That was what I was used to.'

Obree had spent the previous twelve hours trying as best he could to build a protective carapace around himself. He wanted no distractions, just to get back to the velodrome and ride his bike for an hour, in spite of his exhaustion. 'I was physically and mentally shattered,' he admits. 'But I was emotionally emboldened. I came striding in there like Butch Cassidy. On a subconscious level I knew it was just a veneer, and if that veneer got broken I would become that wee mousey person again.'

Obree did only three warm-up laps – he simply didn't have the energy to spare for any more. Then he was ready. But as he pulled up to the start line, he spotted the speaker inhaling a breath. 'I saw the starter's chest cavity rising, I knew he was going to say the same thing to me. I didn't want that. I wanted to be in control. It could break my veneer. So I said to him, very firmly, "Are you ready?" and took control of the situation.'

Obree tells me he would have been willing to die on that track to get the record that day. He set his pace, and refused to drop below it. This time, the schedule was calculated to Moser's figures – it didn't matter what Obree did, as long as he covered more ground than the Italian, even if it was just a single metre. His 5-kilometre time was identical to the previous day's: 5.47, level with Moser. After 10 kilometres he was 8 seconds up – almost half a lap. He drew steadily clear through the ride. And it was excruciating. 'It was a new level of effort. But if it wasn't for the failure, I wouldn't have reached that new level of effort. It's like a toothpaste tube: how much can you squeeze out? You have to imagine your heart is a boiler in one of those Buster Keaton films. You can see it expanding, with the needle bending in the red zone. You've got to be willing to hold it there even if the boiler is going to explode.

'There isn't any conscious thought when you're halfway through the hour record. My eyes went kind of numb round the edges. If you stay underwater in a swimming pool for a long time, then come up gasping for air, the breathing is like that, for an hour.'

He overtook a red flag which had been placed at the point Moser's record stood after 59 minutes and 29 seconds, and had time to add another 445 metres. The new hour record stood at 51.596 kilometres.

The cycling world, apart from the British fans who knew what Obree was capable of, was stunned. Pierre Ballester persuaded his editors of the magnitude of the achievement and *L'Equipe* turned over their first three pages to Obree, pushing the Tour de France back to the middle of the newspaper. Because their photographer had gone home early, the full-length image of Obree that appeared on the front cover under the headline 'L'Incroyable Mister Obree' was actually an image from the failed bid.

British cycling journalist William Fotheringham recalls Pier Bergonzi, the senior cycling journalist at *La Gazzetta dello Sport*, coming over in the Tour de France press room to ask him about Obree before the bid happened, and whether it was possible for him to beat the record. The Italian media and fans were quite protective of Moser's record and status; the possibility of their grand champion being beaten by an unknown amateur was as difficult to swallow as undercooked spaghetti. 'I told him the record was possible, and Bergonzi said to me, "If he succeeds, I will give up journalism and go back to my mamma's place in the country and eat pasta." Then he succeeded, and Bergonzi decided that Obree was his best friend.'

The British mainstream press were less impressed. 'I got the film processed in Hamar, at a one-hour printing shop, phoned all the Sunday papers, and they said no,' says O'Connor. 'It was incredibly frustrating. I wanted to tell people what we'd seen. He'd beaten Francesco Moser's hour record, and nobody wanted to know.'

Not long after he broke the record, Obree broke off his arrangement with Vic Haines. Haines wasn't popular with Obree's wife Anne or her mother, both of whom pushed him to make the decision. There was little friendship involved in the relationship between Obree and Haines anyway. Haines cajoled and bullied Obree into breaking the hour record, and put thousands of pounds into it, and the experience was stressful for him: in the photographs taken after the successful hour attempt, Obree and his helpers wear broad grins, unable to help smiling at the audacity, the surprise and the sheer joy of an underdog's success; Vic Haines lurks in the background, his shredded nerves preventing him from sharing the moment,

his face curiously neutral as he watches the celebrations.
· Haines claims he put £25,000 into Obree, plus another
£20,000 that his wife doesn't know about, and he's carried the
baggage of his involvement for twenty years. It's not the money;
he's more affronted by the missed opportunity than the dent in
his bank balance. He's still got the Burrows bike, and some
other bits and pieces from the bid. But he says he's 'not bitter. If
he rang me up now and said, "Vic, I'm going for the hour
record again, would you help me?" I'd help him, even though
he flicked me. But I want to sell all that memorabilia, because
I'm pissed off about it. The bike is quite close to my heart at the
moment, and I don't want it there.'

About 1,900 kilometres south of Hamar, Boardman's morale
took its final hit when news filtered through that Obree had
beaten the record, although he put a brave face on it. 'I'm disappointed not to be breaking Moser's record – I've been
working on that for six months,' he said at the time. 'But it
changes nothing. He can enjoy it for a week.' Later, he admitted
that it had taken the wind out of his sails. One minute he was
trying to beat the nine-year-old record of one of the most
illustrious one-day racers and time triallists in cycling history.
The next, he was going for a record held by an unknown third-
category amateur cyclist who'd built his own bike for less than
£100 and had set the record on his second attempt in two days.

Importantly, Obree had not beaten the record by a huge
distance. The new mark, 51.596 kilometres, was well inside the
margin of error the Boardman team had set for their attempt.
And Boardman's training was finally going well again, after
fluctuating unpredictably between the national 25-mile
championship and the final trip to Bordeaux. In the last week
before the bid, as he digested the implications of Obree's achievement, he set an unofficial world record over 4 kilometres – 4.24,

from a standing start – did a flying kilometre in under a minute, and completed three thirty-minute test rides, the last of which averaged 52.69 kilometres per hour – a full kilometre per hour faster than Obree's new record. Unlike the Scot, who did an hour-long ride in the week before his official attempt and broke Moser's record, albeit by less than he'd originally thought, Boardman was holding his form at its peak, without wasting energy. He was in such good form that it would have been a disaster for him not to break the record.

Friday, 23 July 1993 dawned hot and humid. Two hundred kilometres away, in Orthez, the riders of the Tour de France were getting ready to set off on the third-last stage of the race. The previous day had been the final mountain stage of the race, and the general classification had, as expected, been more or less decided, with Spaniard Miguel Indurain on the verge of his third consecutive Tour win. Today would be a quiet one.

Ian Emmerson and Doug Dailey turned up in Bordeaux on the morning of the bid. Pete Woodworth's impression is that they hadn't been supportive of the Boardman hour record. 'Doug was morally a hundred per cent supportive, but the BCF had contributed nothing,' he says. 'Chris was almost operating outside the BCF, and I felt there was a bit of resentment there.' His feeling was that they'd been more helpful to the Obree bid, although people in the Obree camp recall that Vic Haines kept the BCF at arm's length. 'They turned up on the morning of the bid and brought BCF T-shirts and asked us to wear them,' Woodworth adds. 'To which we said no.'

To avoid the worst of the midday heat, the attempt was due to start at ten a.m. But the velodrome was like an oven. For the ride itself the arc lights, which had been off all the way through training, had been switched on, raising the temperature. The humidity had risen and the air pressure was high – both slowing factors.

Interest in the attempt was also high, with many of the Tour's journalists having skipped ahead specially to report on the bid. Although the perception of the Boardman camp was that Obree's success had taken the shine off the prize they'd wanted to claim, he'd actually done Boardman a huge favour by putting the hour record on the front page of *L'Equipe* just a week before and creating interest. Only two journalists and a single photographer had witnessed Obree's record; Boardman's attempt was the cycling press's chance to make amends for having missed out on Hamar. As Boardman made his final preparations and did his last warm-up, he was besieged by photographers – a situation that had been anticipated by Woodworth, who'd hired half a dozen security men to keep them at a safe distance.

As Boardman approached the start line, after Keen sprayed him with ethyl alcohol in a vain attempt to keep him as cool as possible, he was expecting a 'major grim ordeal'. At ten, the stadium was hushed, although the silence was broken by a Colombian radio presenter giving live commentary down a telephone line – a detail which Boardman fixed on, according to his accounts of the event. At 10.02, Boardman stood up on his pedals and accelerated away from the line.

Keen and Boardman had agreed on a schedule of 52.5 kilometres. He was a second behind Obree, who'd started fast, at 5 kilometres, but moved a couple of seconds ahead at 10 kilometres. Another 5 kilometres and he was 9 seconds ahead of the record holder, but the red numbers Keen was showing him from his position on the back straight indicated that he was falling behind his own schedule. When his deficit hit 3.5 seconds, Keen switched to the 52.4-kilometre schedule – he had worked out every schedule in 100-metre increments between 52.4 and 53 kilometres. On the home straight, Woodworth had put up a screen showing Boardman's average speed, and it had crept down to 52.3 kilometres per hour. So the higher schedules were abandoned and Boardman paced himself by the screen for the second half of the record attempt.

Phil O'Connor had flown back to France after covering Obree's hour record, but he felt the atmosphere was different for this attempt. 'I knew he was going to get it right from the start. There wasn't the "wow" that Obree had.'

Boardman, however, was suffering in the heat, his pulse sky-rocketing. When he started to feel dizzy, he backed off again. He never experienced the same elemental urge to drive himself beyond his previous limits that Obree did. Nonetheless, he was sailing away from Obree's distance. When the hour was up, he'd covered 52.270 kilometres. The record had gone for the second time in the space of a week. The first time, it had been an unknown British amateur with a notorious bike. The second time, it was also an unknown British amateur and, for the first time for either rider, for once the bike wasn't the story. Which didn't please the PR lady from Corima, who complained to Boardman after his post-record press conference for not mentioning the company often enough.

The first part of Boardman's PR ambush on the Tour was complete: he'd duly impressed the hundred or so race journalists present, as well as two or three team managers who'd also come to see what all the fuss was about. The second part came that afternoon when the Société du Tour de France, having experienced something of a change of heart, invited Boardman to share the Tour podium with Miguel Indurain, the yellow jersey. At that moment, Boardman and Indurain were the two most prominent people in world cycling. Importantly for Boardman, he'd also suddenly just made himself one of the most marketable men in cycling as well.

That night, Boardman and his entourage, plus a few journalists and hangers-on, went for a meal and a celebration.

Even as everyone around him drank beers and toasted the achievement, Boardman sipped from a cup of coffee.

Obree took having his record beaten very well, better than Boardman had taken his having beaten Moser's record in the first place. But the two riders had targeted the record for different reasons. Obree had done so because it was a challenge – an impossible one in many people's eyes. Boardman had broken it because he could; there was never any doubt, once he had achieved certain speeds over certain distances in training, that he would break it. It had started as an academic exercise by Peter Keen; the actual ride was just a confirmation of hypotheses he had already tested. If the hour record hadn't been possible according to their calculations and early tests, they would have set an achievable target instead.

The distance by which Boardman raised the record in comparison to Moser – over a kilometre, and at sea level – showed that it had been a vulnerable record all along. It had enjoyed the reputation of an unmatchable feat, mainly because Merckx's record, before Moser, had always been seen as the pinnacle of the greatest cycling career ever. But Keen and Boardman had never been ones to respect reputations or swallow received wisdom.

The difference between Boardman and Obree was what came after the hour rides. Obree had no idea what he was going to do next – the hour had been an end in itself. For Boardman, it had been a means to an end, and with professional cycling managers now starting to chase his management team, it had been a successful one. He refocused on his next target, the world track championship, while he weighed up his options.

'There was a sense of relief after it,' Obree says, reflecting on his short-lived hour record. 'The pain of failure avoided. What would I do next, to feel good about myself?' The answer actually came quickly. After riding an exhibition pursuit match in Denmark after his hour record, and enjoying the experience, he phoned Doug Dailey to ask how to go about gaining selection for the British team in the individual pursuit. His aim, too, was to become the world champion.

12

Sorry About That

Graeme Obree had to get used to the attention that came with being a world hour record holder, even if it had been for less than a week. When he arrived back at his home he found three camera crews waiting for him. 'I was so naive,' he recalls. 'The French were there, and they said, "We have whisky and a kilt. Where is the castle? We'll drive out to the castle and do some photographs with Old Faithful and the whisky."' Obree went along with it, but he cringes now at the way he allowed himself to be portrayed by journalists eager to play up the angle that he was eccentric. He was, but in a far more complex way than he was presented.

Chris Boardman often observed that he and Obree were very different, that they took different routes but ended up at the same place. On the surface of it, it's difficult to disagree with that – they were opposite characters in almost every way. Obree's plan for breaking the hour record was straightforward, uncomplicated: he'd simply train as hard as he could, then book a velodrome and ride as hard as he could for sixty minutes; willpower would take care of the rest. Boardman would never have allowed a concept as unreliable and variable as willpower to enter into his planning. Evidently, it takes a great deal of the stuff to train for and break an hour record, but Boardman's willpower was born of the confidence that he already knew he could do it.

The press played up to their stereotypes. It was the human versus the robot, the weirdo versus the square. The artist versus the scientist. The loner versus the committee man. The contrast in characters heightened the sense of a classic rivalry.

But they had things in common, too. Both were petrified of failure, even if they dealt with this in contrasting ways. Obree was prepared to risk failure, but when it came, he found it psychologically overwhelming. Boardman avoided it; he set out his career path within the parameters of what was possible. 'I was a bit of a coward and I stuck to things I knew I could do,' he confirms. The reassuring three-digit readout on his pulse monitor told him what was possible, and he obeyed it religiously.

They also trained in a similar way. Neither followed the traditional plan involving a large volume of bike riding, emphasizing high-quality work instead. Boardman and Keen evolved this by applying scientific method and following the latest physiological research, while Obree arrived at his method intuitively. Vic Haines recalls that when he was training for the hour, Obree rode at 30 miles per hour on a static trainer in his cellar for an hour, three times a week. But he listened to his body intently. 'Sometimes, he'd go out for a ride, and two minutes later he'd come back in saying he felt tired and wasn't going out.' So there was no plan as such; he just followed his body's signals, hammering himself to the point of oblivion, then recovering, then hammering himself again, then recovering. It was probably quite similar in structure to what Boardman was doing, in terms of the number and intensity of the efforts, but only Boardman's training would have been plotted out in advance and analysed. Obree, who was less meticulous, just went through one session at a time. And the results were, in the end, just the same.

During 1993, as Obree and Boardman made their hour record attempts then moved on to the world pursuit championship, the rivalry attracted the attention of a documentary-making team who pitched a programme to Channel Four about the two riders. Adam Glasser, the cycling journalist who'd broken the news about Obree making his hour attempt in Hamar, was working on the documentary as associate producer. A former keen amateur racing cyclist himself, Glasser found the rivalry compelling, but also saw as many similarities as differences. 'Graeme was a self-made guy,' he says. 'He found it hard to join organizations and toe the line. He was a fascinating, artistic genius. And so was Chris. These guys were two of the most creative people cycling has known, and there's actually much more in common as intelligent thinkers about racing, and athletes, than people think. They were actually very close to each other in the way they trained and raced. The common misconception was that they were the crazy guy versus the appliance of science. But both gave a lot of thought to what they were doing.'

Glasser had watched Obree's British hour record at Herne Hill, and quickly become fascinated by his character, and his ability. He'd followed his time trial times in *Cycling Weekly*, and realized that though Boardman was the more renowned rider, their times and abilities were quite close. So he wrote a treatment pitching a piece that would follow the two riders through the second half of the season. The executives looked at it just as Obree hit the headlines with his successful hour record, and they immediately gave it the go-ahead. And, as luck would have it, the remainder of the season pitched Obree and Boardman against each other on several occasions.

Glasser, who swung between earning money as a musician,

writer and documentary-maker, identified far more readily with Obree than Boardman, although he also got on well with Peter Keen. 'I became friendly with Graeme. Less so with Chris – he needed friends less and he was obviously well supported by Keen and Woodworth, and the guys around him. Chris was distant.'

Obree certainly made friends more easily than Boardman, but he wasn't very good at keeping them. Apart from Vic Haines, he rarely fell out with people, but he had the tendency of the introspective individualist to let relationships wither on the vine. He was generous to and considerate with his friends, then he'd simply move on. Kelvin Trott supported Obree to his hour record, and Obree was grateful and thoughtful enough to make him that trophy out of his handlebars, which Trott treasures to this day. But he rarely heard from him after 1993.

I spoke to David Taylor, the one British journalist at the Hamar hour record, and he showed me a Norwegian fifty-krone note Obree gave him at the end of the trip. The Scot had scrawled out the zero and written '1.596' over it, so the note now read '51.596' – the distance of his record. 'The one I didn't spend,' he also wrote. It was a touching gift, but Taylor hasn't heard from Obree in years either.

The documentary, which was shown on Channel Four with the title *Battle of the Bikes*, was a low-fi, atmospheric and gritty account of Boardman and Obree's rivalry, and was even-handed in its treatment of the two riders. At the time Glasser recalls that the Boardman camp were less happy with it than Obree. 'I sent Chris a copy and never heard from him. He probably thinks it's a load of old bollocks really,' Glasser adds, laughing.

Great Britain had three slots in the individual pursuit competition in 1993. As Olympic champion, Boardman had qualified by right, while Shaun Wallace, the silver medallist in the previous two professional world championships, had taken the second. The championship in 1993 had been unified, with professionals and amateurs alike now all in one category: elite. The distance would be 4 kilometres – one less than the professionals were used to, but standard for the amateurs.

Boardman had resumed his pursuit training just two days after he broke the hour record, staying in Bordeaux to take advantage of training on the track. The record had made him confident – he was talking up his chances of riding a 4.20 at the world championship. He was also dropping hints about turning professional. 'Being an amateur is going to hold me back,' he said. 'I can't be riding 25s any more, and all the publicity in the world from an hour record is not worth a carrot unless you do anything with it.' The rumours were that three professional teams at the Tour had already tapped him up.

Doug Dailey, who was still the national coach, informed Obree that if he wanted to represent Britain at the world championship, he would have to win the British championship outright first. Obree hadn't ridden a pursuit series since 1990, when he'd come a disappointing tenth in the nationals.

Having trained for and beaten the world hour record he was in good shape for long steady efforts, but a four-and-a-half-minute pursuit demanded a different level of effort. With much of his time being taken up with exhibition races and public appearances, Obree would go to Leicester only hoping that he could convert his hour fitness into a good pursuit series.

Dailey had deliberately set the bar high for Obree in order to expose him to the pressure of having to win in order to make the team. Dailey had watched Obree at all his previous efforts at the national championships, and witnessed him fall just short each time. He felt an affinity with the Scot, though. 'I've always been one for oddballs and wild cards,' he says. 'They fascinate me. Obree was a great rider, with the added interest of the unusual position on his bike. I'd watched him from a distance for some time.' One year at Leicester, Dailey had been particularly impressed with his effort in the pursuit. 'His start was electric – he used to lift the front wheel off the ground. You could tell he was really putting some power through those pedals.'

He'd tried working with Obree in his capacity as national coach before 1993. Most of Obree's racing before then was done in time trials, under the code of the RTTC, the Road Time Trials Council, which was outside Dailey's jurisdiction. But he'd invited him to join the national squad for some team time trial training sessions in the Midlands. 'I picked him up from the station, just him and his bike bag, which had cornflakes, jam, skimmed milk and bananas in it,' he recalls. Obree had been slotted into a team with a few of the other squad members, but he'd touched a wheel during one of their practices and fallen off. 'The boys weren't happy with him. He wasn't a team player and he didn't mix well. There was a degree of rejection by the others because he was on different equipment, with a different style, and a different temperament. He was an individual who wanted to be in control, but you can't be in full control of a team time trial. It wasn't going to work. But to me, talent is talent, and exceptional talent couldn't be ignored.'

At the national championship, Obree breezed through the early rounds, although his opponent in the semi-final, Chris Ball, tried to ambush him. Obree used a much higher gear, which meant turning the pedals at a lower cadence than most pursuiters. His unusual position on the bike, which pitched his weight forward, towards the front of the bike, allowed him to use his weight as well as leg strength to turn the pedals, enabling him to turn higher gears. He couldn't disobey the laws of physics, however: while his top speed was higher, it took him longer to accelerate up to that speed. Ball knew he wasn't a match over 4,000 metres for Obree, so he started very fast, to try and catch him before the Scot could get up to full speed. After two laps, Ball was 3 seconds ahead, but it wasn't enough. Obree got himself up to speed and caught his opponent before the finish, even though he was holding back in order to lull his fellow finalist into a false sense of security.

In the final, his opponent was Bryan Steel, the experienced rider who had given the LotusSport bike its international competitive debut at the World Cup in the run-up to the Barcelona Olympics. What's more, Steel would be riding the Lotus in the final against Obree. The Scot had been the faster rider through the series, however, making him the favourite.

But the violent starting effort that had so impressed Dailey a few years before almost cost him. As Obree accelerated out of the start gate, his foot pulled out of his pedal. His bike shuddered underneath him, his right foot still going round, his left flailing in thin air. It took two pedal revolutions for him to clip his foot back in, while Steel had got off to a smooth start. It cost Obree 3 seconds on the first lap. That was as close as Steel got. Obree's superiority soon saw him back on level terms, then ahead, and he won comfortably. He was the national champion in his first attempt at the pursuit in three years. More importantly, he was going to Norway with the British team.

Obree went back to Scotland to practise all-out starting sprints on a straight and flat stretch of A-road near his home, his brother-in-law driving in a borrowed Citroën behind him.

Before the world championship, Obree and Boardman were both invited to take part in the annual Newtownards Champion of Champions 25-mile time trial, held in August. As we know, it was at this event three years previously that Obree had recorded his only ever win over Boardman in a time trial. But this time the Englishman rode a blinder. In 1990, both had ridden the out-and-back course in just under fifty-four minutes. In 1993, Boardman recorded a 49.36.

Obree might have got closer but he punctured early on, and getting the rear wheel off Old Faithful was a time-consuming process. It was a track bike, and the wheel was bolted in, so it wasn't as easy as just stopping and swapping it for another. He switched to his warm-up bike – just a normal racing bike – for 7 miles while his helper fixed a new wheel to Old Faithful. Once the wheel had been mended, he switched back to Old Faithful, but crashed, his racing tyres not holding enough grip in the greasy conditions. By the finish he was two and a half minutes down on his rival. With only a week to go to the world championship, an important psychological blow had been struck. But it might actually have worked in Obree's favour.

It's clear that Boardman felt that the natural scheme of things involved him beating Obree. In head-to-head competition he had only lost once to him, even though Obree's crisis of confidence in the national 25-mile championship earlier in the year had cost him a second win. The two were not far apart, but the evidence put Boardman slightly ahead, on all terrains: he'd beaten Obree often in time trials, and on the one occasion so far that they'd competed on the track, he'd put over 600 metres into him when breaking the hour record, in unfavourable conditions. When Boardman was interviewed in Northern Ireland about Obree's chances at the world championship, he was dismissive. 'Graeme's just one of so many people I have to beat at the worlds. It's his debut there, and I know what the others can do, so I'm more worried about them than I am about Graeme,' he said.

It's unlikely Boardman was playing mind games. Obree's approach was so alien to him that he didn't understand it, and to acknowledge him as a genuine contender would have been to validate a method he felt was wrong. Boardman was the Olympic pursuit champion, a position he'd reached through years of pulling himself up to the necessary standard by his fingernails. It had taken him many years of slow improvement to win a world-level title. Obree had barely ridden the track; to consider him as having a real chance of gold would have been to cast into question Boardman's own development and methods. As the pair prepared to fly out to Norway, Boardman didn't see Obree as a threat. It just didn't compute.

If he'd known that 5 kilometres into the Newtownards time trial Obree had actually been a second faster than him, maybe he would have been more wary.

Boardman's ambitions for the worlds were high. Dailey expected him to contend for the gold medal, while Boardman himself continued to make noises about becoming the first rider to break 4.20 for a 4,000-metre pursuit. It was a mark of how confident the Olympic gold had made him – in 1991, he couldn't even break 4.30. Boardman rarely made predictions that were based on anything other than empirical facts, and the rumours were that he'd broken the world record in training. It was clear he was expecting to win.

The cycling world had seen pictures of Obree's bike and position from the hour record reports in *L'Equipe* and other publications around Europe. The world championship was the first chance to see it in action. The German press dubbed it the 'Devil Bike', while *L'Equipe*, taking a different angle from their hour coverage, described it as a 'circus bike'. But they loved it, likening Obree to great Scottish inventors of the past such as James Watt, Alexander Graham Bell and John Logie Baird.

Obree saved his warm-up session on the Hamar track until the last possible moment before the championship began. The track emptied as he practised his starts, and riders, coaches and journalists stopped whatever they were doing to get their first sight of the Scot in full flight. Obree gave them a demonstration of his starting effort, sprinting half a lap, then easing up for half a lap before stopping and repeating his effort. As the track started to fill up again, Obree rode continuous laps, cruising past lines of riders, and three things made him stand out. His compact position was odd compared to the relaxed posture of the other riders on their tri-bars, but he looked much more aerodynamic. His gear was noticeably larger, too – his cadence was slower than anybody else's there. And, most importantly, he looked fast – much faster than any-body else riding on the track.

There was no time for competitors to ride themselves into the competition in Hamar. The format was that the qualifying round would put the sixteen fastest riders into four groups. The fastest four – group A – would then contest the two semi-finals. The winning semi-finalists would go on to dispute gold and silver in the final, but the bronze medal would be given to the fastest losing semi-finalist. Just one sub-par ride could put a hopeful medallist out of contention immediately. The margin for error was small.

The three-man British pursuit team attracted a lot of attention because of their bikes. Boardman was riding the Corima, Wallace had a Lotus, while Obree had Old Faithful. Obree had altered his position slightly, after sorting the prob-lem with his pedal that had almost cost him the national championship. Doug Dailey recalls that Obree had come up with a novel solution. 'He generated tremendous force at the start, and the pedal couldn't cope. I expected him to tighten up the spring or buy new cleats, but Graeme doesn't work like that. He thought it through, and came back with an integral shoe and pedal arrangement. He bolted the shoes to the pedal and covered it neatly with fibreglass. Very effective.' By bolting the shoes to the pedal, Obree was able to sit a couple of centimetres lower.

Dailey couldn't have been any happier with the qualification round: all three British riders made it into group A. Obree and Boardman had both recorded 4.24, while Wallace was a couple of seconds slower. Jens Lehmann, the Olympic silver medallist and 1991 world champion, qualified fifth fastest and was out of the fight for a medal. The only complication was that Frenchman Philippe Ermenault had finished his ride in 4.23, meaning that he had 3 seconds to spare over Wallace for their semi. Boardman and Obree would face each other in the other race.

Boardman may have been confident before going to Hamar, but now it had dawned on him that he had a match on his hands. He felt flat, and his stated aim went from winning the gold medal in a world record time to taking a medal. 'I was worn out mentally, and physically I was jaded,' he said. 'The motivation wasn't there.' He'd tried to hold his hour form, but it had suddenly gone, while Obree had had the advantage of an extra week after his hour, during which time he'd been doing a lot of short, explosive races in exhibition events. His qualification round, his first pursuit in an indoor velodrome, had been unexpectedly fast.

Ermenault made short work of Wallace. The Frenchman was clearly faster, so he was able to measure his effort against his opponent rather than get caught up in a fast race and tire himself out. At halfway he was only a second ahead, but Wallace wasn't able to hold his own speed, and Ermenault cruised to victory by 6 seconds, visibly easing up.

Then Boardman and Obree took their positions. British athletes hadn't made such headlines in Norway since Coe and Ovett each set world records in separate events at the Bislett stadium in Oslo in the run-up to the 1980 Olympic Games. The British team had to divide their resources between the two athletes, to avoid any hint of favouritism. 'We decided that Peter Keen would look after Chris, and I would take Graeme,' says Dailey. 'Chris already had his support team in place, and we made sure that they both had equal support from the mechanics.'

The difference in experience between Boardman and Obree was huge. Boardman had grown up racing the track. He had strength, style, efficiency, talent and class. He looked great on his bike, his body's stillness belying the huge physical effort he was able to make, and he knew his body through years of racing and experience. Obree was less endowed with class, but he made up for it with ingenuity and fighting spirit.

There was no better illustration of the gulf between them than Doug Dailey rushing through an explanation of pace judgement and how he would communicate with his rider. Coaches use a technique known as 'walking the line' to get messages across to their rider, who is moving too fast to absorb complex information. Simply put, if the rider is ahead, the coach will move forward from the finishing line; if he is behind, he will move in the other direction. Just before the semi-final of a world championship pursuit is not generally the time or place to explain that sort of information, but Obree was so inexperienced that he hadn't quite learned the signals. To complicate matters, he misinterpreted Dailey's gestures during the race, and was convinced he was behind.

Boardman had gone out fast, but Obree didn't take long to get on level terms, and the difference in their pursuiting styles made it clear that the Scottish rider now had the advantage. Boardman always rode an even pace, whether it was in an hour record or a pursuit. He was able to find his ceiling early on and ride to it, never slowing down. Obree's tactic was different. 'He wasn't like Sturgess, who would let riders go away then catch them with a three-lap purge at the end,' Dailey explains. 'Graeme just ground them down. He went quicker and quicker. His style was to do an accelerating ride.'

Obree stretched to a lead over Boardman, and Boardman had nothing to fight it with. Keen's method of communicating with his man was with a flipboard showing the difference between the two riders in tenths of seconds. He shouted encouragement to Boardman each time he passed, showing him red numbers to indicate a deficit, but the worried looks he was casting up to the scoreboard showed that he wasn't confident.

Obree finished in 4.22, a new world record, and won the race by 3 seconds. Their previous meetings had all counted for nothing in this first encounter on a world stage.

The reaction of both men to the result was curious. One man had established superiority over the other, but both still seemed surprised by the new hierarchy. As Boardman circled the track and slowed to congratulate Obree when he stopped, the Scot apologized to him. 'Sorry about that,' he said. It was an awkward moment, because it seemed both sincere and horribly inappropriate under the circumstances.

Boardman put a brave face on it. 'I wasn't going to beat that,' he said. And as Obree turned away to receive more congratulations, he added, 'Not today.' He had finally accepted Obree as a genuine contender, and he lent his rival his streamlined helmet to wear in the final. 'At least something of mine is going to win a gold medal,' he commented wryly.

Ermenault was still the favourite for the gold, having ridden similar times through the series but not having had to dig so deep in his semi-final, making him fresher for the final. Sure enough, the Frenchman started strongly, and he had over a second in hand after just one lap, but it only took Obree three more laps to get on level terms. He led by 2 seconds at halfway, and again won by 3 seconds in another new world record, 4.20.

Obree was the world champion, and he'd beaten his biggest rival en route to the final. It hadn't been straightforward – he stated that never before had he ignored the warning signals from his body to ease off to such an extent. While Obree gasped for recovery, Ermenault collapsed on a plastic chair, sobbing at his defeat.

Obree was an instant hit with the European media. That night, the journalists were shocked to see him and several British team-mates out at a nightclub. David Taylor, one of the two journalists to witness the hour record, recalls them waiting for Doug Dailey to retire to his bedroom for the night. The windows opened, several riders came out and we all went to a bar. As Obree walked in, they played "We Are the Champions". Obree was wearing his rainbow jersey, and the foreign journalists couldn't believe it.'

Boardman and Obree were now competitors on an equal footing. Each had broken the hour record, and each had won a world-level pursuit competition. Boardman had taken Obree seriously to an extent before, but his comments had always reflected more on what he could achieve if he did things with better planning. Now the final recognition had come, and he admitted that he might have something to learn from his rival. 'After what he's done we have all got to sit back and take a look,' he said. 'I don't relish the thought of changing my position but I have always advocated looking at anything with an open mind. Perhaps we will all have to change.'

Obree had been faster than Boardman. But even more crushingly than that in Boardman's eyes, he'd out-thought him.

13

Welcome to Hell

Lille, France, 2 July 1994

The Grand Départ of the Tour de France is the absolute centre of the cycling universe. It's the singularity from which the biggest race in the world explodes outwards, having fed on all the potential energy built up by the warm-up races and other big events of the year, by the public interest, and by the media stoking the hype around the big names. It's where anticipation just starts to overlap with the actual race.

In the 1990s, the established format for the Grand Départ was a prologue time trial on the first day of the race, the riders setting off at gaps of one minute. It's a time for sizing up rivals and psychological warfare – a light hors d'oeuvre before a chewy main course. Nobody has ever won or lost a Tour de France in the prologue, although the time differences here are usually magnified later in the race.

The 1994 prologue, in Lille, is a 7.2-kilometre loop around the city centre, pan-flat but with a couple of corners that are just above 90 degrees – sharp enough that the riders will need to think hard about their entry speed and trajectory. They'll probably need to feather the brakes. It will cost momentum, and a physically expensive acceleration out, but nobody wants to crash on the first day of the race.

Miguel Indurain, aiming to win his fourth consecutive Tour de France, is the favourite: he's won the last two prologues and is widely regarded as the best time triallist in the world. Tony Rominger, the Tour runner-up the previous year, and Alex Zülle, Rominger's Swiss compatriot, are also in with a shout.

Beside the start house, Chris Boardman sits in a plastic chair, the Gan logos on his tight skinsuit distorted by the stretch in the material. Gan was the team that won the race to sign the Englishman following his hour record the previous year. Boardman's minute-man, Luc Leblanc, sets off, and the Brit, surrounded by photographers, shuffles up the steps to the start house in his cleated cycling shoes. Leblanc had been disparaging about Boardman's hour record the previous year, claiming that 'half the peloton' could break it if an unknown amateur could. Although he claims not to be thinking about Leblanc's words, there couldn't have been a better choice for minute-man than the Frenchman.

Reunited with the LotusSport bike, his team having done a deal for him to use it in time trials, Boardman is held upright on the start line by an employee of the Tour organization in a crisply ironed shirt that's two sizes too big, and bright blue nylon trousers that are worn too high, while the starter counts down, marking each second with a reduced number of fingers in front of the rider's face.

'Trois . . . deux . . . un . . . *pop!*' says the starter, and Boardman is away. Two slow pedal strokes down the ramp, followed by an acceleration in both cadence and speed.

'I think I can do this at fifty-four kilometres per hour,' Boardman had told his Gan manager Roger Legeay. The pair had worked specifically on the course the day before the prologue, Legeay pacing him towards the corners in a team car at 60 kilometres per hour, then pulling off so that Boardman could practise going through them at race speed. Rather than ride the whole course, he rehearsed the technical sections several times. He would learn nothing from the wide flat boulevards between the corners – he already knew what his body was capable of doing. But by practising the corners, he'd built in an extra advantage. When they'd finished, he'd turned to Legeay and said, 'I'm not using my brakes tomorrow.' And, with the exception of a sharp corner just 200 metres from the start, he wouldn't.

Through the streets of Lille, Boardman is in full cry. His upper body is perfectly still, his legs churning a huge gear, only small deviations in direction as he applies downward force with each pedal stroke showing the massive effort he is making. Legeay drives the team car just a few metres behind the rider, the Gan mechanic standing up and shouting encouragement from the sun roof.

And ahead, on the long finishing straight, Leblanc. Boardman is catching Leblanc.

Prologues are decided by seconds and fractions of seconds. For a major contender like Leblanc, who'd come fifth in the 1991 Tour, to be caught in a 7-kilometre time trial is an utter humiliation. As Boardman gains on Leblanc, tight against the barriers along the right-hand side of the road, the Frenchman is looking like a Sunday amateur rider in comparison. He's out of the saddle, time-trialling as if he is climbing a mountain, wasting energy, unfocused. Leblanc looks over his left shoulder, the movement pulling his handlebars slightly left and leaving a gap to his right, which Boardman goes through, straight as an arrow, before Leblanc's even had a chance to digest what he's seeing.

Boardman has a few dozen metres left to ride, and when he stops the clock, he's the fastest rider by 23 seconds. It's taken him 7.49 to ride the prologue, at an average speed of 55.2 kilometres per hour – a race record to this day. As the final contenders come in, only Rominger and Indurain are within 20 seconds of him. Indurain is second, 15 seconds behind. It's the most stunning debut to a Tour de France in living memory. A British rider, just six months into his international road racing career, is wearing the yellow jersey.

Boardman had had an immediate opportunity for a revenge match for the world championship defeat to Obree at the Grand Prix Eddy Merckx in Belgium, in the first week of September 1993 at a 66-kilometre time trial to which the pair had been invited. And if Obree had won the battle at that worlds, it looked like Boardman was winning the war: at the GP Merckx he was riding his first race for his new team.

Gan was one of the biggest teams in world cycling – a major French outfit whose team leader was Greg LeMond, the three-time Tour de France winner. LeMond was past his best, but Gan was still strong, with an unbroken history going back to the early 1900s. Manager Roger Legeay had persuaded Boardman to sign with his team – Woodworth's publicity coup in Bordeaux had worked to a tee. Eight months of specific training and a well-timed publicity campaign had replaced a season or more of grind in the amateur ranks.

So when Boardman showed up in Brussels for the GP Eddy Merckx it was with the full support of Gan – team cars, mechanics, and a few of his new team-mates. Legeay, too, made the trip to watch his new rider's professional debut.

Obree, on the other hand, looked unfocused and out of his depth. While he had a target to concentrate his obsessional behaviour on, he was formidable. But the hour record and world pursuit championship were over, and once again he was struggling to work out what to do with himself. He'd been riding at track meetings throughout Europe, for which he was being paid appearance money, and although he wasn't being courted by the big road racing teams as Boardman was, he had technically turned professional. The problem was that he'd got rid of Vic Haines by this point and there was the impression that his new manager, his brother-in-law Martin Coll, didn't really have the experience to negotiate. It was a precarious and unpredictable way to make a living.

Obree's hour record backer Kelvin Trott was in Brussels to watch him take part in the race and recalls that the Scot's approach was a bit shambolic. Obree and Coll had turned up without knowing anything about the route or the race, and had decided not to stay in the hotel they'd booked, because at £267 for two nights they felt it was too expensive. The final indignity to Obree and Coll had been that the rate didn't even include food. 'Graeme had got a good signing-on fee, but he was very sensitive about money,' says Trott. 'Rather than pay for the hotel, he slept the night on the floor of a room above a grocer's shop, which was owned by a local amateur rider. You're up against the best riders in the world, in peak form – sleeping on a floor can't have helped. They'd have had massage and preparation, while Graeme turned up on the start line in a car, put his bike together and off he goes. He didn't even warm up.'

Obree rode poorly. He'd been suffering from a cough and he was off the pace. Then he crashed after slipping on a drain cover. He scraped into the top ten.

Boardman, on the other hand, settled into the professional cycling world as if born to it. His only concession to his amateur past was that he'd inserted a clause into his contract with Gan that allowed him to race out that season on the Cougar bike he'd used for the first half of the year with North

Wirral Velo. It didn't hinder him in any way: he won the event by a full minute from his team-mate Pascal Lance. The next four riders were all former Tour de France stage winners – Jelle Nijdam, Frans Maassen, Johan Museeuw and Boardman's compatriot Sean Yates. Further down the field there were two riders from the top five of that year's Tour – Zenon Jaskula and Bjarne Riis. Boardman had taken some significant scalps, with beguiling ease.

In the team car, driving behind Boardman, Gan boss Roger Legeay watched his rider participate in a road event for the first time and was happy with what he saw, but not surprised. 'You have a *garçon* who is an Olympic pursuit champion and just broke the hour record. You expect him to win. *Formidable!*'

On the surface, a time trial looks like a purely physical effort, with no real tactics. How complicated can riding from point A to point B as fast as possible be? But Legeay noticed that Boardman paced his ride unusually. While most professionals were able to ride fast through brute strength alone, Boardman thought more carefully about it. 'He managed his efforts very well,' Legeay recalls. 'It didn't look like he was going very fast on the uphill drags, but once he got to the top and over the other side, *c'est parti*! Most riders are strong so they ride fast all the way round the course. Not Chris: he rides fast at some points, less so at others, with great efficiency. And he won the race, so he must have been doing it right.

'We understood that he was a very intelligent kid. Very organized, and very professional. I have never found another rider who was so developed in the science of time trial riding.'

While Obree went off to record a techno pop song at a Belgian recording studio, Boardman prepared for his next race, the Telekom two-up time trial. Anybody looking for a perfect illustration of each rider's career plans could find no better example than this.

*

Chris Boardman was as good at choosing long-term advisers and helpers as Obree was bad at it. Roger Legeay was the final addition to his kitchen cabinet, joining the two Peters, Keen and Woodworth, and Sally Boardman.

I meet with him in a nondescript bar opposite Le Mans station, where we talk over double espressos then milky, sugary hot chocolates served by a waiter who possesses the perfect combination, for his line of work, of brusqueness, efficiency and menace. France isn't what it used to be: the television is stuck on a music channel which loops the K-pop hit 'Gangnam Style' every quarter of an hour or so.

Legeay is a suave, well-groomed and courteous sixty-three-year-old with a smart V-neck jumper, a pair of glasses which he puts on the end of his nose to read, and a face whose default setting is verging on a smile. He's retired from managing professional cyclists, but he bristles with energy, which he's now putting into an anti-doping movement, the Mouvement pour un Cyclisme Crédible, working on the local pro race, the Circuit de la Sarthe, and helping to organize a twenty-four-hour bike marathon which takes place on the Le Mans 24-hour race circuit. Maybe next year, I tell him, when he asks if I'll be accepting his invitation to ride it.

Legeay met Boardman and Woodworth in Cardiff, in August 1993, during the Tour of Britain. He'd been impressed not only by the Olympic gold and the hour record, but by the ability to pick a target on a specific day and succeed in achieving it. 'Organizing his hour attempt during the Tour de France was a good idea. That was Chris – very intelligent. I met them and said, if you want to ride the track, you can ride the track. But I have a project for you. They weren't that excited about it originally.' He laughs.

Legeay was a professional rider himself, although he started riding late, at eighteen. He grew up on a farm in the Sarthe département, near Le Mans, then boarded at his school's demi-pension after his parents split up. Sport was not on the horizon, although he did a bit of athletics at school. After leaving school he did clerical work for Crédit Agricole, one of the major French banks. 'I had a friend in my village who had a bike. I had no bike and no money, so I borrowed his bike for six months. I rode the bike on Sunday, and for the rest of the week I worked.' Legeay improved so fast at cycling that within two years he was selected to ride the French Espoirs (under-23) Championship, which in 1968 were being held in Marseille. He had no car to drive all the way there, so he asked if he could take the Friday off work to take the train for the race on Saturday. 'My boss said no, so I handed in my notice and left.' He was determined to take part.

Legeay didn't win – the victory was taken by future two-time Tour de France winner Bernard Thévenet. But he'd chosen his career path. He raced for another couple of years, did his national service, then turned professional for the Belgian Flandria team and rode the Tour of Italy. He made his Tour de France debut in 1975, with the Jobo team, then rode for Lejeune for three years, supporting Lucien Van Impe to third place in 1977.

In 1979, he joined the Peugeot team, and never left, spending four seasons riding for them as a road captain, then becoming a directeur sportif in 1983, and getting promoted to team manager three seasons later. The team had a series of sponsors after Peugeot – Z, for whom Greg LeMond won the last of his Tours, then Gan, and finally Crédit Agricole, who pulled out of sponsorship at the end of 2008, forcing retirement on Legeay after three decades with the team. As he points out, he both started and ended his working life with Crédit Agricole.

Legeay was aware that Boardman hadn't done much road racing compared to every other rider in the professional peloton. With no exceptions, every professional rider had raced his way up the ranks into a team. Boardman had time-trialled his way in. 'I told him, with the motor you have, you do not have the right not to try this out. I knew he was going to be good. A rider who beats the hour record has a big engine. There was no doubt in my mind,' Legeay insists.

Legeay had a soft spot for anglophones. He'd signed Greg LeMond at the end of 1989 in the first ever million-dollar cycling signing (it was a huge, groundbreaking figure at the time, although spread over three years). When Legeay had ridden for Peugeot in the 1980s, the team had been famous for its 'foreign legion' of Brits, Aussies and Irishmen. Robert Millar, Phil Anderson, Sean Yates and Stephen Roche all rode for Peugeot. All had come through the feeder team ACBB, which tried and failed to tempt Boardman over to Paris to race as an amateur. When Legeay signed Boardman in 1993, the team got their man in the end.

Cycling Weekly editor Andy Sutcliffe noticed the difference with Boardman immediately. 'The Gan machine kicked in,' he says. 'He had team clothing, team tracksuits, nice bikes and blue shoes. He'd gone into a real French team, not some third-string Belgian team as a domestique. And he hadn't gone in on a starter salary, either. He wasn't earning the same as Greg LeMond, but you could see the team meant it – they really wanted him.'

After the GP Eddy Merckx, Boardman only rode time trials for the rest of the 1993 season. For the Telekom race in Baden-Baden he was paired with Carrera rider Claudio Chiappucci, who'd twice finished second in both the Tour de France and Giro d'Italia. The Telekom Two-up was a time trial in which riders rode as a pair rather than individually around the course. The riders would tackle eight laps of a 9-kilometre circuit.

Chiappucci was one of the major stars of professional cycling at the time, and to be put in the same team as him was a mark of how highly Boardman was regarded by race organizers. They were very different riders and characters, though. Chiappucci was a crowd-pleasing, amiable hot-head whose primary tactic in cycling was reckless attacking. He seemed to enjoy losing spectacularly more than winning safely – the polar opposite to Chris Boardman; he was an Italian 1990s Raymond Poulidor to Miguel Indurain's Jacques Anquetil. Photographs of the event show how extreme Boardman's aerodynamic position on a bike was. Chiappucci was shorter than Boardman, but on the bikes, the Brit was several inches lower – hc was giving Chiappucci hardly any shelter when he was on the front.

Chiappucci wasn't a great time triallist, although he was a very strong rider and former King of the Mountains at the Tour, but on the hilly Baden-Baden course he put Boardman in trouble on the climbs. Boardman had done most of the work for the opening 3 kilometres, which were flat, but then Chiappucci took over on the main climb. 'That pushed me over the threshold nicely,' said Boardman. Boardman then had to change bikes after his experimental electronic gears went hay-wire, but his spare bike had no bottle on it. He was starting to feel dehydrated, so Chiappucci gave him his bottle, but that was filled with concentrated glucose, which Boardman wasn't used to, and it made him feel worse. He came round for the last few laps, but the damage had been done and the pair were second behind Gianni Bugno and Maurizio Fondriest, also both major stars of the sport at the time. Chiappucci thinks Boardman's bike change cost them the win. 'He was running electric shifting that was causing him a lot of problems and he had to stop twice to change bikes. We had a good rhythm – Chris rode on the flats and me on the hills.'

It had been Boardman's first exposure to many of the top riders. Chiappucci had been friendly – he even asked Boardman for a signed racing cap, which he has kept to this day – but some of the other riders had been less welcoming to the newcomer. Boardman had nodded a greeting to Tony Rominger and Zenon Jaskula, second and third in the Tour de France that year, but they hadn't nodded back.

By the end of the season, Boardman had achieved three wins, a second place and a fourth, the last of which came in the biggest time trial of the year, the Grand Prix des Nations. Meanwhile, Graeme Obree was still suffering from a lack of focus. He'd been a poor fifteenth in the Grand Prix des Nations, and pulled out of the Duo Normand (which Boardman had won with his team-mate Laurent Bezault). Martin Coll was talking about putting together a media pack to see if a corn-flakes or washing machine company wanted to sponsor Obree, and also claimed that three Italian teams had approached him to ride for them on a similar programme to Boardman's at Gan. There was also talk of consultancy work on a feature film that had been proposed by the French company Gaumont, with the funding coming from the USA. If there was any conclusion to draw from Obree's schedule and interviews in the two months following his world championship win, it was that he didn't have a clue what direction to take next. Boardman was adjusting to success better than Obree was.

We like to think that sport at the top level follows the same logic as sport at school, the only difference being that the practitioners have different skill levels. But professional cycling is different. It's professional in the pure sense of the word: cyclists are moving billboards for the company that sponsors them, and conformity to orders from the people providing the money is strict. Personal ambition is to be sacrificed for the good of the team. Obree didn't have a chance in a world like that. He was riding his own bike for a start, which meant manufacturers weren't interested in getting involved. Had the Olympic Games remained amateur, he could have carved out a career as a successful Olympian, but Barcelona was the last amateur Games and in the open era he would fall between the cracks. He'd been mainly racing in plain kit in 1993, although the Bic company had supported him for the Grand Prix des Nations and he'd worn their colours there. When *L'Equipe* asked four prominent professional team managers whether they would sign Obree, the response was a unanimous 'no'.

Roger Legeay says much the same thing when I ask about why he was so keen to hire the Olympic pursuit champion and hour record holder but not another rider with a world pursuit title and an hour record. '*Non. Ah, non*, it wouldn't have worked. Obree, no. Boardman, yes. I saw him, but he had a different philosophy, especially in terms of his position and his way of doing things. I might be wrong, but I don't think he could have done it. He was an individual. Chris was capable of adapting to team life.'

'I wasn't a natural road racer,' Chris Boardman insists.

His results in that autumn of 1993 had been impressive, but they had all been achieved in the comfort zone of his speciality: time trialling. In spring 1994, he'd make his debut in the continental road races, where he would be by far the least experienced rider in the bunch. Just a year before, he'd been riding mainly time trials, doing a lot of training, and taking part in the occasional road race. He'd be going from the Tour of Lancashire in 1993 to some of the world's biggest races in 1994. He was expecting, in his words, to get his head kicked in.

Phil O'Connor went out to photograph Boardman's first race of the year, the Tour of the Mediterranean. The early season races in France were renowned for being very competitive and tough, held on the poor-quality, gravelly, narrow, twisting roads of rural Provence. 'The first stage was a team time trial, and that went OK,' says O'Connor. 'Then they did a road stage and I remember seeing him afterwards and he was shocked. He'd never been in a bunch of two hundred people hurtling down little lanes. I think he had some self-doubt then. He warmed up to it, but I think it was a shock, plus he would have known absolutely nobody. It was like a big party, and he'd crashed in as the hour record holder, which probably meant for some of them they wanted to make life difficult for him. Welcome to Hell.'

Boardman did manage to have one good day at the Tour of the Mediterranean. He'd been feeling vulnerable and uncomfortable in the bunch, so he joined an attack off the front of the race during stage six, although it came to nothing in the end. Every day he filled in a questionnaire given to him by Peter Keen in search of feedback on what was a new environment for both of them. The final question on the form was the refreshingly naive 'Why didn't you win today?', which Boardman answered on most days with the words 'not good enough'.

But just one week after the Tour of the Mediterranean, Boardman had achieved his first wins of the season, albeit both in time trials. He took the prologue and the final time trial of the Tour of Murcia, although he missed the race-defining move on a hilly stage in the middle of the race. The wins were good for his confidence, but they were even better for his standing in the bunch. With wins came acceptance by his peers. 'The yellow jersey is a passport to the front of the race,' he explains. 'In my first races I couldn't get to the front – you don't get let through. It's very Darwinian. I won the Murcia prologue and suddenly I had a passport to the front. In an echelon, when people are looking for somebody to push out of the way, they'd leave me and do the next person. I got cut slack.'

The Murcia prologue also gave him ideas. Originally, Boardman had not intended to ride the Tour de France in his first season – the rigours of racing for three weeks in the hardest event in the world were intimidating. But with Gan's leader Greg LeMond continuing to show indifferent form, Legeay and Boardman came up with an alternative plan: ride the first week or ten days of the Tour and target the prologue and the first long time trial of the race. The training would fit well with Boardman's other targets for the year, the world pursuit championship and the inaugural world time trialling championship, which would take place in Sicily in August. There was also an excellent piece of timing: the Tour was due to visit England for only the second time in its history, for two stages in the first week of the 1994 event. If Boardman could win the prologue and Gan could defend the lead in the team time trial, he could carry the yellow jersey to his home country.

However, for all that Gan had historically been a welcoming team for anglophone riders, through 1994 there was a bit of tension between the French riders, and some of the management, and the foreign contingent. The team's most experienced rider, Gilbert Duclos-Lassalle, was renowned for his chauvinism. It was rumoured some senior riders were unhappy when English-speakers actually spoke English within the team. According to Pete Woodworth, LeMond's poor form, and the fact he was on the highest salary in the team, caused problems with the French. 'There was no animosity, but they weren't interested. A lot of people were fed up with non-French riders, and that transferred to Chris. It was a tough first few months.'

There was one more background issue in 1994, which Boardman had not been exposed to but which was starting to become common knowledge.

The first half of the year was being dominated by the Gewiss team, from Italy. Their rider Giorgio Furlan won the Milan-San Remo Classic, while Evgeni Berzin, who'd won the 1990 world individual pursuit championship ahead of Boardman, won Liège-Bastogne-Liège, before trouncing Miguel Indurain, who'd won the last three Tours de France, in the Tour of Italy. But it was the Flèche Wallonne race which underlined the team's marked superiority. Three of their riders – Furlan, Berzin and Moreno Argentin – simply rode away from the rest of the peloton to fill the podium at the finish. Normally that would never happen in a bike race – every team in the peloton would work together to chase down an escape formed of riders from one team. But the Gewiss riders were so superior that normal rules didn't apply.

The team's doctor was a man called Michele Ferrari, who would later coach Lance Armstrong and be banned from the sport for life. Ferrari gained notoriety when he was interviewed by *L'Equipe* and stated that EPO, which was rumoured to be gaining a foothold in the peloton, was not dangerous in itself, only the abuse of it was.

EPO boosted haematocrit, which is the percentage of red blood cells in total blood volume. Normal values for an adult male would be expected to be in the range of 35 to 45 per cent. An Italian journalist, Eugenio Capodacqua, got hold of the haematocrit levels of the Gewiss team, and there were readings as high as 60 per cent – a figure that would be impossible to reach naturally. Berzin was showing 53 per cent. With no test for EPO available, there was widespread cheating going on, and the effectiveness of the drug was such that clean riders had very little chance against those who chose to dope. Boardman had entered the sport at probably the worst moment in its history.

Boardman, for his part, had a clause written into his contract allowing him to walk away if it was ever suggested to him that he take performance-enhancing drugs. 'It was made plain to Roger that Chris wasn't ever going to go down that path no matter what,' Pete Woodworth says.

By the middle of the season, Boardman had definitely noticed the difference, and heard the rumours. He wrote about the form of the Italians in his monthly column for *Cycle Sport*, using phraseology that was either serendipitously accurate or knowingly tongue-in-cheek: 'There have been all kinds of reasons put forward for their recent success, ranging from new training methods, to discipline, to better medical health supervision. Others have said that the popularity of cycling there has a lot to do with it, and this, coupled with the history of the sport, means that winning is in the Italians' blood.'

The Critérium du Dauphiné Libéré was the race in which Boardman booked his place in the 1994 Tour de France. The Dauphiné is an eight-day-long stage race held in the Alps in June every year; it's seen as the final tune-up to the Tour de France, and covers many of the same Alpine climbs as the bigger race. Boardman had good form coming into the race, having been fourth in the Tour de l'Oise behind defending Tour de France champion Miguel Indurain. He duly won the prologue, then won the time trial three days later. He tried to defend his overall lead, but was dropped on the final climb of the hardest stage, to the Collet d'Allevard. Boardman was already considered one of the best time triallists in the world, but on a summit finish in a mountainous race he had been found out by his more experienced rivals.

On the final stage, Boardman had sore legs on the start line, but his pulse had been low – an indication that he was on a good day – and he managed to get into a break with three other riders. They might have been left alone to contest the stage, but when two more riders joined, the ONCE team started chasing them down. When the gap was closed to under a minute, Boardman attacked again, and stretched his lead, this time on his own. It was the same method he'd used in virtually every road race win he'd ever achieved – open a gap and time-trial to the finish. He held off the pursuers to win by two minutes. It was his third stage win of the week, and one of the race sponsors was a chocolate company that awarded the stage winner his own weight in its product, so Boardman also left the race with 210 kilos of chocolate.

The final stage win looked coldly calculated. In fact, it had been planned for a very specific reason. 'Chris had a plane to catch,' recalls Legeay. 'He said in the morning meeting that he needed the stage to be fast, then he could get an earlier flight. He rode the whole stage off the front, very fast. After the finish, I took him to the airport, he got changed in the car and he got his plane.'

Boardman wasn't the finished product yet. He was still having trouble riding in the bunch and was nervous when there were too many riders in close proximity to him. Gan started putting a rider each side of him to give him more confidence. He took part in one more race before the Tour de France, riding a few days of the Tour of Switzerland, where he won the time trial, and then flew home to Hoylake to complete his final preparations for the prologue of the Tour, in Lille. Just a week before the Grand Départ, he rode the Chester Road Club 10-mile time trial and set an unofficial British record of 18.21.

The Lille prologue was the third great publicity coup of Chris Boardman's career, following the Barcelona Olympics and the world hour record. The only question after his resounding victory was, could he carry the yellow jersey to Great Britain?

'It wasn't super!' laughs Legeay about the team time trial, which took place three days after the prologue, and the day before the race crossed the Channel. 'We were still sixth or seventh, but we wanted to take Chris to England with the yellow jersey – it was the one chance in his life to do that. *C'est la vie.*'

Gan were already tired from defending the jersey for two days, and a combination of poor planning, judgement and bad luck contributed to a disastrous day. Boardman's handlebars worked loose. Jean-Claude Colotti and Thierry Gouvenou were too tired to work effectively and were dropped. Jean-Philippe Dojwa suffered two punctures and lost minutes. Even Greg LeMond was dropped on the run-in, and two of the riders came close to crashing on an innocuous bend near the finish, skidding round and having to stop. A team time trial needs every rider to work together efficiently, but Gan looked like nine men who'd never met one another before.

Boardman had to stop to have his handlebars tightened, and when he caught his team-mates again and went past, he immediately put them in trouble. There was confusion when LeMond told the team to take it easy up a climb, while Legeay was shouting for everyone to start riding hard again. The crucial point came in the middle third of the stage, over a series of headlands, where the wind was three-quarters behind the riders. That meant that while the stronger riders were still riding hard, the weaker riders behind were getting less shelter. Boardman later described it as a shambles. 'Our lack of team-work showed that day. My form was so good that I could have done the course quicker on my own. I just wanted them to get out of the way and let me get on with it. That sort of mess could have been avoided with a more scientific approach but it would have taken a tremendous amount of work from the team and I'm not sure they would have been prepared to trust each other enough.'

To show up to a race unprepared for its specific demands was a cardinal sin for Boardman. However, he was as much a part of the problem as everybody else, only his fault was to be too strong for the team, rather than not strong enough, as some of the other riders were. Francis Moreau, another rider who'd suffered, claimed that he'd been OK, except when 'certain members of the team' put in hard accelerations. Boardman had tried to compensate for the weakness of his team by trying to ride more strongly himself, but all he'd done was burn off his team-mates. Instead of riding faster, he should have ridden longer turns at a slower speed, to allow his team-mates to recover. He lost the yellow jersey.

Boardman was still relatively new to the team, which meant he'd been reluctant to impose his opinion. But after the team time trial, he changed his stance. 'Up until now I've sat and watched and thought, "This doesn't seem quite right." Now I'm ready to say, "Now, here's my opinion,"' he said. 'In the future we're going to have to make some changes.'

Boardman pulled out of the Tour on stage eleven, suffering from fatigue after the longest stretch of racing he'd ever done. He'd managed a telegenic and crowd-pleasing escape on the first British stage into Brighton, finishing fourth, but was a disappointed fifth in the long time trial in Bergerac, losing over five minutes to Indurain.

With LeMond faltering, Boardman was evolving into the team leader, but he gave an interview after he'd pulled out in which he made a statement that would haunt him for the rest of his racing career. 'It looks feasible – not definite, but feasible – that I can put in a serious challenge for the Tour next year,' he said.

Although the words were circumspect, Boardman had discovered his next great target: the general classification of the Tour de France.

14

One Man Banned

They'd all laughed at Graeme Obree's tuck position. Then they copied it.

Francesco Moser, a man whose prodigious ego and entourage of yes-men had allowed him to develop that self-perception beloved of some retired sportsmen and most sports administrators that he was to be treated as some kind of aristocrat, announced that he was going to try to break the hour record again, a decade after his first record, at the age of forty-two. Photographs of him circling a velodrome using a modified version of Obree's position were released – he'd added a chest support pad attached to a strut. His official aim was to beat the figures he'd recorded in 1984, but as Boardman commented at the time, why was he going to all the expense of having several different bikes made, working with his old mentor Dr Conconi, having the Italian paint and adhesives company Mapei paint a strip of varnish on the testing track and going to Mexico if he didn't secretly want to break the actual world record?

He came close, riding 51.840 kilometres in Mexico City in January 1994. He'd beaten Obree by 250 metres, using the same position (albeit at altitude, which was worth a kilometre or more), and fallen just 430 metres short of Boardman's record.

Moser wasn't the only professional to dabble with Obree's position. Tony Rominger also had a look at it over the winter, testing it in San Diego. And Boardman had returned to the Bordeaux velodrome in November 1993 to grit his teeth and test it out. In the evenings, he made appearances at the Bordeaux Six-Day race, including a best-of-three pursuit match with Graeme Obree which hadn't gone the way the organizer had intended. The idea was for each rider to win one race each, on the first and third nights of the event, with a grand decider on the fifth night. The trouble was that Boardman won the first two, leaving the organizer wondering how he was going to sell the final race (he got away with it by offering double points for the final night's race, and it was Obree who won).

But in the mornings, as the cleaners brushed away the plastic beer containers from the previous night's entertainment, Boardman was testing bikes: his Corima, a Cougar with a bodged-together Obree position, and a bike with a classic 'Merckx' position, complete with what Boardman described as a 'bunch of bananas crash hat' – an old-style leather ribbed helmet. 'It's a sad day,' said one of his entourage as Boardman wobbled away to try a bike set up in the Obree position. They'd already described the sessions as 'lose-lose': if the bike wasn't more aerodynamic, it meant that Boardman had to find another 3 or 4 seconds on Obree to beat him in the world pursuit championship; if it was, he'd have to start using the position. He'd probably have chosen the physical pain of the former over the psychological pain of the latter.

Boardman rode the Obree bike and his Corima in back-to-back 4-kilometre tests and the results were close, with too many variables to draw a conclusion, other than that the Obree position certainly wasn't any slower.

Keen worked out the power Boardman would need to produce to ride 52.270 kilometres for an hour (the world record he'd set in July) on the different bikes. On the Merckx bike, Boardman would have to maintain 473 watts to equal his hour record, a figure some 16 per cent higher than the 409 watts which Boardman needed on the Corima bike. On the Merckx bike, Keen estimated that Boardman would be able to ride 49.5 kilometres at sea level – further than Merckx did in Mexico City in 1972. The Obree bike turned out to be almost 4 per cent more efficient again: Boardman would only need to average 394 watts for an hour to equal his hour record. If Boardman made an hour record attempt using the Obree position, and could hold the 409 watts he was capable of that summer, he'd ride 53.180 kilometres, Keen estimated.

The advantage was mostly, but not solely, aerodynamic; the Obree position also gave riders a more stable pelvis, allowing them to put out slightly more power. It was biomechanically more efficient, as well as more aerodynamic.

But while Moser and Boardman were finding out that if they adopted the position they'd probably ride faster and further, cycling's governing body, the UCI, were starting to take an interest. As early as 1992, after Boardman had grabbed headlines with the Lotus bike, the UCI's president Hein Verbruggen had begun drawing a distinction between athletes and the technology they were experimenting with. 'I'm a conservationist in this respect,' Verbruggen said. 'I believe the man on the bike is more important than the bike. With the attention on Boardman at the Olympics I have a fear that the bike will become the more important. This may be OK for motor racing, but it isn't for cycling.'

Verbruggen, the man who presided over the doping crisis of

the 1990s without raising the slightest concern about whether it was damaging the sport, apparently seeing it as a PR failure rather than a moral one, rarely allowed consistency to interfere in his ambition for the sport to become a global (and therefore lucrative) business. According to Doug Dailey, while holding the above opinion about the primacy of the athlete, Verbruggen found the time to write a note to Obree after his hour record and world pursuit title to congratulate him on his refreshing approach to the sport. 'He wrote that it was great to see something new in the sport,' recalls Dailey. 'Then, a few months later, they outlawed the bloody position.'

Obree suspected the governing body was out to get him, and he thinks that Moser's failure to break the hour record in Mexico, using his position, was a contributory factor. 'The UCI thought I'd just bowled out of the Highlands, some half-trained amateur cyclist. They never saw me and Chris Boardman doing battle since 1990. They thought I was a third-category rider in a strange position with a twenty-five per cent advantage.

'I can see their perspective,' Obree adds. 'Before Francesco, there were spoked wheels, round tubing, dropped handlebars, from 1920 to 1984. In those years from 1984 to 1992, you go from that to aero helmets, aero tubing, carbon frames, disc wheels, skinsuits. Then I came along with a different position. Then Francesco came with a chest support. They hit the panic button.'

Obree had spent the winter of 1993/94 racing in exhibition events and pocketing as many appearance cheques as he could. He'd competed in a similar selection of late season time trials as Boardman, but unfocused training, poor form, disorganization, illness and a busy schedule conspired to prevent him equalling his rival's impact. Fourth in the Chrono des Herbiers, which was won by Boardman, was as good as it got. With the world championship in September 1994 his next major target, he could afford to slacken off the training and appear at as many events as he could, along with Old Faithful, which was starting to show signs of wear and tear. But once Obree heard rumours that the UCI were looking at banning his position and bike, he decided that he would try to beat Boardman's hour record without delay.

The opening salvo was launched by the UCI as early as February, when they banned Obree's position in road events. At a rushed press conference at the world cyclo-cross championship in Belgium, Verbruggen announced that the position would be banned in time trials until the Technical Committee could report on its legality, adding that he felt the position was unsafe.

Obree's hour record in 1994, 52.713 kilometres, was a marked contrast to his first. It appears his heart wasn't in it as much, even though he beat his 1993 record by over a kilometre. In his autobiography, the initial hour record takes up two chapters, while the second is shoehorned in among various winter track meets, and he doesn't even record the distance he rode. While the first record was an all-out attempt to justify his very existence to himself, the second, at best, was getting his retaliation in first against the UCI. The impact on his career was a positive one, but it had much less import for his emotional well-being. The closest it came to the angst of the first attempt was a minor falling-out between the promoters of the record, Gerald Oberson and Daniel Perroud.

Perroud thought Obree wasn't taking the bid seriously, and the preparation had started late. Oberson suggested the bid should go ahead at the end of April, to pre-empt any chance of the UCI banning the position on the track. 'At the end of January, maybe February, I thought I'd better get on the case,'

Obree says. 'To be ready for April the twenty-seventh I had a couple of months.

'Daniel told me a couple of weeks before the bid that he wasn't paying me. "You're just here for the beer and the money," he said.' Perroud had agreed to pay the Scot, but was now telling him he wouldn't hand over a penny. If Obree wasn't resolved to beat Boardman's record before, he was now.

But there was a curious lack of emotion about it compared to Hamar. Obree was confident he'd break the record, and wanted to break it, but the knowledge that he was capable of doing it took the unpredictability out of it. He hadn't quite turned into Chris Boardman, but it was a far less career- and life-defining event. 'In terms of needing to do it for my emotional survival, I don't think I desperately wanted it, to the point of burying myself,' Obree explains. 'There wasn't the same sense that I was ready to go to the edge of death for this. But I'd learned to draw the energy out without thinking I needed to die. Once you've stretched yourself that far, you can do it again.'

Obree broke the record in Bordeaux, in front of huge cheering crowds. It was the last significant result for the tuck position: just a few days later the UCI outlawed it. Jean Wauthier, one of the UCI's Technical Committee, claimed that Obree wouldn't have ridden further than 46 kilometres in an hour if he'd used a normal bike. Obree's records would stand, but future attempts in the position wouldn't count.

Ian Emmerson, the president of the BCF, and also a UCI vice-president, clarified that the problem was the position of the saddle and handlebars. 'The new rule is to stop any further move by riders to the prone position,' he stated. Jim Hendry, the chief executive of the BCF, defended the position, and wrote to Verbruggen saying that the bike should not be banned, and that the BCF should be part of any consultation process. But the decision had been made.

The UCI approved a proposal to change Article 49 of their technical rules, which was the article protecting the 'classical' riding position. Their ruling stated that the tip of the saddle must be 50 millimetres behind the centre of the bottom bracket. Obree's saddle was virtually over the bottom bracket.

But the illogical part of the ruling was that bike dimensions were proportional, rather than linear. A short rider, in the same position as a tall rider, would have a saddle nose much closer to the centre of the bottom bracket. There would be no advantage, because the position was identical, but because the UCI had specified a set distance, rather than an angle, some riders were inadvertently breaking the rules in entirely normal positions.

The UCI came up with some ludicrous claims. Marco Bognetti, the president of the Technical Committee, stated that the Obree position allowed riders to access 25 to 30 per cent more power. 'In my opinion it has not got much to do with the athletic performance of the cyclist,' he said. Verbruggen also claimed that by removing his arms from the equation, he'd eliminated 25 per cent of the total wind resistance. Wauthier said that research had been done demonstrating an unfair advantage, although he was unable to provide evidence. 'If the Obree position is allowed, you'll get contortionists breaking the records without being real champion cyclists. A mediocre cyclist could become world champion.'

The UCI may have declared that they had studies which they were unable to cite or produce that demonstrated a 25 to 30 per cent advantage for the Obree position, but Keen and Boardman's studies had indicated a less than 4 per cent advantage, some of which was biomechanical, some of which was aerodynamic.

The suspicion, given weight by Wauthier's words about mediocre cyclists, was that Obree's face had not fitted in the pantheon of champions that the UCI wanted for their sport.

He was not in the usual mould of hour record holders like Jacques Anquetil, Eddy Merckx and Francesco Moser. So they banned him.

As defending champion, Obree had automatic selection for the world pursuit championship in Sicily in August 1994. The second berth would go to Boardman, who'd ridden ten and a half stages of the Tour de France then pulled out specifically to go and train for the worlds at Lyon velodrome, site of Colin Sturgess's world championship win five years before. The Boardman camp had identified Lyon as the ideal place: the velodrome there was a bumpy outdoor track, and the temperatures were stifling – exactly the same conditions as they'd face in Sicily. Both riders were in the pursuit team, and both riders were also down for the time trial.

Obree wasn't beaten yet. He intended to ride his own bike in the pursuit at the world championship, and still make it legal. He had pushed his saddle as far back as it would go, then cut the nose off it. He just managed to make the minimum 50-millimetre distance, and dubbed his saddle the 'UCI rule buster model'. He rode and won the British pursuit championship without a hitch, because the BCF hadn't adopted the new UCI rule 49 yet anyway.

Boardman, for his part, was in superb form. He entered a local club 10-mile time trial for fifty pence on the start line and rode 17.54 – an unofficial British record. With Obree riding a legal bike, and Boardman in top form, the British team could anticipate a repeat of the previous year's gold and bronze medals, perhaps even an improvement.

But the UCI weren't finished.

They rejected five different saddles submitted by Obree the day before the competition. They wouldn't allow the saddle with the nose cut away, and another one, which he'd made out of a leather strip at home, was disallowed for not being available on the commercial market. He finally solved the problem by using a child's saddle and pushing it as far back as it would go, and the UCI had no choice but to accept it, under their regulations.

Even then, an hour before Obree was scheduled to do his qualifying ride the UCI informed the British team that they had introduced a new rule, *that morning*, which dictated that there had to be a 'certain distance' between the chest and the handlebars, and 'daylight' must be visible between the chest and the arms.

The BCF immediately lodged a complaint, but it was rejected. As Obree started his ride, the track was lined with UCI officials with red flags, squinting at the rider as he went past. Obree was sat right on the tip of his saddle, trying to get as far forward as possible, but there was no doubt whatsoever that the new rules were beating him, and the red flags were repeatedly raised. He finished his ride in 4.32, the third-fastest time of the day, but he was immediately disqualified.

Obree was livid. He tells the story in his autobiography that Hein Verbruggen himself had attempted to step on to the track three-quarters of the way into the race, and physically prevent Obree from finishing. Obree just rested his chest on his handlebars and maintained his momentum, riding straight at the Dutchman, who was forced to jump out of the way.

The UCI had repeatedly changed their own rules in order to prevent Obree from using his position in competition, and each time they had done so Obree had managed to make enough adjustments to conform. Changing the rules on the morning of the competition, and failing to inform the British team until it was far too late to change, was a clear indication that their main motivation was not the spirit or letter of the rules governing cycling, but to get the Scot's position out of the sport.

While the dust settled on the sensational qualifying round,

Chris Boardman was picking his way through the competition with a confidence that had been missing in Hamar the year before. He qualified fastest, in 4.29, 3 seconds clear of Obree. In the second round he beat Spaniard Juan Martínez, finishing in 4.25, then beat his old rival Jens Lehmann in the semi-final. In the final, Boardman was up against his Gan team-mate Francis Moreau, and he won by 12 seconds to take his first world pursuit title.

He then won the world time trial championship just a week later, for a double that has never been repeated. Obree rode, but his heart wasn't in it and he was well down.

The score between Obree and Boardman was now two hour records to one in favour of the Scot, one world pursuit championship each, plus an Olympic gold and a world time trial rainbow jersey for Boardman. On the track they were well matched, but on the road, Boardman, who had almost always beaten Obree in time trials, was stretching away.

But Obree has the last word on the 1994 world pursuit championship. 'Chris transgressed the rules as well, according to the UCI's wording,' he tells me. 'The rule was that you had to have daylight between your hand and your shoulder at all times. Well, Chris won the championship at night. There was no daylight there.'

15

All Out

Chris Boardman's most famous quote came in an interview with *Cycling Weekly* in 1992. The interviewer, Luke Evans, asked innocuously, 'Do you like riding your bike?' The answer: 'Not particularly, no.'

There was always something a little disdainful about Chris Boardman's relationship with cycling, as if it were manual labour and he was a white-collar office worker. Being good at it and being extremely competitive were entirely different things to getting enjoyment from the act of riding a bike. In that 1992 interview, he said he had managed to reduce his riding hours, including racing, down to about eight a week, and the inference was that that suited him just fine. While his rivals were out for twenty hours a week or more, he was focusing on quality, not quantity.

The accepted wisdom in training, into the 1990s, was that the best way of getting good at riding a bike was to ride a bike. Long rides were the staple diet of road racers. Even the international professionals, with just a few forward-thinking exceptions such as Greg LeMond, did lengthy rides through the winter, then raced themselves into shape in the early season races in February and March. The long steady miles of the off season were supposed to be fun and enjoyable, a chance to look around and appreciate the scenery. The act of cycling is inseparable from the landscape in which it takes place, and that's what gets many people into the sport in the first place.

Boardman wasn't interested in any of that. Not liking riding a bike might seem like the worst possible character trait for a professional cyclist, but it gave him sufficient distance to be able to ask what type of training would make him the best he could possibly be, without any emotional attachment to scenic rides in the countryside getting in the way. When Peter Keen substituted quantity of riding for quality over a period of years towards 1992 and 1993, Boardman had no objection to trying it out. And when it worked, it encouraged them to try to cut back even more. The conservative cycling establishment couldn't work it out, although as Keen's methods started filtering through into the Great Britain team's riders, the standard and results began to improve for them too.

Training eight hours a week was fine while Boardman's events were no longer than an hour in duration, but both men acknowledged that there would have to be some concession to longer hours to prepare Boardman for the rigours of the Tour de France, and the eighty or more days of racing he'd face each season. By the end of 1994, Keen was prescribing many more long steady rides over the winter. Boardman was going out for training rides into North Wales with a local cyclist, former national professional road race champion Mark Bell, who was the brother of journalist Tony Bell, and the only rider in the area willing and able to venture out with Boardman. Even on Boardman's steady rides the pace was uncomfortably high for most cyclists.

When Boardman was an overly serious teenager and Mark Bell a chippy and aggressive racer in his mid-twenties, the older rider had detested the younger. Boardman was prone to imparting advice earnestly, even when he was fourteen, and it rubbed some of the more experienced cyclists up the wrong way. But Boardman and Bell seemed to reach some mutual understanding as the years passed, and Bell now tolerated the daily torture with the younger rider, although he didn't particularly enjoy it. Tony Bell recalls his brother fretting over those long rides. 'I remember Mark saying he was riding to meet Chris, and he was dreading it because he knew the next five hours were going to be purgatory. When Chris went out training, there wasn't much time or energy for talking.'

It was almost a traditional training schedule, but Keen and Boardman being Keen and Boardman, they also had a new development for 1995. The target now was the Tour de France, and Boardman's training was geared to doing well in the race. In 1994 it had been more straightforward: he'd basically trained for the prologue and the subsequent pursuit world championship; as he had pulled out of the Tour before the race hit the mountains, there had been no need to train for the climbs. For 1995, he'd need to do some climbing training, and as there were no mountains near the Wirral, Keen came up with an alternative – a treadmill, tipped up at a gradient of 9 per cent, upon which Boardman would ride his bike for up to an hour at a time, trying to simulate the demands of racing up Alpine and Pyrenean passes. It was a typically unorthodox solution to the problem, although it attracted curiosity and ridicule in equal measure.

Meanwhile, during the off season between 1994 and 1995, the question of what Boardman would be capable of at the Tour wouldn't go away. Gan manager Roger Legeay felt that just finishing the Tour in 1995 would be the most important step, irrespective of what position he ended up in. But Boardman, while being at pains to point out that he'd never said he *could* win it, only that he'd try to do his best, said that he was hoping to finish in the first twenty.

Boardman's racing season, too, was based entirely around peaking for the 1995 Tour de France. He'd had his practice run at the event the year before. The good news was that he'd worn the yellow jersey; the bad was that he'd been extremely tired after only a week of racing. Even if he'd always planned on pulling out after ten days, he hadn't anticipated the level of cumulative fatigue, nor losing five minutes in the long time trial a week into the race, even if only three other riders apart from winner Miguel Indurain had finished ahead of him.

Illness and a virus after his world championship win meant a low-key end to 1994. Boardman competed in the Grand Prix Eddy Merckx and Grand Prix des Nations just as he had the year before, but twelfth place in the former and sixth place in the latter were disappointments compared to his impressive professional debut. He wasn't winning races as early in 1995 as he had been the year before either. He'd been keen to get early wins under his belt in his debut full year, but with bigger targets further down the road, he could afford to ease himself into the season.

Professional cycling in 1995 was being dominated by a few key figures. Indurain, the tall, phlegmatic Spaniard with sleepy eyes, lungs like bellows and legs that looked as if they'd been carved from oak, had now won four consecutive Tours – only the second man in history to have done so. Winning in 1995 would make him the first to win five in a row. Indurain's biggest rival was Tony Rominger, the Swiss time trial specialist with his mercenary and unromantic attitude to the sport. He looked like an accountant, and rode his bike like one, too. Rominger was a late bloomer: six years of decent results in small races and mediocrity in the Grand Tours had been followed by three consecutive Tour of Spain wins (and he would be victorious in the Tour of Italy in 1995). Laurent Jalabert was another rider who'd undergone a mid-career transformation in the mid-1990s. After having his features resculpted by one too many bunch sprint crashes, his wife persuaded him to change tack and he'd developed into a Classics and short stage race specialist, seemingly winning at will, going on to place in the top five in the Tour de France, and winning the Tour of Spain.

These were the riders against whom Boardman was hoping to measure himself, although they were unnaturally strong. There were also riders like Johan Museeuw, from Belgium, Swiss rider Mauro Gianetti, and Lance Armstrong. Classics specialists, but men whose ambitions overlapped with Boardman's in the shorter stage races.

Boardman took a beating from Jalabert in his first big race of the year, the Critérium International, a three-stage race featuring a flat section, a hilly section and a time trial, which would normally have suited the British rider down to the ground. He also suffered through the Tour of the Basque Country, a tough hilly race in northern Spain. It wasn't until May that Boardman started winning, with time trial victories in the Four Days of Dunkirk and Tour de l'Oise in France. Then his confidence was boosted by beating Indurain in the time trial stage of the Midi Libre stage race. But it was in the Critérium du Dauphiné Libéré in mid-June that Boardman's perception of himself as a Tour de France contender reached its zenith.

Just as he had in the same event the year before, Boardman won the prologue. He'd prevailed over Indurain, but the Spaniard returned the favour in the stage three time trial around the vineyards of Tain l'Hermitage, beating the Brit into second by a minute.

The next day, the race went into the mountains, with an ascent of Mont Ventoux before the finish in Carpentras.

Boardman neither shone nor completely capitulated. He conceded just over a minute to Indurain and a handful of other rivals, but the time he'd gained in the time trial meant he was still second overall.

Boardman was expected to concede more time on the most mountainous stage of the race two days later, which crossed the Col du Galibier and the Col de la Croix de Fer, two of the Tour de France's most difficult mountains, before a 7-kilometre climb to the finish in Vaujany. But he hung on, basing his tactics on Indurain rather than Richard Virenque, a climbing specialist whose modus operandi was to attack repeatedly. The Frenchman was often more annoying than he was effective at actually winning races, and his stop-start rhythm certainly wasn't comfortable for Boardman. Indurain, however, refused to follow Virenque's attacks and rode at a steady, diesel-like pace, so Boardman followed him. He'd been in trouble on the first climb, the Galibier, but the race had settled down, giving him a chance to catch up with the leaders again. Boardman was one of five survivors to contest the sprint for the stage in Vaujany, and even though he was fifth, he didn't concede any time to his rivals. This was new territory for the Brit – he'd stayed with the best climbers in the world over the hardest mountains of the Tour. Add that to his time-trialling ability, and he was looking like a genuine Tour contender.

On the final day, when Indurain stretched his legs over the final climb, Boardman was one of only four riders who were able to stay with him. His form was holding, and he finished second overall. Indurain, the best stage racer in the world, had won, but Boardman was close behind him, just over two minutes down. If he could match that effort in the Tour de France, he wouldn't be far from the podium.

'I maintain that Chris had the capacity to do an extremely good Tour de France,' says Roger Legeay. 'All the great champions of the Tour were, first and foremost, *rouleurs* – time triallists, not climbers. Indurain wasn't a climber. LeMond wasn't a climber. Hinault wasn't a climber. Thévenet could climb, but he was an all-rounder, not a climber. Anquetil was a *rouleur*. All these riders were *rouleurs*. Big engines, who treated the mountains like time trials – they didn't follow the attacks, but just neutralized them instead. Wiggins, in 2012, won the time trials and then rode the mountains as if they were time trials. Cadel Evans won the year before Wiggins, and isn't a climber. Only rarely do climbers win the Tour – like Lucien Van Impe, [Marco] Pantani and Federico Bahamontes.'

As Boardman readied himself for his second Tour de France, the cycling world wondered what might be possible, and he tried to play down expectations. 'In the past, journalists have asked, "Would you like to finish in the top ten of the Tour?" and I've always said, "Yes, that would be great,"' he said. 'Then the next day I open the paper and it says "Chris Boardman says he can finish in the top ten". It's not the same thing at all. What I would say,' he added, 'is that I reckon I can get to the finish in Paris. I'm confident I can do that.'

He spoke too soon.

The Tour prologue in 1995 took place in St Brieuc, in Brittany. It was an unusual course compared to the straightforward wide and flat roads in Lille, with a significant climb and descent to tackle. It was also held at an unusual time of day – the evening. That wasn't popular with the riders, who needed to rest, recover, eat and have a massage after each stage and who would now be finishing several hours later than normal. But the organizers wanted the spectacular effect of night-time racing, live during primetime, rather than daylight cycling in front of fewer viewers in mid-afternoon.

Unfortunately, the weather changed from sunny in the

afternoon, to rainy through the late afternoon, to a full-blown storm by the time the final riders were set to head out. Boardman and Legeay didn't know what to do. 'I had driven behind all the other riders – I did the course nine times that day,' says Legeay. 'There was sun, for the start, then it got a bit overcast, and there was less nice weather for each rider. Then rain. Our directeur sportif Serge Beucherie was looking after Chris and I said to him, "What is he going to do?" "It's up to him. If he goes à fond, all out, he goes all out. If he doesn't, fine." Each time I passed, I asked, "What will he do?" and each time the answer was, "We don't know."'

The time came for Boardman to take the start line, and he decided to go for it.

Gan hadn't had a great season until that point. Both Boardman and Legeay deny that the subject was raised, or that a yellow jersey on day one of the Tour would rescue a mediocre season, but the temptation to try and repeat what had happened the year before was too strong.

Boardman had spent the whole day watching the weather deteriorate, and the nerves had been building, but once he was on the start line, he committed himself. The second-last Gan rider to go out, Didier Rous, who rode in the rain, told Boardman he'd only dropped 30 seconds to the current leader, Jacky Durand, who'd ridden in the dry. Rous egged on Boardman. If *he* was only 30 seconds down, he pointed out, Boardman could win.

It wasn't ideal, because Boardman had had to compromise on his tyre selection. As the rain set in, he'd decided he wanted heavier, grippier tyres, but with so many riders all competing and setting off at different times, the supply of tyres and wheels was tight. He was forced to go out with an ordinary road tyre on the front and a slick time trial tyre on the rear wheel. That meant his front wheel had more grip than his rear.

On the start line in 1994, he had looked focused and aggressive. A year later, with his skinsuit already soaked by the teeming rain, he looked anxious and frightened.

Through the town before the climb, the course was very technical, with some sharp bends, which were incredibly slippery. But somehow Boardman managed to get through them without crashing. He later recalled thinking, 'I can't believe I just got round those.'

Boardman was the ninth rider Legeay had followed round the course, so the Frenchman knew it by heart now. As Boardman crested the hill, just a couple of seconds down on his team-mate Francis Moreau, who'd also ridden in better conditions and was only 3 seconds in turn behind Durand, Legeay knew that Boardman was set fair for the win. 'I said, *calme, calme*, it's OK. He'd passed all the tricky bits and there was a downhill and flat section to the finish.'

But there was one slight left-hand bend on the descent – barely a change of direction, but in the dark and the pouring rain Boardman's bike suddenly slipped out from underneath him as if he'd hit a patch of ice. The British rider slammed into the tarmac, and he and his bike slid across the road into the barriers on the opposite side. Boardman later estimated that he'd been travelling at about 80 kilometres per hour when he fell. 'He was riding on a rough bit of road, but then there was a smooth bit of tarmac. When he hit that, his bike slid out,' explains Legeay, who only just managed to stop the car before hitting his rider, who was sitting prone in the road.

Boardman quickly remounted and rode a few yards down the road, but it became clear he was in serious pain. He'd sustained a shattered ankle and broken wrist. His Tour was over after just a few minutes' racing.

Legeay doesn't regret the way things happened. 'Chris is a great champion. Great champions don't hold back just because

TOP: Boardman composes himself ahead of the first stage of the Tour of the Mediterranean, a team time trial, in spring 1994. The world of international road racing would be a steep learning curve for him.

MIDDLE: With the Gan team manager, Roger Legeay. The pair first met during the Tour of Britain in 1993, and the Frenchman was particularly impressed by Boardman's intelligence.

BOTTOM: Three-time Tour de France winner Greg LeMond was the Gan team leader, but Boardman soon took over that role.

ABOVE: Boardman wins the prologue of the 1994 Tour de France, in Lille. Luc Leblanc, who suffered the humiliation of being caught by him in the 7.2-kilometre time trial, is in the background.

BELOW: Boardman became the first British rider since Tom Simpson to wear the yellow jersey, but couldn't hold on to it by the time the Tour crossed the Channel to Dover four days later.

TOP AND MIDDLE: Boardman considered himself a contender for the general classification in the Tour de France in 1995, but a fifty mile an hour crash on the wet roads of Brittany put paid to that ambition.

BOTTOM: The Tour's private jet flew Boardman home from Dinard airport, but he was in obvious agony from his injuries, including a shattered ankle and broken wrist.

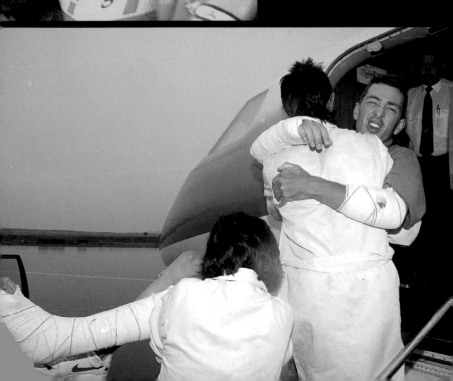

TOP: Catching Laurent Jalabert. By finishing third overall behind the ONCE rider and Lance Armstrong in the Paris-Nice race in 1996, Boardman showed he could compete with the best on the road.

MIDDLE AND BOTTOM: The heat and humidity in Atlanta in August were overwhelming, but Boardman still managed an Olympic bronze medal in the time trial to go with his track gold from Barcelona. Miguel Indurain of Spain took the gold, and his compatriot Abraham Olano silver.

The hour record had passed from Obree to Indurain and then Tony Rominger, but Boardman set an astonishing mark of 56.375 kilometres in Manchester on 7 September 1996, adopting Obree's Superman position. Peter Keen was walking the line, doing entire circuits of the track.

LEFT: Boardman's career had reached its zenith on the track, but competing on the road in the doping-fuelled mid-90s could be an uphill task. Here he struggles on Mont Ventoux, losing four and a half minutes, during the 1996 Critérium de Dauphiné Libéré.

BELOW: Boardman still dominated the Grand Départ though, taking the yellow jersey again in Rouen in 1997.

ABOVE: Toasting the Cannibal: Eddy Merckx and Boardman.

TOP AND MIDDLE: Victories in regular road race stages were a rarity for Boardman, but you can see both exhilaration and exhaustion etched on his face as he crosses the line to win in the PruTour in Newcastle in 1998.

BOTTOM: Another Tour de France prologue victory followed in Dublin in 1998, but life on the road had already begun to lose its allure, and 1999 would be Boardman's final Tour as a rider.

RIGHT AND MIDDLE:
Manchester, 27 October
2000: Boardman's final
hour. With Keen at his
side as ever, Boardman
broke Merckx's 1972
'athletes' distance record
by ten metres, pushing
himself to the limit like
never before.

BELOW: Boardman's
effort was so intense that
his wife Sally, pictured
applauding her husband
here during his Bordeaux
hour record, even went
to the trackside to urge
him on.

it's raining. It's a huge compliment by Chris to the race, and indicative of the grandeur of the Tour de France and its riders, that he didn't hold back. I said to him that it was his choice, and he said he would go for it. That was the mark of a huge champion. It rained, he went à fond, and the possibilities from that moment were two. Either he would win, and it would be extraordinary. Or he would fall and crash out, and that would be extraordinary too. Of course, it was disappointing that instead of winning he was in the hospital. But there are no regrets. What regrets could we have? We could have regretted it if he'd come eighth after not trying. If he'd done that, he'd spend the rest of his life wishing he'd gone à fond. No regrets, just frustration. And it was a serious crash, but it's now part of his notoriety. He was courageous, and he accepted the challenge like a toreador in front of a bull. It's why cycling is so magnificent – because there are magnificent champions. It was his choice, and I respect it. I think it's normal that an athlete tries to take his destiny in his hands.'

Legeay then adds a note of levity as he looks back on what they might have done differently. 'I'd have done the same thing in his position. So would Chris now, I think, except he'd probably just ride a foot to the left of where he actually did.'

As the next rider on the road, Maurizio Fondriest, slithered through the gap left between the Gan team car and the barriers, Roger Legeay picked Chris Boardman up in his arms, carried him over to the car and put him inside.

'That was a strong moment,' Legeay recalls. 'It wasn't fair.'

The next day, Boardman was taken to nearby Dinard airport to be flown home in the Tour's private twin-engine jet. William and Alasdair Fotheringham, covering the race as journalists, guessed where he was flying from and waited at the airport to get the final glimpse of Boardman before he left the race for good. 'We sprinted across the airfield when the Crédit Agricole car appeared,' Alasdair recalls. 'He was screaming with pain when they put him on the plane. They jarred the stretcher against one of the doors. I was trying not to look.'

Had Boardman been unnecessarily bullish? The yellow jersey contenders all rode conservatively – Miguel Indurain completed the course on his road bike, rather than a time trial bike, conceding 30 seconds to Durand. He went on to win the Tour, while Boardman, who'd taken a lot of risks and got found out with the very last one, wouldn't get the chance to see how far he could have gone in that year's race. The pressure of having won the prologue so convincingly the year before meant that the expectation for him was to win again in 1995. He'd been within a few seconds of Durand over the climb, which he would have taken back in the final flat, uncomplicated couple of kilometres. If he had done so, he'd have been hailed as a hero. So fine is the line that divides recklessness and glory.

Boardman had found himself riven by two conflicting urges on the start line. He wanted to ride like a Tour winner, and he wanted to ride like a prologue winner. The two aims, on that day, were completely incompatible.

16

Superman

Chris Boardman's 1995 season might have been blown apart, but no one could take away from him the blessed end to 1994, with its yellow jersey and world championship pursuit gold medal. Which is more than can be said for Graeme Obree, for whom things just got worse following his disqualification from the world championship. First, his hour record was beaten, initially by Miguel Indurain, next by Tony Rominger. Then, in October 1994, his brother Gordon was killed in a car crash.

Obree, with a busy schedule of exhibition races, didn't allow himself the time or space to grieve. He'd also signed a contract with a professional team, Le Groupement, a new outfit sponsored by a sales company called GEPM (Le Groupement Européen des Professionnels du Marketing). As well as Obree, they'd signed the new road world champion Luc Leblanc, a nine-time Tour de France stage winner; Jean-Paul Van Poppel; and Obree's fellow Scot Robert Millar, a former King of the Mountains at the Tour de France.

GEPM sold household goods, clothes and cosmetics to a forty-thousand-strong network of part-time sales representatives who then tried to sell on to friends, acquaintances and neighbours. GEPM's head, Jean Godzich, was the son of Polish parents who were displaced during the Second World War, and who emigrated first to France, then the USA. Godzich came to France as an adult and set up GEPM in 1987. He encouraged a slavish devotion among the sales reps and organized huge motivational rallies to encourage them to bring in more reps, who were in turn similarly encouraged, while flogging books and videos. It was a classic pyramid sales operation, with the added complication that Godzich also had links to a right-wing evangelical church in the United States. Godzich had pledged £20 million over five years for the cycling team.

Obree describes his employment with Le Groupement as the 'shortest ever professional career'. His contract officially started on 1 January 1995. By midday that day, he'd been fired.

He'd irritated the management by missing the first team get-together, in Florida in early December 1994. Then he'd gone on holiday to the United States before being summoned by the team to attend another meeting on 23 December. 'I'd just flown in from Arizona via Chicago to London, then to Paris, and I was dog-tired,' Obree says. From Paris, he was picked up by his team-mate Robert Millar and driven the 200 kilometres to Lille. They arrived late, and the team's manager, Guy Mollet, informed them they had missed dinner and would not be getting fed. 'There was food there,' Obree bristles, still feeling the injustice of it. 'The other riders were still eating.' The two Scots ended up sharing some cornflakes that Obree had smuggled in.

Unfortunately for Obree, just after Christmas he started experiencing the delayed shock of his brother's death, which pulled him into a spell of depression. Then he came down with the flu and he subsequently missed the next team get-together, on New Year's Day. He was instantly dismissed.

Obree alleged that a Le Groupement team-mate told him

that as a squad member he'd have to pay £2,000 a year for 'medical back-up'. Doping in cycling may have been growing ever more organized, scientific and institutionalized in the mid-1990s, but this still shocked Obree and he refused to pay.

There was one last problem with Le Groupement: Obree despised most of his new team-mates. Marcel Wüst, a German sprinter who became friendly with Millar and had always gravitated to the English-speaking members of the peloton, told him that many of the French riders were mocking him behind his back. 'I hated hanging around with them,' Obree says. 'They were ignorant; they wouldn't even grunt at me. But I think the reason I got fired was because I wasn't going to take the kit.'

He needn't have worried too much. GEPM went bankrupt in 1995, and the cycling team folded in late June, before they'd even had a chance to ride the Tour de France. GEPM ended up being designated a cult by the government, and Godzich later spent three years in prison for misuse of corporate assets.

It had been a terrible start to the new year for Obree. 'I had no sponsorship, no team, no hour record, no world championship and no riding position that I was allowed to use. My brother died, I was full of the flu, and I was feeling seriously depressed. That was the start of 1995.'

One day in April 1995, Doug Dailey's telephone rang.

'Hello, Doug,' said the voice at the other end, and Dailey immediately knew it was Graeme Obree. Obree pronounced Dailey's name the Scottish way, to rhyme with 'moog', not 'mug'. 'I've developed a new position, and it's even faster than the old one,' he continued.

Obree had pulled himself out of depression and had started experimenting with tri-bars. 'I thought, Boardman has been doing this since 1989 or 1990, he must know what he's doing, so I'll copy him. I went out with these low-slung handlebars and it felt awful. It didn't feel right.' He decided to look at the position more broadly, realizing that there were more tri-bar positions than people had realized, ranging from arms all the way back, and bent at the elbow, all the way through to a full extension of the arms. He worked from both ends to see which would suit him. 'I tried with my arms outstretched as far as I could, like Superman. It was ridiculous, and I thought, "You cannae do that."' But he did. He built the stem and bars up, and went to test the bike.

'I made sure nobody could see me, and I thought, this is brilliant. I've worked out since why the new position was so good, and it wasn't just aerodynamic. From the elbows as a support point, going through your upper arms, shoulders, spine and to your coccyx, it's an arch, so you are locked in place. In the normal tri-bar position, you can shimmy forwards and back, because there is nothing locking you in. In this position, you are locked in, and not losing any power.'

Over the phone, Obree told Dailey about the new position and said he had entered a ten-minute individual pursuit match against seven others, including up-and-coming rider Rob Hayles, at the Herne Hill Good Friday track meet. Dailey promised he would go to the event and watch.

It was no contest. Although it boiled down to a two-man race, between Hayles and Obree, Hayles caught the Scot well before the finish. 'He was good enough not to say anything as he went past,' Obree jokes. But Dailey recognized that Obree was on to something. 'It was the old Graeme,' says Dailey. 'The position was terrific, you could see it. It was another first for him. He loves to think outside the box.'

Dailey told Obree that if he could get fit, he would select him to ride the individual pursuit in the upcoming World Cup fixture in Athens.

While most of the other cyclists at the Good Friday meet had reacted at best with amusement and at worst with derision, Dailey had seen something to work with. His greatest asset was his ability to identify talent, in both coaches and athletes, and give them the space in which to operate. He'd done that with Peter Keen and Chris Boardman, and he knew it was also the best way to deal with Obree.

'Doug was instinctive,' Obree recalls. 'He would never tell me what to do or what not to do. He knew that if I was left to my own devices, most of my ideas would be bollocks, but that there would be a gem in there. Doug stuck his neck out and selected me for Athens. You'd never get away with that these days – the rules would prevent it.'

Obree trained hard in the four weeks leading up to the Athens World Cup. The format was strict: one qualifying ride would put two riders into the final. He qualified fastest, in a time of 4.32 – 3 seconds clear of the second-fastest rider Dietmar Müller of Austria. Although it was 12 seconds off the world record he'd set in Oslo in 1993, Athens was an outdoor track and the race was being held on a windy day. He made short work of Müller in the final, winning the event and repaying Dailey's trust.

Dailey kept on selecting Obree for World Cup events through the 1995 season; he was a one-man Team GB, taking himself and his bike bag to the German, Australian and Japanese rounds of the competition. In Germany, he unshipped his chain and didn't qualify. He won the Australian round in Adelaide, beating Philippe Ermenault, his rival in the 1993 world championship final. A week later the tables were turned, and Ermenault beat him after Obree had overslept with jet lag.

In August, while Boardman was convalescing from his Tour crash, Obree entered the national track championship, which was being held in the new Manchester velodrome. His form was getting better and better, and in qualifying he rode the 4,000 metres in 4.22 – just a couple of seconds outside his own world record, after having started on a slower schedule. Nobody was anywhere near his standard, and he wrapped up the series easily, winning his third national pursuit championship by beating Bryan Steel in the final. There was no hope of a world record this time as the temperature rose in the velodrome, making fast times less likely.

Whether deliberately or accidentally, the person the BCF had lined up to present the medal and champion's jersey was Chris Boardman.

While Obree's ex-Le Groupement team-mates were scrabbling around trying to find employment for the rest of the season and for the next year, Obree was contemplating likely selection to represent his country at the world championship, which would be held at high altitude in Colombia. Indeed his 4.22 made him an immediate favourite for the title. But at the Manchester round of the World Cup, a new contender emerged – the Italian Andrea Collinelli. With Ermenault absent, Obree and Collinelli were the two fastest. Both rode 4.24, then the Italian prevailed narrowly in the final.

While Obree did his final few weeks' training for the world championship, Doug Dailey went off to Colombia to recce the location. The track championship would take place in Bogotá, while the road race and time trial, the latter of which Obree was also entered for, were happening a few hours' drive away in Duitama, in the province of Boyaca.

'It was an armpit of a place,' recalls Dailey.

He booked hotels in both cities: the road riders would stay in Boyaca, while the track riders would be based in Bogotá. But then, while Dailey was driving through Duitama, he spotted a sports stadium in which he thought he could just see a velodrome. He asked the driver to stop and climbed over the wall to have a look. 'It was a bloody cycle track,' he confirms. 'It was in pretty awful condition, maybe two hundred and fifty metres round, and concrete, but it was marked out. There were no changing rooms, no toilet, just a derelict building. I thought that instead of having two camps in two different places, I'd bring all the riders to Boyaca. I knew I'd have a riot when they saw it, but the Bogotá track wasn't finished yet, so we could train on this track.'

With the championship taking place at an altitude of 2,625 metres, acclimatization would be necessary, and Dailey decided to send the British team to Breckenridge, in Colorado. A contact had put him in touch with an expat who rented out apartments and houses in the area, and who was willing to let the team use one of the empty properties for their camp.

The British cycling team of the mid-1990s was a far cry from the modern British cycling team, with its huge budget and military organization. Obree recalls that the operation was run on a shoestring. When, after a long training ride over Vail Pass, the riders found a restaurant serving an all-you-can-eat buffet for five dollars, the whole team piled in. When they went back the next day, the owner told them they were closed.

Simon Lillistone remembers Obree turning up to the camp a few days after the other riders. 'He got off the plane, unpacked his bag, and asked us, "Does anybody have a turbo trainer?" Then he got on it, no warm-up, and nearly killed himself. He did four Ks absolutely full on.'

Eccentric training or not, Dailey recalls Obree's form getting better and better. When they transferred to Boyaca and started training on the old concrete track there, he was measuring himself against the team pursuit squad, and riding faster than them. The only problem was that he had developed a toothache. 'I was a bit annoyed about that because he'd obviously brought that problem over with him from Britain,' says Dailey. 'We found a dentist, who wanted to give Graeme a complete dental makeover. Graeme thought he was great. I asked how much it was going to cost, and he mentioned this huge number. My attitude was, bloody hell, that's the food money. I told Graeme I'd pay fifty per cent of it, and he got the complete makeover. It took away the pain, and he started riding even quicker. He was absolutely flying.'

Generally, pursuit series follow sporting logic. Once the qualifying round has been ridden, the hierarchy is fairly predictable. Riders tend to go as hard as they can, in order to secure an easier draw in the subsequent rounds. Hold back in the qualifier, and a rider runs the risk of coming up against a strong rival earlier in the draw. But that's what Obree did in the 1995 world championship. He'd identified that the quarter-final would be the championship-deciding ride for him. The quarters came soon after the qualifying round, then the semi-final and final were the next day, separated by an hour. Obree calculated that a decent qualifying ride followed by a very fast quarter would give him three things: momentum, an easier opponent, and an advantage in scheduling. If he was the fastest quarter-finalist, he would ride against the slowest quarter-final winner, in the first semi-final. That would give him an extra ten minutes of recovery time, which was crucial in the thin air of Bogotá. The man he really feared was Collinelli; without these extra advantages, Obree couldn't be confident of having a chance against him. 'Being the first to ride in the morning was pivotal, because basically, Collinelli was faster than me, and that was a problem,' Obree says.

This intelligent scheming is interesting because the common perception of Obree is that he had a chaotic approach to the sport, which contrasted with Chris Boardman's meticulous planning. Obree contributed to this perception by playing up to his image. Photographer Phil O'Connor recalls that the Scot seemed very aware of the camera being on him. He'd photographed Obree for a shoot for Specialized not long before his hour record attempt. 'He always knew when the camera was on him. He would strike a pose. I was hanging around in Norway, and he got this book about Moser's hour record out, and sat there reading it, so he'd be photographed reading it. There would be a pile of jam sandwiches ready – was it for me to photograph, or was it part of the myth? He was very savvy.' Cycling journalist Adam Glasser shares another story, about Obree sitting in the pits at Herne Hill, eating jam out of a jar with a spanner as he chatted to his fellow competitors. He performed to the crowd, without a doubt, but it's not clear where the performer ended and the real Obree began – they were virtually the same person. He played the clown effortlessly, but sometimes consciously.

In Colombia, Obree qualified third fastest, in 4.26. It was quick, but he'd held a lot back for his planned assault on the quarter-final. Collinelli was the fastest qualifier, in 4.24, with Australian Stuart O'Grady second in 4.25. Behind Obree, a full second behind, was Philippe Ermenault. In Obree's quarter-final, he dispatched Spanish rider Juan Martínez easily, but the time was the important thing. 'I didn't treat it as a race, I treated it as a time trial,' he says. 'I was thinking, "If I don't go faster than Collinelli here, I can forget about winning."' There was a fraction of a second in it, but Obree qualified fastest. The semi-final line-up would be Obree versus Ermenault, followed by Collinelli versus O'Grady.

Obree had been keen to avoid the Italian. He'd also been keen to avoid the Australian. 'I respect Philippe, but he was a known quantity, and predictable. What he did in qualifying, he would do against me. I told Doug before my semi-final, "Don't even tell me what Philippe is doing, just tell me where I am with my schedule." Philippe rode to his pace, I rode to mine. It wasn't an easy ride, but it was simple. I did a standard ride at a pace I knew I could win it at to get to the final.

'Collinelli was up against O'Grady, who I definitely did not want to race. You never knew what he was going to come out with. If I'd been racing O'Grady ten minutes after Collinelli, I would have lost the final. And against Collinelli, O'Grady came out with this phenomenal ride – Collinelli had to fight to the end. Meanwhile I was getting my recovery in. Collinelli was flat on his back getting oxygen at the end of the ride. I thought, "I'm having you."'

O'Grady had changed his tactics completely for the semi-final and gone out extremely fast, drawing an energy-sapping ride out of his rival. It took a 4.22 for Collinelli to beat the Australian, but in spite of this draining fight he was still dangerous to Obree.

Obree, using a much bigger gear than his rival, started slowly in the final, but went into the lead after two and a half laps. Collinelli edged ahead after a kilometre, then Obree led by 0.2 seconds at the halfway point. On the tenth and eleventh laps (of twelve), Collinelli picked it up, and with one 333-metre lap to go, the pair were virtually level.

'I'd told Doug again, it's not about the other rider, it's about me. I didn't want a signal until halfway. When it came, it was the worst possible signal – level. Then I went up. Then level. Then slightly down. Then level. On the last lap, it was like storming a machine gun post. I don't know if there's something inside me that comes out at that moment, but that last lap was at the point of pain of drilling your own teeth out.'

On the infield, the British team mechanic Sandy Gilchrist turned to Yvonne McGregor, a member of the women's team, and told her, 'That's it. He's lost.' He knew Obree wasn't usually capable of a sprint finish.

But Obree found the speed from somewhere to cross the line

first, by half a second. He'd won his second world individual pursuit championship, just a year after being disqualified in Sicily. A measure of how well organized his series had been was that over the course of the rides Collinelli had gone faster than Obree, but in the one race that counted, Obree had outwitted and outridden him.

The pursuit was over with but there was still the time trial to go, and Dailey was confident that Obree could pull out another big ride, in spite of the fact he'd always faltered against international competition in road events. 'He was flying, and he was revelling in the riding at altitude. The food there was crap and the accommodation wasn't great, but he was used to it, and living off skimmed milk, cornflakes and bananas. And in the run-up to the time trial, he was going better and better. Chris had shown us the year before that it was possible to win the pursuit and the time trial. In training, two of our road riders, Jonny Clay and Simon Bray, couldn't even hold his wheel, let alone go past him. He was awesome.' Moreover, the time trial course was a straightforward linear one between two towns. All Obree had to do was hold his form for another week and he could even win a medal.

Unfortunately, the focused Obree of the pursuit series was replaced by the disorganized and unfocused Obree of stereotype. 'One of the sponsors whisked him away after the pursuit to do some adverts and he was gone for bloody days,' recalls Dailey. 'They paid him well, and the advert was on television. He'd have been put up in a nice hotel and they'd have loved him – he'd have kept them entertained with all his stories. We didn't see him for days, then he came back and he was riding like a dog.'

Obree rode the time trial and finished a distant twenty-first, almost six minutes behind the winner, Miguel Indurain. But Dailey knew better than to get frustrated with him. He knew that without the Obree who disappeared for days in the run-up to the time trial, there couldn't be the Obree who won the pursuit final.

17

Keen

On the other side of the Atlantic, Peter Keen and Chris Boardman were already busy getting ready for a full 1996 season. As always, they were doing it together. Indeed, to understand Boardman, you need to understand Keen. The career of one makes no sense without that of the other.

I'm waiting for Keen at St Albans station, and watching the station clock. 'Peter will meet you at 10.30,' his PA had written. The clock clicks over to 10:30:00 and he's not there. But it's only a few more seconds before he walks in.

'You're four seconds late, Peter. I'm disappointed,' I tell him, and he laughs, but I think he's already worked me out.

The picture I've built up of him, from reports, interviews and anecdotal evidence, is the same as everybody else's: Keen is a scientist and planner – he introduced elements of both into cycling that were way ahead of, or on a completely different level to, what anybody else had been doing. The photographs of the white-coated boffin measuring Boardman's physical output in a lab were so memorable, fresh and striking at the time that fourteen years of coaching and human relationships has been boiled down into this one image.

There was truth to the stereotype, too. If he'd really wanted to contradict it, he'd have shown up at 10.35. (I'm pleasantly surprised he's here at all, to tell the truth. My requests for interview had been politely but firmly turned down throughout the course of my research. In fact this book was well over halfway towards completion when at last he consented to meet me.)

My impression of Keen was reinforced when he was quoted immediately after Boardman's 1993 hour record in Bordeaux. He was pleased, of course, but he also expressed regret that he had not had the opportunity to get a core temperature reading immediately after Boardman had finished. Only Peter Keen's first instinct after one of the greatest athletic achievements in cycling history would be to stick a thermometer up his rider's arse, rather than give him a hug.

'We were kids,' he tells me over a skinny latte in a St Albans café. 'We weren't able to counter that one-dimensional storyline with anything smart enough to challenge it. Graeme the clown, me the white-coated egghead and Chris the machine.'

But Keen's not just a scientist. He's a historian and a philosopher of science, too. Our interview is peppered with mentions of the British philosopher Karl Popper and the psychologist Mihaly Csikszentmihalyi. The American science historian Thomas Kuhn is referred to indirectly. He tells me about the light-bulb moment he had in his early twenties when he realized that science was not about sitting in classrooms absorbing facts and being able to repeat them. Most people consider science as a source of certainty and answers; Keen sees it as creative and uncertain, more about probability and method than received knowledge. 'It was about posing questions and figuring out what was going on,' he says. When he made that mental leap, he spent the next few weeks being the last person to leave the library while he read the works of Popper.

Keen is at pains to point out that the contrast built up between Boardman and Obree, the idea that their approaches, characters and methods were diametrically opposed, was a false one, that the reality of their lives and the uncertainty imposed by all the different variables of cycling made their stories far more complex than the reports would have us believe. One of Popper's most famous works is *The Poverty of Historicism*, in which he criticizes the assumption that history develops predictably along logical lines and can therefore necessarily be used as a predictor of the future. Any assumption that Chris Boardman's career was reducible to a simple narrative, a few easy stereotypes and a bit of armchair psychology would be, in Keen's eyes, flawed.

It's the same with Keen. I'd known he was a schoolboy champion cyclist. I hadn't known how poorly he'd done academically.

Keen describes his background as 'spectacularly average'. The second of three children, he grew up in High Wycombe, where his father was a draughtsman working in the print industry, transposing images on to rollers to print stamps. His mother brought up the children, then worked as an office clerk. I had assumed that at school he gravitated towards the sciences, hung around with the nerds and was a star pupil. 'You're wrong,' he says. 'My school reports, if there is any academic prowess there, point more towards the arts and humanities.' Keen dropped out of A-level biology and left school with a D and an E at A-level maths and physics. After telling me this, he adds, 'You can render down the next three hours to two words: luck and logic. If you want to understand me, Boardman, performance and everything we've been involved with, there's an awful lot of logic behind it. And luck plays its part.'

Keen's way into cycling had been similar to Graeme Obree's. He went on a bike tour with a friend during the Easter holidays in 1977, going to Wales and back in six days and staying at youth hostels. He came back a different person, he says. He joined the Cycling Tourists' Club, got interested in racing and found a local coach, Gordon Wright, whose methods intrigued him. Wright had a busy job, so he trained hard and smart, rather than in volume. He didn't race very often, but when he did, he usually won.

In 1980, Keen won the national schools 10-mile time trial, which Boardman himself would win four years later. Conditions and the different locations of the race make comparison between years impossible, but Keen's 21.30, recorded on a normal racing bike, wasn't beaten until 1991, and only four more times since. He was good.

He made it into the national squad, but it didn't work out. He needed coaching, but all they gave him was racing. He was invited to a training camp in the Peak District along with eight or ten others, including Adrian Timmis, who would go on to ride the Tour de France (and, some speculate, ruin his career, having been thrown into the biggest race in the world too young). 'The overriding memory is that they all seemed to know a hell of a lot about what they were doing,' he recalls. 'They had the kit, their dads all raced.' Keen had ridden one road race in his life. He was completely out of his depth. He likens the experience to being put on a football pitch and not knowing the rules. He did what was asked of him, which was train hard and race a lot, but the guidance wasn't there. He was being asked to do, not to understand.

If he was honest with himself, road racing didn't suit him, in two ways. The tactics and variables of the discipline frustrated him, and more importantly, he didn't need to win that badly. 'I can remember times when I was riding in races, and some kid would be sat on my wheel for forty miles, quite happy to sit there and do absolutely nothing, and every lap you'd have his dad shouting, "Sit on him! Sit on him!" That's not right. I'm very black and white like that. For me, sport is about the rules and the sense of winning the right way. And for most of the time since then when I've thought about it, I've just felt I wasn't sufficiently narrow as a person. I never really wanted to win that badly. I loved training, I loved riding, and I was probably most comfortable when the variables were known.'

Keen got little guidance, trained too hard, was underweight, and got ill a lot between the ages of sixteen and eighteen. At the same time, his A-levels were sacrificed on the altar of his ambitions to be an international cyclist. But that lack of a firm guiding hand in cycling cost him. 'If there's a psychoanalyst in you, I'm sure you'll conclude that's what's driven me to want to make it so for others,' he comments.

'I'm very comfortable with the idea that I didn't make it as an athlete, because I am curious about other things. I became very curious about studying science. I am very curious about music and love jazz. What I see in Obree and Boardman is a willingness to narrow life to such an extent that you can reduce the errors to the point where you outpace everybody else. I honestly don't think I could have done that.'

Keen walked into a careers office in High Wycombe at the age of eighteen, wondering what he was going to do with his life. One phone call later, he'd enrolled on a sports studies course at University College, Chichester. His teacher was Professor Tudor Hale, who changed the way Keen thought about science. Keen studied the history of sport, sociology and a whole range of linked subjects. 'When I got in the lab with an excellent teacher and had a reason to study, which was that I wanted to understand, I was a completely different person.' In the space of a year, he went from having scraped a couple of poor grades at A-level to winning the Sports Council's Dissertation of the Year award in 1985.

All the cycling world saw of Keen was his work with Boardman and the British cycling team. He was the national coach between 1989 and 1992, and was the first Performance Director of British Cycling from 1997 to 2003. But right up until he took the performance director's job, he had a full teaching and research load at Chichester, and then the University of Brighton. Occasionally, the two jobs helped each other out – in Chris Boardman, he had a prime test subject for his research. But at other times, the workload and stress were severe, and he wasn't getting rich from it. The national coach's job from 1989 to 1992 was essentially voluntary, with a small expenses budget.

At the final training camp for the Barcelona Olympics, he selected the team, which included going to each rider's room individually to tell them face to face whether they were in or out. 'It was not a lot of fun,' Keen recalls. 'Most went, three didn't, and they weren't happy. One in particular reacted very negatively, or rather his parents did, so I knew that when I got off the plane in Heathrow I was going to get an earful. I was driving home, about an hour after getting an earful from an irate father, and suddenly had an almost heart attack level of anxiety. I got a physical response in my thorax. I'd convinced myself that I'd left an entire set of exam scripts from the students' physiology finals in the seat pocket in front of me on the plane. I'd been sat there marking them.' It turned out to be a false alarm – the scripts were in his bag – but he'd been so preoccupied he couldn't even remember putting them there. 'That,' he adds, 'was British sport back then.'

When Keen became Boardman's coach in 1987, replacing Eddie Soens, like had not been exchanged for like. 'Eddie was the traditional coach. He was there with you, if not always literally then emotionally, in your head. He was very intuitive in the way he operated and he was a real physical and emotional presence. I was just a source of technical advice at the beginning, albeit at a rapidly expanding level.'

Boardman was Keen's perfect subject. The innate seriousness and literalness with which the cyclist saw the world might not have made him a scintillating dinner party guest (although his friends universally describe a dry sense of humour that is more knowing than it comes across), but the clarity of his feedback was first-rate, and was just what Keen needed. Boardman's honesty, which got him into trouble when he thought out loud to journalists and had his words interpreted, accurately or otherwise, was an asset in the lab. 'I learned faster with him than with anybody else I worked with, because he was such an exceptionally good and honest communicator,' Keen tells me. 'To this day he tells the truth as he sees it. He's very honest, and it's not everybody's cup of tea. He's not flamboyant or amusing, but he calls it as he sees it. "Great training session." "Crap training session." "It doesn't make sense, Pete, explain it again."'

Keen could see at the time that Boardman was good. But it's only with the benefit of hindsight that he has identified the most important bits of information. He was measuring Boardman physically, and witnessed his results, but it was the rate of improvement and ability to respond which really set him apart. 'By 1989, he'd pulled away from the pack, and I'd seen something that very clearly stood him out. I don't think as a physiologist I can explain that, but as an armchair psychologist I think it's got a lot to do with the learning style and what Mihaly Csikszentmihalyi describes as an autotelic personality.'

It was the renowned professor of psychology who came up with the concept of 'flow', a state of full mental and physical immersion in a task such that it's performed almost at a subconscious level. It's what athletes who describe themselves as being 'in the zone' might be experiencing, or a piano player who has the ability and technique to play a piece without thinking consciously about it. Both are products of many hours of practice and focus rather than any special innate physical talent. According to Csikszentmihalyi, autotelic personalities can achieve this state of flow more easily than others. Their character traits include high levels of curiosity and persistence, with less focus on the rewards that are a product of success than on the process itself.

Keen uses the examples of the three best pursuiters from Britain during his early years as a sports scientist. He considers Boardman and, especially, Obree as autotelic personalities who, importantly, had to fight their way through before emerging as dominant racers. The third, Colin Sturgess, who was one of the first cyclists Keen ever tested at Chichester, was different. 'There is limited literature on this, but trace back through the profile of some very successful Olympic-level winners and the pattern seems to be that they were in the pack, but they weren't winning. They were there or thereabouts, but they weren't necessarily dominant. That's the problem with prodigious talent. Colin was extraordinary, but I'm not sure he understood that or had complete ownership of it. He wasn't able to grow. Maybe he wasn't such an autotelic personality.'

But what Keen seems most eager to impress on me is that the false perception of the contrast between Boardman and Obree grew out of a one-dimensional interpretation of a much more complex situation. The narrative of the scientist Boardman versus the disorganized Obree was, on one level, the wrong way round. 'Obree is as much a natural scientist, in the more meaningful sense of the word, as most people have ever met,' he insists. 'I'm talking about effortful thinking. What he came up with was not intuitive in the sense of it flying out of his subconscious without him knowing anything about it. He built the persona of an eccentric innovator, which was amusing and attractive, and he was comfortable with that. But the Graeme Obree I saw and spent time with was absolutely a better scientist than most, in terms of asking questions and forming hypotheses, then testing them. And with Chris, we were very organized and structured in a relative sense, but what we were dealing with, in terms of his life, was chaotic. He had a growing family from the age of eighteen, and his life was probably not much less chaotic than Graeme's.'

Keen and Boardman pulled a con trick on cycling. They put up a smokescreen of success, fostered the perception that they knew exactly what they were doing, but behind it all they felt out of their depth. That was the point of their approach. They were dealing in uncertainty and asking questions, not in certainty and definite answers. 'Most of the time, when the results came it was a relief,' Keen admits. It's ironic that in those images of the white-coated and studious-looking Keen, Boardman on an indoor bike, tubes protruding from every orifice, and numbers cascading down computer screens, while they looked impressively assured, the reality is that they weren't.

But they learned fast. World and Olympic pursuit titles, the hour record, Tour prologue and time trials – their approach certainly led to success. They could operate outside the mainstream, just show up at races and win.

At the Tour de France, however, it didn't work.

18

The Beginning of the End

'I can tell you the exact point my career ended,' Chris Boardman told me. 'October twenty-second 1996, around four p.m.'

That was the date of Boardman's annual debrief with his kitchen cabinet. In the meeting, they analysed the successes and failures of 1996, a season that had panned out like a microcosm of Boardman's career. He won early season time trials and did well in shorter stage races, even winning one. He took a hammering in the Tour de France. Then he produced a pursuit and hour record of extraordinary, unbelievable brilliance. Everything he could do and could not do had been encapsulated in that one season.

They then looked ahead to 1997. When Boardman realized that in their planning for the coming season, for the first time ever they were talking about how they could do the same thing again rather than how to get better, the penny dropped. 'I think we realized we'd looked under every stone,' he said. 'That was what we were going to get out of this body. That was it. In that one instant I lost interest in the whole thing.'

*

With his ankle healed, Boardman had managed to fit in a couple of races at the end of 1995, including a farcical head-to-head against Obree at the Bercy velodrome in Paris, where the Scot's starting effort pulled the bottom bracket clean off his home-made frame. Boardman's plan for 1996 was halfway between those of his first two seasons as a professional. In 1994, he'd aimed to get good results early, in order to demonstrate his worth to the team and boost his self-confidence; in 1995, with the focus on the Tour de France, he'd started his season late, treating the early season races as training events. In 1996, he decided to hit form for the important early season races, so there would be insurance in case of disaster at the Tour. He'd felt that the lack of results in the first half of 1995 had put undue pressure on him to try and win the prologue. After a break from racing in May, he'd build again to peak at the Tour.

Boardman's path through the early season would take him to the Tour of the Mediterranean, where he'd made his first appearance for Gan in a non-time trial event in 1994, through Paris-Nice to the Critérium International. All three were French races, and therefore important to the team's sponsor. From Boardman's point of view, every good result would mean less pressure on the start line of the Tour.

It went well. At the Tour of the Mediterranean, which features an annual summit finish on the steep Mont Faron climb above Toulon, Boardman came seventh overall. Next up was Paris-Nice, and as it finished with a flat 20-kilometre time trial, he would start the race as one of the favourites. Boardman's main rival would be Laurent Jalabert, whose ONCE team seemed to be winning as many early season races in 1996 as Gewiss had in 1994. In the Tour of Valencia, the top five places were all filled by ONCE team members, and their Spanish rider Melchor Mauri won the Tour of Murcia. Jalabert had finished fourth in the previous year's Tour de France – an unusual result for a rider who'd always been seen as a Classics and short stage race specialist, and a sprinter before that.

Jalabert attacked on the first uphill finish of the race, a 3-kilometre climb to Chalvignac in the Massif Central, and only five riders could stay anywhere near him: Lance Armstrong, Laurent Dufaux, Luc Leblanc, Frank Vandenbroucke and Boardman. Boardman conceded 16 seconds. Much the same thing happened the next day, on a harder climb to the finish at Millau. Boardman was distanced and slipped to fourth overall, 1.09 behind the rampant Jalabert.

Going into that final time trial, a 20-kilometre run from Antibes to Nice along the Mediterranean coast, Boardman was confident of doing a good ride, describing the situation as 'win-win'. 'If I do a bad time trial I'll be third overall, if I do a good one I'll be second, and if I do one like in the worlds in 1994 I'll be first,' he reasoned. He actually did better than that, riding the fastest time trial ever seen in professional cycling, a tailwind-assisted 56.199 kilometres per hour, even faster than the Lille prologue in the 1994 Tour. Unfortunately both Armstrong and Jalabert had done good rides too, and they held off Boardman's challenge overall. On the podium it was Jalabert first, Armstrong second and Boardman third. It was as prestigious a result as his second place in the Critérium du Dauphiné Libéré the year before.

Seventh in his first race of the year, third in his second. It was the kind of linear progress towards a goal that Boardman and Keen thrived on. Keen made the trip out to the Tarn region of France, east of Toulouse, for the Critérium International – his first ever visit to a professional race – two weeks later. With Jalabert and Armstrong both non-starters, Boardman was the hot favourite.

Gan dominated the race, keeping it together on the opening

flat stage, then setting up Boardman to attack the finishing climb on the Pic de Nore. It was an aggressive and fragmented race, with thirteen riders, including Boardman, separating themselves from the rest of the bunch on a climb before the final one, before Mauro Gianetti then attacked on the Pic de Nore. Boardman's team-mate Didier Rous rode tempo up most of the climb, keeping his leader as close as possible to the Swiss rider. With a kilometre to go, there was a 25-second gap, but Boardman turned himself inside out to claw back 10 seconds, leaving him coughing badly in the cold air.

In the time trial the same afternoon, the result was predictable. Boardman was second to Rous, but he beat Gianetti by a lot more than the 15 seconds that separated them, winning the overall classification by 5 seconds. While the French press busied themselves trying to make Rous say that if he hadn't had to work so hard for Boardman on the uphill finish he'd have been the rightful winner of the race, Boardman celebrated his first ever stage race win as a professional rider.

His next major target was the Dauphiné. He'd won three stages there in 1994, then come second in 1995, and initially it looked like he might continue his run of success. He won the prologue, but three days later, with the race climbing Mont Ventoux, Boardman faltered badly. As Jalabert and Richard Virenque went away to finish first and second, and even Miguel Indurain found the going hard and lost a minute, Boardman conceded four and a half minutes. There was another warning sign in the time trial the next day, when both Indurain and Tony Rominger put time into the British rider. But in the high Alps stage, to Briançon, Boardman limited his losses by riding conservatively, and by the finish he was up to fifth overall, over five minutes behind.

Losing five minutes to Indurain was disappointing, but most

had been in one stage. Boardman still felt he had the Tour's measure. In the run-up to the event, he stated that with the data they had, he and Keen felt the top twenty was realistic, and 'maybe the top ten'.

The Grand Départ of the 1996 Tour took place in 's-Hertogenbosch in the Netherlands. There was no climb and descent, but it was a technical course around the city, and as luck would have it, it rained again. Not wanting to repeat the experience of the year before, Boardman took it extremely easy on the bends. '1995 had an enormous influence on his prologue in 1996,' says Roger Legeay. 'He went much faster round the corners in 1995, but a year later he had learned fear. I have more regrets about 1996 than I do 1995 – he should have won in 1996.' Boardman ended up losing by just a couple of seconds to Alex Zülle of the ONCE team. Both had ridden in the rain, but Boardman's crash was too fresh in his mind for him to risk a repeat. The Brit had ridden the 1995 prologue with the success of the 1994 prologue pressuring him into a mistake. He'd ridden the 1996 prologue with the failure of the 1995 prologue constraining him.

Gan, however, had a good first week. Their sprinter Frédéric Moncassin won a stage, then Stéphane Heulot took possession of the yellow jersey after getting into a break.

On stage seven, the race went into the mountains, with a summit finish at Les Arcs in the Alps. The rain had followed the Tour from Holland all the way through the first week, and the first Alpine day was particularly cold and wet. Heulot was still in the yellow jersey, while Boardman was tenth overall, in a cluster of overall favourites including Zülle, Indurain and Rominger, just over four minutes behind.

On the Les Arcs stage, Boardman was aiming just to finish his first ever mountain stage of the Tour de France, with the hope of remaining within sight of the leaders. The day's route climbed the Col de la Madeleine, one of the hardest mountains in the Alps, followed by the less severe but still difficult Cormet de Roselend ascent, and then the final climb to the Les Arcs ski station.

Things went badly almost from the start. Boardman was distanced on the Col de la Madeleine, in frigid sleet. No disaster: as his group descended the other side and rode up the valley towards Albertville, they slowly closed the three-minute gap on the group of favourites. But on the next climb, he disappeared off the back for good. Ahead, Miguel Indurain was in the process of losing his battle for the yellow jersey, being dropped for the first time since 1990 and conceding four minutes. Boardman struggled to the finish almost half an hour behind the winner, Luc Leblanc.

In one day Boardman lost a couple of kilograms in body weight, but he had lost far more than that: he'd gone from potential Tour contender to also-ran. In a double blow to Gan, Heulot had had to pull out of the race with tendonitis before the finish in Les Arcs.

For the middle week of the Tour, Boardman performed quite strongly. He was eighth in the mountain time trial to Val d'Isère the next day, and in the final Alpine stage to Sestriere, which was cut short owing to snowstorms over the high mountains, he was twentieth. During the Massif Central stage to Super Besse, he even had the confidence to get into the early break, and still salvaged seventh place on the stage after the group of race favourites caught his group. He'd moved back up to thirty-first overall. A strong ride in the Pyrenees might yet put him in the top twenty.

But it wasn't to be. On the summit finish to Hautacam, where Bjarne Riis was riding up the climb at 30 kilometres per hour and retaining the yellow jersey, Boardman conceded nine minutes. And the next day, the Brit suffered a defining experience on the bike.

That seventeenth stage, to Pamplona in Spain, unusually long at 260 kilometres, and over several mountains on a kiln-hot day, is what Boardman always refers to now as the hardest thing he ever had to do on a bike. It stretched across his career like a recently opened fissure, dividing the ambition of his early years from the realism of his maturity.

Boardman was off the back after 5 kilometres and spent the entire day fighting to stay in contact with the *gruppetto*, the back group. Ahead, the top eight had ridden away from the rest, finishing eight minutes in front of the next fifteen riders; there were another twelve minutes to the group after that. It was a brutal day of racing. Boardman's group finished three-quarters of an hour down.

Sixth place in the final time trial in St Emilion, only two and a half minutes down, was probably Boardman's best ride of the entire Tour apart from the prologue. He dragged himself into Paris in thirty-ninth place overall, almost an hour and a half behind Bjarne Riis, the winner. The top twenty, let alone the top ten, were well out of reach. It was an unbridgeable gap.

Why did Boardman have such a hard time at the Tour de France when he was capable of finishing second in a mountainous race like the Critérium du Dauphiné Libéré? Certainly endurance and recovery were a problem for him compared to other riders. He never strung together a good performance in a three-week race, before or after 1996.

This was linked to the second reason, which was the obvious problem of doping in the mid-1990s. Bjarne Riis later confessed to having taken EPO in order to prepare for the 1996 race. There were very few riders in the top ten that year who weren't associated with doping in one form or another;

anecdotally, it was rife. A clean rider wouldn't stand a chance against the superior endurance and recovery of a cyclist who'd doped with EPO.

There was also a third reason, identified by both Peter Keen and Roger Legeay, which is Boardman's skill on a bike. Legeay refers to it as a rider's *bagage technique*, the stock of technical skills he or she must have in order to be able to handle him- or herself in a bunch of riders. 'Chris's biggest problem was that he spent a lot of energy riding in a group,' Legeay explains. 'If you know how to stay in the peloton, sheltered, you barely need to pedal. But he became tired in a longer race because he wasted energy every day. Instead of riding in the bunch he was riding a time trial beside the peloton. It's not his fault – his background was as a track rider and time triallist and he didn't do much road racing as an amateur. With the motor he had, I think he was capable of winning a Tour de France, but he was very handicapped by his lack of technical experience.'

Keen recognizes that this was a serious deficiency in Boardman's skill set. 'The one thing I couldn't coach Chris with was what it was like to ride in a peloton at eighty kilometres an hour. I'll never forget when the phone went during the first Tour of the Mediterranean, and he was terrified. The Tour of Lancashire doesn't prepare you for the start of the European season. He did pretty well for a guy who went in at twenty-five with a limited skill set and experience. He was prepared to do it, and that speaks a lot about the strength of character he had to show to be able to do that.'

Keen's memory of the 1996 Tour is of the almost daily phone calls reviewing Boardman's form and results. They were mostly pretty gloomy. 'The 1996 Tour was brutal. Chris should have won the prologue, so he started well, but the moment it went uphill, he lost ground very quickly. It didn't just hurt him physically. Psychologically it was devastating. We spoke most evenings and he had some real long dark nights of the soul. It was obvious he was completely out of his depth.

'The stage to Pamplona, when he had seven hours in the *gruppetto* in forty-degree heat, was probably a definitive point in his cycling life.' Boardman asked Keen if he should pull out. They considered it, but once Boardman had got through Pamplona, the worst was over. And as he rode the final few stages to Paris, his form started picking up again.

Keen felt that the overload of the Tour would bring Boardman some good form in the weeks following the event. If he was right, the British rider would have a good chance of performing well in both the Olympic Games, which started the week after the Tour's finish, and the world track championship a few weeks after that. 'What I'd got good at by then,' says Keen, 'was having the confidence about the training loads and waiting for the recovery and the breakthrough. He'd banked an insane amount of overload against a whole load of people who were doing something else, and you could see what he was going to do. His form started coming up.'

In Atlanta in August, Boardman was focusing on the time trial. The format was unusual. They'd decided to hold the race in town, on a circuit that the riders would cover four times. Because of the potential congestion of having all the riders out on the circuit at the same time, they split them into four groups of ten, with an hour separating each group, so there would only be ten riders on the road at any one time.

Unfortunately for the second and third groups, there was a torrential downpour in the middle of the day which meant the riders in those groups had no chance of an Olympic medal. The city roads were slippery and greasy with a mix of oil from the road and rainwater. But by the time Boardman was off, in group four, the surfaces were drying, and the heat and humidity were overwhelming.

Boardman was immediately riding very well. After one lap, he led the Spanish pair of Miguel Indurain and Abraham Olano by 17 seconds. But his fast start was his undoing. Boardman always found hot conditions testing, and he began to feel faint, just as he had done during his Bordeaux hour attempt. He was forced to ease off a little. 'Chris's form was phenomenal but he couldn't cope with the heat,' Keen recalls. 'Normally his pacing was spot on, but it was thirty degrees and ninety per cent humidity. His legs were fantastic, but he cooked.' At the halfway point Boardman still led, but he was only 3 seconds ahead of Indurain. Another lap and the Spaniard was in the gold medal position, while Boardman was barely ahead of Olano. By the finish, the Brit had slipped to bronze.

Back in the cooler climate of the UK, Boardman started running tests on the track. He tried out Obree's Superman position, and the results were so good he began to talk about an hour record attempt immediately after the world championship, which was being held in the Manchester velodrome. The position was so beneficial that he was predicting a 4,000-metre time of 4.16 or faster. 'When I was training for the pursuit, we did some tests at Manchester and it looked like the hour record might be possible,' he said. 'The stretched-out position makes a big difference. I'm as confident as you can be in sport that I've got a good chance of beating the record.'

Since Obree's 1994 record of 52.713 kilometres, both Indurain and Rominger had improved it. Indurain began preparations for an attack on the record after his 1994 Tour de France win. The Spaniard was not an experienced track rider, and his position on the bike was considerably less aerodynamic than Obree and Boardman's, but he made up for that by being able to put out huge amounts of power.

Indurain's build-up was less than ideal, however. His form was starting to drop off from the peak of the Tour de France, and he was training in a slightly lower position, which was giving him back trouble. He was also having problems following the black line on the track. Still, at Bordeaux velodrome, the Spaniard managed to raise the record by just over 300 metres, taking it to 53.040 kilometres.

Two months later, Tony Rominger made two separate attempts on it. He eclipsed Indurain's record easily with the first one, riding 53.832 kilometres behind closed doors. Then, just a week later, he added almost 1,500 metres to that mark, raising it to 55.291 kilometres. It looked like the Swiss rider had put the record on the shelf for ever: after Boardman, Obree and Indurain had in turn squeezed a few hundred metres more out of the hour, Rominger had just added six laps to it. But Boardman's post-Tour form, and the new position he was cycling in, made him and Keen think the record was surpassable.

Before any attempt to emulate Rominger's feat there was the world pursuit championship to focus on. With Obree suffering from poor form, Boardman was Britain's main hope, and it was clear that as in 1995, Andrea Collinelli, also now riding in the Superman position and fresh from having won the Olympic Games pursuit, was going to be the main opposition.

Boardman firmly installed himself as the favourite during the qualifying round, when he demolished the world record, riding 4.13. It was an astonishing time, given that he'd rarely gone below 4.25 in the past. He'd even caught and passed his old rival Jens Lehmann. Both Boardman and Collinelli then breezed through the quarter- and semi-finals.

Before the final, in front of a packed home crowd, Boardman rode tight circles on his road bike in the track centre, while Collinelli lapped the track slowly, rolling around the banking as he psyched himself up.

Keith Bingham reported the event for *Cycling Weekly*. 'It was an amazing final. Edge-of-the-seat stuff,' he says.

Boardman started more slowly than Collinelli. The Italian rode the first kilometre a second and a half faster. The crowd waited for the gap to close. And waited. But after 2 kilometres, the Italian was still almost a second clear.

'Collinelli led all the way,' Bingham recalls. 'People were wondering, when is the fightback going to start? It got down to the closing laps and it looked like Boardman was starting to fight back. But it wasn't that at all. What he was doing was holding an absolutely dead-level effort and speed, and it was Collinelli who blew and had to come back. That's what they'd counted on him doing.'

The gap slowly but surely decreased. 0.558 seconds . . . 0.071 seconds . . . and then Boardman took the lead with four laps to go. Keen knew at that point, with only a kilometre left to ride, that his man had won.

'You can't set off like Collinelli did,' Bingham continues. 'You can't exist for four kilometres at that speed. But we didn't know that. Pete Keen once told me that once Boardman has reached top speed, he's never known him fall away. Boardman's split times for the final were 1.08 for the first kilometre, while he got up to speed, then 1.00, 1.00, 1.00 – within hundredths of a second of each other. The point is that Boardman couldn't have gone any faster. If he'd done a faster kilometre earlier on, he'd have cracked. We had the impression Boardman sped up, but he didn't. They knew Collinelli couldn't hold that effort.'

Collinelli cracked spectacularly in the final kilometre. From leading most of the way, he gave up and faded to 4.20, which still would have won him the gold medal in most other years.

Although Boardman did win easily in the end, it hadn't been an easy ride. Keen had been walking the line during the ride to indicate where Collinelli was in relation to him, and he'd been worryingly static on the wrong side of the line for a long time. 'I was pushing and pushing harder,' Boardman said. 'Pete still wasn't edging back. But suddenly he was running down the track. That was when Collinelli parked up in the last kilometre. Thank God.'

Boardman's time was another new world record. He'd ridden 4.11, a time that wouldn't be beaten until Jack Bobridge of Australia rode 4.10 in 2011, a decade and a half later.

The week after that was spent holding form for the hour record. Boardman went back to the GP Eddy Merckx the weekend after his pursuit win and took his second victory in the event, this time winning it easily, with Lance Armstrong second, 90 seconds behind. Then it was back to Manchester for the final few training sessions.

His sparring partner for these was his old clubmate Simon Lillistone. 'We spent the week leading up to it with him driving over to Manchester. I was sorting bikes out, going on bike rides and gophering. Peter Keen was sending over the programme, and one day, with about three or four days to go, he said Chris needed to do twenty minutes at hour record pace. His session was to do fifty-five and a half kilometres per hour for twenty minutes and he couldn't do it. It nearly killed him to do it – for a third of the time he needed to do it for a few days later. The hour-and-a-half-long drive back to his house in the Wirral was absolute silence.'

But Boardman experienced no such problems on the night. He added more than a kilometre to Rominger's record, riding an astonishing 56.375 kilometres in the allotted time. He led Rominger by 3 seconds at 5 kilometres and continued to hold his speed for the entire hour. As Keen walked the line to show how far ahead Boardman was, he was doing entire circuits of the velodrome. His record had beaten Fausto Coppi's by 10 kilometres, and it was 5 kilometres, or twenty laps, more than Francesco Moser's, his original target three years previously.

Boardman's career had reached its zenith. Physically and psychologically, he would never achieve those heights again.

19

The Final Hour

The career trajectories of Boardman and Obree reflected their temperaments. Although it couldn't have been planned in advance, Boardman's was a steady, sober progression from strong junior to strong senior to strong international amateur to strong professional rider. Apart from a blip in 1995 when he crashed out of the Tour, and then a more serious dip in 1996 when he took a hammering in the event, the curve described its way to a peak in 1996, with the hour record and pursuit world title. Then it started to dip, and began a controlled descent towards his retirement.

Obree's career trajectory was less smooth, the highs followed by plateaus at best and lows at worst. The 1993 hour record and world championship win were followed by a mediocre 1994 as his position was banned and he struggled to capitalize on his successes. The curve rose again in 1995, but once more when he reached his goal he hadn't really considered what should come next. 'I just thought once I broke the hour record, stuff would happen,' he explains, 'good things would happen, but I didn't know what. I didn't have a clue, whereas Chris was much more planned.'

For Obree, the goal was the thing. For Boardman there were goals too, but there was always an understanding of their place in the plan and the process. When Obree won the world pursuit title for the second time in 1995, he didn't get a single offer from a professional team – partly, he thinks, because he'd been given a bad reputation among team managers after falling out with Le Groupement.

You also get the impression with Obree that he only ever needed to prove himself once. Doing the same thing twice carried far less meaning for him than doing it in the first place. In 1995, he had the motivational impetus of his new position. In 1996, it was just the same as before. Far less exciting.

That's not to say that the Scot didn't ride well in 1996. He just wasn't riding brilliantly. He came second, fourth and third in successive World Cup pursuits, whereas the year before only mechanicals and jet lag had prevented him winning such events. His times hovered around the low 4.30s. He needed to find 10 seconds more compared to the previous year, and that was assuming – wrongly as it turned out – that nobody else improved.

Obree did win his fourth consecutive national pursuit title in 1996, and the national 25 championship – surprisingly his only triumph in the event. He thrashed the opposition, beating Rob Hayles by 1.48. But he seemed to be more pleased by having beaten Chris Newton, who was another 15 seconds back in third.

There was a suggestion of tension between Obree and Newton. Obree says that the national 25 championship that year was the only instance in his entire career when he felt motivated to win a race by dislike of another competitor. Newton was a young member of the British national team, a track specialist who also excelled at time trialling and road racing. He'd been on a trip to a World Cup event in Milan, during which an incident took place which was recalled by Obree in his autobiography. One of the riders had urinated in the Scot's bed, as a practical joke. Since he had been mercilessly and horrifically bullied as a child, the incident was an unpleasant flashback for Obree.

Unfortunately for Obree, his desire to beat Newton had overridden his concern for his health: he'd come down with a chest cold in the days leading up to the 25 championship, and the winning effort exacerbated the condition. With the Olympic Games, for which he'd been selected for the pursuit and the time trial, less than two months away, Obree's already stuttering preparation had suffered another setback. A week after the 25 he was laid flat out in bed with a viral infection.

Obree rode one more World Cup event before Atlanta – in Cottbus, Germany, where he came seventh. His form refused to return, and in the background he had to put up with rumours and speculation that Boardman, whose form was coming round after his bad Tour de France experience, was offering to take his place in the GB squad.

Atlanta was a disaster for Obree. He rode 4.34 in qualifying – a terrible performance just a year after he'd won the world title. Andrea Collinelli was the fastest qualifier, posting a 4.19 – faster than Obree had ever ridden, and on an outdoor track. The Italian, who had adopted the Superman position after being beaten by Obree in Colombia the year before, went on to win the gold. Philippe Ermenault took the silver. Obree pulled out of the time trial and went home.

'It didn't happen,' recalls Doug Dailey. 'I don't think he was hungry enough. He'd done it already, he'd won the worlds the year before, and even though the Olympic Games is a massive challenge, it didn't seem to fire him. He wasn't eating, sleeping and drinking the Olympic Games.'

Certainly during the period when Boardman was winning the world pursuit championship and smashing the world hour record, Obree was beginning to talk like somebody whose heart wasn't in it. 'Pursuiting is like the table cloth trick,' he said. 'You've got to be totally committed for it to work.' The inference was that he was less than totally committed.

The final nail in the coffin came in October 1996, when the UCI banned the Superman position. A new directive was issued by the Technical Commission stating that the handlebar could not extend more than 15 centimetres ahead of the hub of the front wheel. It was the second time in three years that the UCI had allowed one of Obree's innovations to be used in competition, then subsequently banned it.

Obree's career didn't end that month. He raced into 1997, sporadically winning time trials, almost gaining world championship selection and winning the BCF national time trial championship. In 1998, he was selected as a reserve for the British team pursuit squad but didn't ride, and he fell out with the new Lottery-funded World Class Performance Plan when he claimed his living grant from them amounted to just £430 for the year. Even through 1999 and 2000 his name popped up occasionally in the results pages of *Cycling Weekly* for one time trial win or another, but the absences grew longer and longer.

Doug Dailey reckons the Atlanta Olympics was the end of Graeme Obree as an elite athlete. 'I was half-expecting him to ring me again for months afterwards with some new position, but he never did. My feeling is that he could have achieved more in pursuiting. There was a marvellous time trial ride in there somewhere, but we couldn't bring it out on an international occasion.'

Several years later, Dailey did hear from Obree, out of the blue. After the 1996 hour record was set, the UCI split the record into two categories: Boardman's 56.375 kilometres was now designated the 'best hour performance', while the 'athletes' hour record' was put back to Merckx's 1972 figures: 49.431. The idea was that everybody from Francesco Moser onwards had used increasingly efficient aerodynamic aids, and that reinstating Merckx as the holder would restore athletic integrity. Obree wanted to give the athletes' hour record a go, using the normal racing position without tri-bars, some time in 2004 or 2005. He came to Manchester velodrome to do some testing on the track, riding laps while Dailey shouted out the times. 'He was off the pace,' Dailey recalls. 'He stopped and had another go, and he still wasn't on the pace. Stopped, rested, and went again. That was it. He said he'd go away and think about it and do more training. But I got an email from him saying it wasn't going to happen and he abandoned it. I was glad he took the decision. Lightning wasn't going to strike three times, and I think he saw that.'

So Obree rode on into the twenty-first century, but his knowledge of the drugs that were skewing performances and results on almost every level made him angry with the sport. He now sees his racing career as just a small step in a journey of self-acceptance and understanding. 'I was told in 1995 that just about every Tour de France rider was taking EPO, but I was arrogant enough to believe that I would keep winning without it,' he says. 'I underwent the five stages of grief. Denial – that was me at the 1996 Olympics. Anger – I just thought I'd ride hard and ignore it and still win. Then negotiation – I thought I'd do the hour record again. Then depression. And then I finally reached acceptance.

'But there's a sixth level. After acceptance, I think there's another stage – indifference. We waited seventeen years for the truth about doping to come out, and now I've got to that stage about it – complete indifference.'

*

Chris Boardman had one more serious crack at the Tour de France, in 1997. Although he'd acknowledged he probably wasn't going to improve on the level he'd reached in the late summer of 1996, there was still the irresistible feeling that if he could nail the recovery, or climb better, there was a good Tour de France ride in him. In terms of pure numbers, his power output, for an hour on the track, should have been enough to be able to ride up the mountains of the Tour not far from the favourites. At 70 kilos, however, he was slightly heavier than the specialist climbers. Keen and Boardman's solution? Try to maintain the same power output, but lose weight.

Keen says that Boardman was putting out 430 to 440 watts when he broke the hour record in 1996. Assuming he was at his racing weight of 70 kilos, he would have been putting out about 6.2 watts a kilo. To put that number in context, the very best riders in the Tour de France these days rarely get anywhere near that output, although the comparison is not exact, because stages of the Tour last longer than an hour, and the circumstances and context of the effort are different. In the mid-1990s and into the 2000s, EPO and blood boosting allowed riders to raise that number to 6.7. If Boardman could lose 3 kilos and put out 430 watts at 67 kilos, he'd be racing at 6.4 watts per kilo.

Keen did some sums using the Col du Tourmalet, one of the hardest Pyrenean climbs. He calculated that if Boardman lost 1.5 kilos, he'd save 46 seconds on an hour-long climb, and seven minutes overall. And it wasn't only the actual time savings that would be an advantage: the less time a rider loses on a climb, the less energy he spends catching up the riders who dropped him.

It was the kind of evidence-based plan Boardman loved, and he bought into it. But, uncharacteristically, he got carried away. Keen's weight loss plan involved carefully cutting back on calorie intake and losing a kilo a month over three months.

Boardman was actually enjoying the training and tracking the numbers, and started overdoing it. If the schedule said ride for two hours at 300 watts, he'd ride two and a quarter at 330. On rest days, he went out for a little spin, just to burn up the calories. He recalled one ride near the end of which his power-meter was recording that he'd used 2,985 of the 3,000 calories he'd been scheduled to burn, so he rode the last 500 metres of his ride with the brakes on, to make sure he reached the 3,000. He ended up losing the 3 kilos in a month. It was too fast. He simply wasn't eating enough for the training he was doing. 'I was right on the limit of what the body can take before the metabolism starts to protest and slow down, and this affects your hormone and testosterone levels,' he admitted later.

The immediate results were positive, however. Boardman started the 1997 season late but was good enough in May to come second in the Tour of Romandy. He won both the prologue and the final time trial, but couldn't quite match eventual winner Pavel Tonkov in the mountains. Tonkov was going into his main target for the season, the Giro d'Italia, as defending champion, so for Boardman to finish close to him was a strong result. He conceded 1.40 to Tonkov on the hardest mountain stage, but took a minute of that back in the time trial.

But instead of being a foundation for better form, Romandy turned out to be as good as it got. Boardman had ambitions of winning the Dauphiné Libéré, but after winning the prologue he first conceded two minutes in the long time trial, then pulled out in the mountains after suffering big time losses. The weight was off, the power was good when he was fresh, but the recovery had dropped right off. Instead of setting him up for a good Tour de France, Boardman's enthusiasm for the weight loss programme had actually compromised his chances further. His recovery had been poor in comparison to the other Tour contenders before; now it was even worse. At the Tour of Catalonia, the same thing happened: a win in the prologue was followed by severe time losses in the mountains.

With the evidence in hand, Keen and Boardman must have concluded that a good finish in the Tour de France would forever be beyond the Brit. But Boardman still allowed himself to hope, and Roger Legeay needed him to target the general classification, to help justify his status as Gan team leader. 'People around me are talking top ten,' he said a week before the Grand Départ in Rouen. 'I think that's ambitious, but nonetheless possible.'

Boardman admitted he was feeling the pressure at that 1997 prologue. His time-trialling form was good – he'd won six out of eight that year before Rouen – but the nagging problem of his poor form made him far less prepared for it than he had been in the previous three years. To make things more complicated, there was a climb early on in the course, a 700-metre-long rise that threatened to seduce the unwary into going too hard too soon. Boardman had visited the course months before to select his gears and decide his strategy, but he spent the Friday before the race looking over it again. 'I know it better than I know the names of my kids,' he said, but he was not confident.

He started steadily, and didn't put in his terminal effort until after the top of the hill, which he felt he'd taken too slowly. He described it later as not being a good ride. But it was enough: he won by a single second to take the yellow jersey for the second time in his career, and a fourth day in total after his three days in yellow in 1994. It was a win based more on experience and technique than strength and fitness, but a victory all the same.

This time he spent only a single day in the race lead: Mario Cipollini, the Italian sprinter, had finished close enough to

Boardman in the prologue that he was able to assume the top spot when he won the first road stage, along with a 20-second time bonus.

Boardman, unlike in 1994, was the designated and unambiguous team leader from the start of the 1997 Tour. The primary tactical aim of the Gan team was to protect him in the flat stages and try to put him into position for a strong ride in the mountains for his general classification ambitions. For a team to do that, total self-sacrifice is required on the part of every rider. Personal ambition must be subsumed to the cause, whether it's to keep the bunch together for a sprinter, or to pace a GC leader. Given that racing cyclists tend to have competitive personality types, managing the tension between riders' urges to do well for themselves and the need for discipline can be something of a challenge for team managers.

Boardman had taken over leadership of the team from Greg LeMond almost immediately in 1994. LeMond's form had been so bad in that Tour that Boardman's taking of the yellow jersey had effectively dictated the new situation. LeMond hadn't reacted well, saying, 'When Chris came on the team and was riding well, Roger Legeay basically ignored everyone. Roger was like a puppy following his dad. It was exciting and everyone was happy Chris was winning, but Roger has to be a diplomat, he has to realize that there are nine riders racing.'

The arrangement is rarely as harmonious as teams might like to portray it. If a leader wins a race, it's traditional to split the prize money between the team riders – loyalty has a price. If the leader is riding badly, team riders are much less keen to sacrifice themselves for him. This had already happened to Boardman once in 1997: he recalled being dropped by a group in the mountains of the Critérium du Dauphiné Libéré while a team-mate disappeared up the road, calling, 'Come on, Chris!'

Now, at the Tour, one of the Gan riders, Cédric Vasseur,

decided to go on a break on stage five, without mentioning it in the team meeting. Tactically, it didn't help Boardman – it left him one man short in the bunch, which might have been a risk. Vasseur stayed away all the way to the finish, won the stage and ended up with the yellow jersey for a week. The sponsors couldn't be unhappy with that, but Boardman was secretly miffed. 'Someone should have said, "Nice ride, but what the hell were you doing?" ' he said.

In retrospect, it turned out to be a positive thing for the team. Boardman crashed heavily in the first mountain stage, injuring his back and losing half an hour. The next day was the toughest day of the Tour, 252 kilometres long, with several hard mountains. Boardman finished in the *gruppetto*, forty-three minutes down. 'It was like eight and a half hours of someone sticking a poker in my back,' he commented. After that, Boardman struggled through the long time trial in St Etienne, losing almost seven minutes to Jan Ullrich, then suffered the indignity of being caught by his two-minute man Frank Vandenbroucke. He pulled out the next day, his ambitions for the Tour in ruins.

Soon after the Tour, Boardman re-signed with Legeay. In spite of his fallibility in the general classification of the Tour de France, he'd been courted by other teams for 1998, most notably ONCE. There was also a story flying around during the Tour de France that the US Postal Service team were interested. They'd got into the 1997 Tour on a wildcard entry, with their highest finisher Jean-Cyril Robin in fifteenth place, but they had bigger ambitions for 1998. Lance Armstrong was signing for US Postal for his planned comeback from cancer that year, for a start.

US Postal never did sign Boardman, a member of the management telling journalists that the asking price was too high. That was news to Pete Woodworth, who recalls that the interest from other teams was primarily useful as leverage for their own negotiations with Roger Legeay. 'Chris had inklings of what was going on at ONCE, and there was no way he would go,' says Woodworth. Nonetheless, they made it clear to the Gan staff that they were talking with the other team.

'With US Postal,' Woodworth continues, 'Oakley phoned me, because they sponsored Chris and Lance. Armstrong was close with one of the directors of Oakley. They said Lance was very interested in having a meeting. If there's any doubt about who was running that team, it wasn't the manager, it was Lance.' Woodworth tried to make contact but was told Lance wasn't available and that they'd get back to him. They never did, and the planned meeting never took place. 'The next thing we saw in the paper was that Boardman wasn't signing for US Postal because he wanted too much money. We didn't even have a meeting.'

Boardman's season stuttered to a close. He went to the Tour of Spain in a half-hearted attempt to build form for the world championship, but the racing was so brutal, and his form so poor, that he barely lasted a week. A bronze medal at the world time trial championship was a brief highlight in the final months of what he described as his 'worst season ever'.

On top of that, his working relationship with Peter Keen was about to get more complicated. In late July 1997, the British Cycling Federation had advertised a job vacancy for perform-ance director. It was a new post. The successful candidate would be responsible for managing a £900,000 budget for the new World Class Performance Plan, funded by the National Lottery. 'You will have imagination, vision, energy and enthusiasm, as well as the courage to be innovative and the maturity to seek advice,' read the ad, which was basically a love letter to Peter Keen, who was one of three men interviewed for the post in September, along with Scottish national coach Steve

Paulding and Paul Sherwen, an ex-professional rider who spread his time between doing PR for cycling teams and television commentary. But Keen was evidently the man for the job. He took what turned out to be a very long sabbatical from academia, and relocated to Manchester.

Keen's plan was audacious: he'd spend the money with the aim of getting Great Britain ranked in the top ten of all UCI-recognized events, and cycling to be regarded as a major sport in the UK. In 1997, those twin targets were a long way off. Keen mainly focused the funds on track racing. There was the correct perception that success in road events at world championships and Olympic Games was difficult to plan for and predict, and doping was still rife (although the Festina scandal of 1998 put a brief check on it). The track had far fewer variables. His years working with Boardman had given Keen the experience to be able to try the same experiment, this time with a team of riders.

By 2000, the British team had won a gold medal in the kilometre time trial, with Jason Queally, plus a silver and two bronzes. By Athens in 2004 it was two golds, for Bradley Wiggins and Chris Hoy; Wiggins was also part of the pursuit team that won silver, and he paired with Rob Hayles to win bronze in the Madison. Then Beijing and London saw a cascade of medals for the British cycling team – fourteen in China, eight of them gold, then eight more golds in 2012. Only in his wildest dreams could Keen have wished for a profile as high as the sport of cycling enjoyed in the wake of those achievements. All this success was built on the foundation of the plan that he had set up in 1997, and that in turn was a product of what he'd learned over a decade coaching Chris Boardman and, for a couple of years, Yvonne McGregor. Without Boardman, there could have been no Bradley Wiggins winning the Tour de France.

So from the outset Keen's appointment was good news for

British cycling, but for Boardman back in 1998 it meant his coach was stretched. The impression Boardman gave over that season, and through 1999, was that he was bored and tired. Certainly very little went right for him.

He'd found a reason for the terrible recovery issues he'd experienced during the Tour de France: a pre-season health test in 1998 identified low testosterone levels, and low bone density. He was diagnosed with osteopenia, the precursor to osteoporosis. Various explanations of Boardman's suppressed hormone levels have been given over the years. For a while before diagnosis he'd noticed consistently low testosterone readings, which suggested that he had naturally low levels. Keen theorized that the years of trying to compete with doped athletes could have worn down Boardman's system, but 'we don't know if the bone mineralization loss that we uncovered was because of that. What I can't say is whether Chris had unnaturally vulnerable hypothalamic pituitary axis function, or if it was the suppression of it that we see in the literature if you train too much.' In short, the probability was that Boardman had naturally low levels, then made things worse by trying to compete as a professional cyclist. Either way, his system was extremely vulnerable, and the only treatment involved hormone replacement therapy – a banned process under the anti-doping rules – and the UCI wouldn't authorize it.

1998 was almost a carbon copy of the previous year. There was an early season struggle, a few odd time trial wins, plus an unusual result for Boardman – a win in a road stage, at the PruTour, as the Tour of Britain was briefly called at the time. His form felt bad, but somehow he won another Tour de France prologue, this time in Dublin. The victory was accompanied by an unusual feeling for Boardman: elation. 'I was convinced I wasn't going well enough, and I rolled across the line thinking, "Nope." But the soigneur [team assistant] told me

I'd done it. It was a real surprise, and that result gave me happiness.'

Boardman rarely expressed happiness with his wins, preferring his version of the emotion: satisfaction. But this one seemed unusual, exceptional. His poor form and increasingly serious health problems had convinced him he didn't have a chance, but some spark of muscle memory deep inside his being enabled him to pull out one last yellow jersey ride.

There was something else, too. After Boardman won the prologue in Dublin he was interviewed for Channel Four by Gary Imlach, and he seemed to be struggling to control his emotions. As he described the win, he sounded like he was on the verge of tears. Then, awkwardly, but earnestly sincere, he turned to the camera and said, 'I don't usually dedicate my wins, but this one is for my wife, without whom I would not be here.' It was a rare display for the normally stoic and outwardly unemotional rider.

During my interview with him, Keen alluded to Boardman's commitment to cycling starting to waver by this point, for non-professional reasons. I'd mentioned to him that Boardman's heart hadn't seemed to be in it from 1997 onwards, and he gently but firmly admonished me for not seeing the broader context. 'I'll give you a brief and general answer,' he said. 'It is tempting to want to look at athletic performance in terms of stats and facts and what science may be able to shed on it. But Chris is a human being, with a life, ambitions, failures and a whole load of stuff in his life, which it's not for me to share with you. But there are other reasons why people succeed or don't in sport.'

When he retired, Boardman gave an interview to *Cycle Sport* magazine in which he talked about suddenly realizing the dangers of obsessive behaviour when he was targeting the Tour de France. 'I didn't think about anything else, apart from the Tour, about my training, getting the diet right, and making sure that everything would be perfect in July,' he said. 'I became obsessive about it, and if a psychologist had seen me then, he would have heard alarm bells ringing.

'It nearly trashed my marriage,' he added.

What nobody knew was that a week before the Dublin prologue, Boardman and his wife Sally went to Amsterdam, without telling Legeay. 'When Sally told me there was a problem, I said, "Why didn't you say something?", and she said, "I have been saying something for years," but I just hadn't listened. From that point on, I didn't care about anything else. I wanted to rescue my marriage because that was the most important thing.'

So much for the obsessive robot. Real life was starting to leak into Boardman's armoured existence. He might not have been achieving the same excellence in cycling that he'd been used to for a decade, but he was starting to become a much more rounded person.

Boardman crashed out of the 1998 Tour just two days after taking the yellow jersey. He fell off after touching a wheel on a flat stretch of road, still in Ireland, breaking a wrist and suffering concussion. The Festina doping scandal was awaiting the race on its return to France, but Boardman was already on a ferry home to Liverpool. Another abandoned Tour of Spain and a lacklustre twelfth in the world pursuit championship and eleventh in the world time trial championship reinforced the impression that the next contract Boardman signed – a two-year deal with Legeay's new sponsor Crédit Agricole – would be his last.

1999 and 2000 saw Boardman's slow decline continue. He was unable to figure in the Tour de France prologue in 1999, then ground his way round France to complete the race for only the second time in his career, finishing 128th overall.

There was a brief highlight when he again took bronze in the world time trial championship that year, but the writing was on the wall when Legeay opted not to select him for the 2000 Tour. 'He wanted to do the Tour as normal,' says Legeay. 'He was going OK. But I took the decision not to send him. I said, "Listen, Chris, we're not going to put you in the Tour team this year." I said I'd call him in a week.'

Once Legeay had given Boardman the time to digest the news, he called and put a plan to him. 'We'll do the hour record, with a normal bike,' he said. This was the newly labelled 'athletes' hour record' (Merckx's 49.431 kilometres), as stipulated by the UCI, not Boardman's own 'best hour performance' of 56.375 kilometres. Legeay thought it would be a good end-of-year target for him. Boardman thought it over for a few seconds, then said, 'It's a good idea.' Legeay left it there to brew a little in the rider's mind but got straight on to the UCI's Technical Committee to work out exactly what was permitted. 'He called a few days later and said, "*On y va*" – let's go for it,' Legeay adds. 'He also said it was going to be very, very hard.'

Boardman would attack the hour at Manchester velodrome, on a regular track bike with drop handlebars, no tri-bars and spoked wheels, in mid-October during a free session at the world championship. The size of the task that faced him became apparent as the specialized training got underway. He wasn't hitting the numbers. 'He did as much training as reasonably possible,' Pete Woodworth recalls, 'but it was difficult because he couldn't really do it. He'd start a session on the track, and stop, saying he couldn't do it, and have to go home and rest. Even Peter Keen was saying he didn't think it was going to happen. At Bordeaux, we knew he had the form and could do it. It was hot there, but we had a margin of error. At Manchester, it was touch and go. There was no margin of error.'

Keen comments, 'There were so many things wrong with it in terms of his build-up, his life, the equipment, you name it. It shouldn't have been doable.'

Boardman and Keen had designed a schedule that called for a 70-metre beating of the record. But gone was the confidence that had characterized the previous two attempts, both of which easily beat the extant marks. As Boardman took the line in front of the Manchester crowd for his last hour of professional cycling, he thought he probably wasn't going to beat the record.

Eddy Merckx had started his record too fast, but Boardman's schedule had allowed for that. He was behind after 5 kilometres, but by 20 kilometres he'd drawn level, and at 25 kilometres Boardman went ahead of the Belgian for the first time. The crowd roared him on.

Phil O'Connor photographed the event for *Cycling Weekly*, and recalls the attempt starting well. 'Pete Keen was walking the line, and we knew that as long as he was ahead of that start line, he was on track. At one point, he was way ahead, right on the other side of the track. Then we noticed he was coming back.'

They say that the halfway point in an hour record comes between forty and forty-five minutes. Boardman had done a test the previous week where he'd ridden for half an hour at 49 kilometres per hour, and it had been an ordeal. Doing that, slightly faster, then having to do it again for another half an hour was going to be unspeakable. 'We hadn't done the work in the death zone of the last twenty minutes, which everybody faces if they take on the hour,' Keen admits. 'There is a cascade of fatigue, which starts in the arms, with g-force from the bends every six and a half seconds. Your lower back will start to go because it's trying to compensate for your arms. Your ability to stabilize the pelvis in the saddle goes, so everything that keeps you pedalling smoothly goes. It's a cascade of pain going down you.'

O'Connor tried to work out how fast Keen was coming back. 'Looking at the clock, and seeing where Pete was, you could visualize it – he was going to go past the line. I was shooting on instinct, just watching the numbers and the clock and Pete. It was painful. And you could see it was killing Boardman. He was in pain.'

At 33 kilometres, the average speed was 49.501 kilometres per hour – bang on the schedule that had him finishing 70 metres ahead of the record. But at the forty-five-minute mark the speed had dropped to 46.446 kilometres per hour – just 15 metres ahead.

'With ten minutes to go, people realized he might not do it, and the noise really started,' recalls Keith Bingham, who was covering the event for *Cycling Weekly*. 'Louder and louder. They were screaming at him to get going.'

Boardman started to slip behind. And he kept on slipping. With five minutes to go he was 52 metres behind Merckx. Sally Boardman went to the trackside to urge him on. The entire velodrome was willing him on, this broken body fighting unimaginable pain, the numbers, pulse rates, power outputs and schedules now forgotten.

With three minutes to go, his face twisted in agony, Boardman sped up, imperceptibly. 'He was looking in my eyes as he lapped for the last ten minutes, and there was something there telling me he was OK,' says Keen. 'He knew he was dying, but that he was going to do it.' When Boardman passed now, Keen was walking back up the track towards the finishing line.

The average speed continued to edge up: 49.401 kilometres per hour, then 49.406, with just a minute left. The number on the scoreboard crept up too, towards Merckx's figure of 49.431. It read 49.407, then 49.411 . . .

When the commissaire shot the gun to signal the end of the hour, Boardman had ridden 49.441 kilometres – 10 metres further than Merckx.

'The place erupted,' says Bingham. 'Just noise. More than when he won the worlds there, and Sally had had to take the kids out because the noise was frightening them. When he finished, you could tell that he'd pushed himself, hurt himself. When he stopped they had to lay the bike down, with him on it, and extract the bike from under him. He couldn't stand and he couldn't sit. I was over there, trying to get to him. As a cyclist, you know not to get too close to people immediately after an effort like that, but I wanted to see as much as I could. I could see his eyes were closed, and the lines on his face told me he'd pushed it perhaps further than ever before.'

Peter Keen's comment that he saw something in Boardman's face that made him think he was going to succeed, in the fraction of a second that he could see it every lap, is an interesting one. The most tempting narrative is that Boardman's three-minute surge to get back on terms with, and then over-take, Merckx's record was some kind of instinctual fight, beyond the level of what should have been possible. But it was still based on experience, numbers and pace judgement, just like every other ride Boardman did. It was just much closer to the limit than he'd previously gone.

'In that one hour, you saw everything you needed to know about Chris Boardman,' Keen states. 'He had the courage not just to ride through, but to hold back enough to feed off the minutiae of information I could give him. It was an extraordinary human performance, because he had everything to lose and little to gain, and he still came through. I can't imagine a better ending than that. There was a sense of who he had been, and who he was.'

There have been few more compelling moments in the sport

of cycling than Boardman's final hour record. After an entire career of flattening out the highs and lows, worshipping at the altar of numbers and sports science, gauging his efforts according to three digits on a screen and meeting targets, his last ever competitive ride humanized him. And then we realized he'd actually been like that all along.

20

Peak Performance

It is impossible to write about cycling in the 1990s without considering doping. The abuse of banned performance-enhancing drugs was as much part of the landscape as fluorescent cycling clothing. It's a matter of record that every Tour de France winner between 1996 and 2007 has been found to have doped, or has admitted doping. Before 1996 there were many suspiciously strong performances, in the Tour and in every other top-level race.

The 1994 season, as we've seen, was dominated by the Gewiss team, whose high haematocrit levels could only have been caused by artificial means. The low forties is a typical percentage of red blood cells in total blood volume for a rested male; the rigours of training and racing tend to lower the number. Some factors, such as altitude or dehydration, can raise it a little, but the Gewiss riders were in the high fifties and even sixties. In short, that's impossible, unless there's something seriously wrong with you.

The evidence is anecdotal, but Gewiss's domination of the early season in 1994 kicked off an arms race which led to some extraordinary and unbelievable performances.

One example: Mauro Gianetti spent nine seasons before 1995 as a professional, during which he won one minor race. That year he won Liège-Bastogne-Liège and the Amstel Gold race, two of the biggest one-day races of the year, on consecutive weekends. (Three years later, he collapsed during the Tour of Romandy, after allegedly having injected himself with perfluorocarbon metabolites, an experimental blood substitute.)

Another example: Bjarne Riis turned from a donkey into a racehorse, winning the 1996 Tour in dominant fashion, having endured years of mediocrity before suddenly rising to fifth in the 1993 Tour and third in 1995 (riding for Gewiss). Riis's nickname was 'Mr 60 Per Cent', although the haematocrit ascribed to him in 1994 was 56.3 per cent. As the medical expert called in by a Danish television documentary to assess the reading stated, either he was on EPO or he was extremely sick.

The year after Riis's Tour win, his young team-mate Jan Ullrich won the Tour easily. He didn't test positive that year (the tests were infrequent and inadequate), but he was banned after his blood was found stored in the office of Eufemiano Fuentes, the doctor at the heart of the Operación Puerto doping investigation in 2006.

EPO was first manufactured for distribution in 1989 by American company Amgen. When it came into the peloton is a matter of debate since the people involved are hardly likely to confess to it, but 1990 is a good guess, judging by the rumours surrounding certain performances that year. By the mid-1990s, the most pessimistic analysis was that just about every professional cyclist was using it. The advantage conferred by EPO was significant, the testing was sub-par, and the culture of doping became ingrained.

This was the state of road cycling when Chris Boardman

turned professional. Boardman's reputation was good, among fans, journalists and other riders, including Nicolas Aubier and Gilles Delion of the Casino team, who in 1997 in a feature by *L'Equipe* described widespread EPO abuse in the peloton. Aubier stated he had been offered EPO by someone outside the medical personnel of his team consisting of seven ampoules to be injected under the skin for a month. 'You had to stuff yourself with aspirin to keep your blood liquid,' he added. (One of the problems of raising the concentration of red blood cells in the bloodstream is that the blood itself becomes thicker. There was a spate of deaths among competitive bike riders in Belgium in the early 1990s, allegedly caused by EPO abuse, where the blood had become too thick for the heart to pump. As Aubier testified, riders kept themselves alive by taking aspirin, which thins the blood, and by setting their alarm clocks to wake them in the night so that they could stretch and raise their heart rate.) Aubier refused to go along with the EPO abuse. 'Frankly,' he added, 'I can hardly imagine a rider in the first hundred in the world who does not use EPO, growth hormone or other products. I have known one – Chris Boardman. I ask myself how he can compete.'

Sometimes badly, sometimes well, was the answer. Boardman won time trials throughout his career, and achieved top fives in some of the most prestigious stage races in the world, but he could never sustain the effort over three weeks. The primary effect of EPO and the cocktail of drugs alleged to have been widespread in the mid-1990s was improved recovery. Daily exertion at the level of the Tour de France would normally cause a physically damaging build-up of fatigue, but riders taking EPO would be fresher than those who didn't. The fact that Boardman's system was so run down by the middle week of the Tour de France while the general classification contenders seemed only to be warming up suggests that he was riding clean. In contemporary photographs, the striking thing is just how tired and worn down Boardman looked when he was racing – huge bags under his eyes, his complexion grey and pale.

'We have a system with Vélo Club de Paris [Gan/Crédit Agricole's owning organization] where every rider signs a separate contract which states that if they are caught using any performance-enhancing drugs they are out of a job,' Boardman said in 1998. 'I have never been offered drugs. I can categorically say that I've never taken anything or been offered anything.'

Graeme Obree also enjoyed a good reputation. He made himself extremely unpopular with many professional cyclists when he gave an interview to French news magazine *L'Express* in which he first told that story of being asked to donate £2,000 to the medical fund at Le Groupement. 'There is a feeling now at the top level that you have to do it, just to compete on an equal basis,' he said.

While I was researching this book, I got an email from somebody on the inside who claimed Boardman was not the only one riding on bread and water alone. 'I really hope you're not writing the "Chris was the only clean rider in 1996" book,' it read. 'Chris would have been one of the best time trial riders no matter what. And more red cells don't help you nearly as much as better aerodynamics on the track.'

There's only one period in Boardman's career during which his performances stand out. From 1992 to 1995 he was clearly a world-class rider, following a steady curve of improvement, but nothing, not even his 1994 Tour prologue win, looked incongruous compared to what had gone before. He may have beaten everybody by a large distance in that event, but he'd been training specifically for it, while his rivals were training for the rigours of a three-week race. He was the best short-distance time triallist in the world, beating endurance-trained athletes in a short-distance time trial.

Boardman's 1996 hour record and pursuit championship stand out above all, however.

All athletic achievements are explainable in terms of numbers, so let's look more closely at the figures involved in Boardman's 1996 records. From contemporary reports, we know certain things. When Boardman tested Obree's tuck position in comparison with his normal position, he and Keen worked out what power outputs were necessary to maintain his hour record speed of 52.27 kilometres per hour. In his normal position, he needed to hold 409 watts, which Keen stated was at 87.5 per cent of his VO2 max of 88 (VO2 max is the maximum amount of oxygen the body can process, measured in millilitres per kilogram per minute). On a regular bike, he would need 473 watts (if he'd ridden 409 watts for an hour on a 'Merckx' bike, he would have ridden 49.5 kilometres, Keen said). And in the tuck position, he only needed 394 watts to hold the speed, which meant that the tuck position needed 3.8 per cent less power than his normal tri-bar position to maintain 52.27 kph. If he rode for an hour in the Obree tuck position, at his hour record wattage of 409, he'd have covered 53.18 kilometres. Some reports stated that Obree's position, which tipped his body forward, was also more biomechanically efficient, with the weight distribution helping to add a percentage of power.

Various factors affect speed in pursuit matches, including altitude, the position of the riders and whether the velodrome is indoors or outdoors. Graeme Obree rode a 4.20 pursuit in the 1993 world championship in an indoor velodrome, at sea level, in the tuck position. Two years later, he rode a 4.22

pursuit at altitude, outdoors, in the Superman position. There are too many variables at play to compare the Superman and tuck positions in these results, although they do suggest that the advantage of the Superman position isn't huge over the tuck.

Andrea Collinelli went from 4.22 at altitude, outdoors, in a normal position in the 1995 worlds, to 4.19 at sea level, outdoors, in the Superman position at the Olympics, to 4.16 at sea level, indoors, in the Superman position in the 1996 worlds. He also went on to test positive in 2000.

Boardman's own pursuit series over the years were remarkably consistent. He would probably have ridden around 4.24 in the 1992 Olympic final (outdoors, sea level), and he recorded 4.25 in both 1993 (indoors, sea level) and 1994 (outdoors, sea level). In 1996, with the Superman position, indoors at sea level, he recorded 4.11. That is a huge improvement – 13 seconds faster than his previous fastest 4,000 metres, which was 4.24 in 1992. Was the Superman position that much better that it resulted in a 13-second improvement for Boardman?

According to Keen, yes it was – to a point. There were certain other factors which were relevant in 1996 – for instance, Boardman had survived a brutal Tour de France, but was now benefiting from the recovery, and coming into the best form he'd ever experienced. But 13 seconds is still huge. Compare Collinelli's rides in the 1995 and 1996 worlds. If the factors that 1995 was at altitude and outside and 1996 was at sea level and inside cancel each other out (which they won't exactly, but will to a certain extent), then the Superman position gained Collinelli approximately 6 seconds – a lot fewer than Boardman. And Collinelli's record was not that of a clean athlete.

The hour record was another massive improvement on

Boardman's previous figures, although he'd been hampered by the heat in Bordeaux in 1993. Even compared to the original Bordeaux schedule of 53 kilometres, 56.375 seems an extraordinary figure.

Keen tells me that the Manchester track was extremely fast in 1996. Air pressure was low, which would increase air density, but it was dry and cool, which suited Boardman. He also says that Boardman 'probably averaged between 430 and 440 watts' during the hour. To get from 52.270 kilometres (Boardman's first hour record) to 56.375 requires either 25 per cent more power or 25 per cent less aero resistance (or a combination of both). If Keen's 440 watts figure is right, the position still needs to be worth another 70 watts.

Here we need to understand another factor: CdA, which measures aerodynamic drag. Cd is the drag coefficient, multiplied by A, which is the frontal area. In short, the lower the CdA, the more aerodynamic an object is. A cylinder would have a CdA of 1.0 (and would not be considered an aerodynamic shape), while a sphere would have a CdA of 0.5 (and would be considered more aerodynamic than a cylinder, but still not very aerodynamic). A cyclist with a very good position in tri-bars might be at around 0.2.

For Boardman to have ridden 56.375 kilometres at a power output of 440 watts, he would have needed a CdA of about 0.17, which, in the words of the aerodynamicist who explained these numbers to me, would be 'remarkable'. In a paper submitted to the *Journal of Applied Physiology* in 2000 that studied Miguel Indurain's hour record, Sabino Padilla estimated Boardman's 56 kilometres hour record CdA at 0.18, but with a power output of 462 watts – much higher than Keen's actual assessment. Assuming Keen's 440 is close to the mark, if Boardman weighed 70 kilos, the watts per kilo figure would be 6.28 – an extraordinarily high number, higher than anybody in the Tour de France has reached for a sustained period since the blood passport came into force, and not far from what Lance Armstrong was expressing at his peak. And there is a 5 per cent drop-off between climbing and time trialling in terms of watts per kilo, since more energy goes into overcoming wind resistance on the flat. Add 5 per cent to 6.28 and you get almost 6.6. That's even more extraordinary.

'The story of the fifty-six-kilometre ride is incredible form coming off the suffering of being battered in the Tour,' Keen insists. 'Exploiting that position, and knowing the difference it made. Good conditions – it was twenty-four and a half degrees, perfect for him, dry air, bit of low pressure, but probably not more than twenty watts higher than Bordeaux, where he died because he cooked, and the Corima bike was shit. It was a perfect day, a great crowd, the form of his life. Is it possible for someone of his shape and weight and training experience to hold four hundred and thirty watts when you can lie on the bike? It's doable. People occasionally do extraordinary things, and the tragedy of our age is that there is such scepticism now in cycling.'

Was it doable? Well, he did it. Did Chris Boardman take performance-enhancing drugs? He's been asked the question before, and he's vehemently denied it, and we should take him at his word. He rode 4.11 for a pursuit in the Superman position, and the world record is now 4.10, set in a traditional tri-bar position (albeit with much better equipment and clothing). But there was a marked fall-off in Boardman's results after 1996 in non-prologue events. He never again got anywhere near the sort of form that allowed him to ride 56 kilometres in an hour, or even 4,000 metres in 4.11. His hormone deficiency and the onset of osteopenia were always cited as major reasons for this.

If he was clean, he was possibly cheated out of Tour de

France wins, and definitely cheated out of stage race wins. The history of cycling from the early 1990s on tells us that results were falsified and no performance can escape scrutiny. Every race win and exploit is open to question.

Epilogue

The Revolution

In 2013, with a British Tour de France winner and after two consecutive Olympic Games of British dominance in cycling events, we can also ask: how would Graeme Obree and Chris Boardman fare in the modern era?

It's safe to say that Boardman would have slotted right in to the philosophy and process of marginal gains applied by British Cycling and Team Sky. After all, these two operations are being run on a template for which Boardman's career was the blueprint. Obree, on the other hand, was the last of a kind. A free-thinking maverick capable of both terrible indiscipline and extreme focus, Obree was more effective on his own terms than anybody else's. He lasted no more time than it took to miss a training camp at Le Groupement. British cycling was lucky to have a coach as good at handling unusual talent as Doug Dailey – he not only recognized Obree's ability, but crucially also understood how to bring the best out of him. Dailey was instrumental in Boardman's international career too, introducing him to Peter Keen and allowing them to operate on their own terms.

Here's another interesting question: how much did

Boardman and Obree need each other? 'A lot' is the answer, although in different ways.

Great riders who dominate are not always emotionally engaging for fans. Miguel Indurain rode like clockwork to five Tour de France wins, but his racing was impressive rather than enthralling. Merckx was equally dominant, but aloof, his super-human exploits creating distance between him and the public. Bernard Hinault was more human. He was top dog in his hey-day, but it was only when he came up against a worthy opponent – Laurent Fignon or Greg LeMond – that the public was able to empathize with him.

But great riders who have a great rival are automatically more accessible. Having the option of picking sides means fans are more engaged. Without Obree on the scene – and without him conveniently seeming to be his opposite in so many ways – Boardman might not have pushed himself as hard.

For Obree, it was even more necessary to have a rival. Cycling journalist Richard Moore, whose book *Slaying the Badger* tells the story of the rivalry between team-mates Greg LeMond and Bernard Hinault at the 1986 Tour de France, com-pared the two sets of riders. 'Like LeMond and Hinault, Obree and Boardman's rivalry validated their achievements,' he told me. 'But there was a difference. Boardman was rattled by an external threat, whereas Obree thrived on that. Hinault and LeMond's manager Cyrille Guimard said that Hinault was a boxer – he needed an opponent to bring out the very best in him. LeMond, on the other hand, was focused on himself, and his biggest fight was against his own demons. Boardman was similar. LeMond and Boardman, like Bradley Wiggins now, were control freaks. They needed a plan, because having a plan was a way of being in control. If anybody deviates from the plan, these people get really rattled.'

If this assessment is accurate, Obree needed Boardman more

than Boardman needed Obree. Boardman would probably not have had a dissimilar career to the one he did have if Obree hadn't appeared on the scene, even if Boardman has made occasional references to Graeme forcing him to up his game. Obree, on the other hand, enjoyed the fight, although in direct competition he lost against Boardman a lot more than he won. In competitive head-to-heads he only beat him twice: in the 1990 Newtownards Clash of Champions time trial, and the world pursuit championship in 1993 (plus a few exhibition races).

It also wasn't a fair rivalry. Although on the surface Boardman versus Obree was a compelling narrative, especially between 1989 and 1993, the reality was that it was more a rivalry between Obree and Boardman plus Peter Keen. Boardman was the physical vessel of the latter pair's ambition. Obree had to provide the brawn and the brainpower all by himself.

It was a happy coincidence that both turned up at the same time, both excelling at the same disciplines. Obree was three years older, but his comparatively late development as an elite athlete meant that he and Boardman emerged almost simultaneously.

It was also a happy coincidence that they seemed so different. The cycling press exaggerated their characters in order to create more of a sense of opposition. William Fotheringham followed Chris Boardman from his time-trialling days all the way through to the end of his career in Europe and admits that he was initially taken in by the stereotype. 'I had this clichéd idea that Boardman was a numbers robot, a cold fish who was impenetrable,' he says. 'It was only after a while that I understood that there was passion, not in the racing but what went behind it. All the ideas and different ways of doing things, like training on a treadmill or diet – that's where he and Pete put their passion. It was just directed in a different way from what we were used to. I think Chris resented a little the fact that people felt Obree was much more human and that he was like a robot. We love contrasts, and it was an easy one for people to make, but it wasn't quite fair on Chris. Nor on Graeme.'

Retirement was initially kinder to Boardman than it was to Obree. He didn't need to work again, so immediately after he left the professional cycling scene for good he poured some of the energy and commitment he'd put into the sport into scuba diving. He's become a dab hand at television punditry, his dry, analytical approach ideal for explaining the sport clearly to viewers. He spent much of the 2000s setting up a bike company, and working in the British cycling team's research and development department. Most of the technical innovations that helped Team GB win so many gold medals in recent years have passed through Boardman's hands at one point or another.

He also slowly accustomed himself to life as a normal person. His friend, the television commentator and author Ned Boulting, acknowledges that Boardman will always be an unusual individual, but much more human than his reputation had it. 'He always says "I'm not a people person", but he's actually a very keen observer of human nature, and he takes a passive interest in everybody and everything,' he says. 'He absorbs information like blotting paper, and he can't help analysing. But you shouldn't underestimate his passion for road racing and his sense of affection for the cultural side of cycling. He gets it. He's a fan of cycling.'

Obree, on his retirement from international cycling, battled with successive waves of depression and mental illness. Sporadic comebacks, during which he'd train with the intensity and focus of the height of his career, were interspersed with periods of futility, dislocation and self-loathing. In December 2001 he made a third attempt on his life, hanging himself in a barn not far from his home in Irvine. Only extremely fortunate circumstances meant that he survived: a fifteen-year-old girl discovered him by chance, called for help, and the man who cut him down was trained in resuscitation. Obree was a minute from death.

When he recovered and published his self-written autobiography, the cycling world was shocked. Obree had been so adept at hiding his illness that almost nobody had suspected he would be capable of or was desperate enough to attempt suicide. The happy-go-lucky clown, the rider who lived off jam sandwiches, the kooky outsider who didn't always shave his legs – it turned out that this man suffered from dark periods of depression. We thought we'd known him well, but in fact we hadn't known him at all.

Both riders were stereotyped early, and neither did much to break the public's perception of them, in spite of the fact that they were both far more complex than those portrayals had it. Boardman even wondered aloud, in an interview just before the 1996 Tour, whether people were right about him. 'I keep on reading about me being arrogant and I've read it so many times I suppose I've got to accept that it must be true, although I don't see it,' he said.

At the height of their rivalry, both riders hogged the headlines. In 1993, especially, they seemed to drive each other to greater heights. Obree set his British hour record, while Boardman broke the national record for 25 miles. Then the Englishman just pipped the Scot to the national 25 title, before Obree struck back with national records at 10 and 50 miles, and then broke Moser's hour record. Boardman beat his record in turn, and then took Obree's scalp again in the Newtownards Clash of Champions time trial. Then Obree won the world pursuit championship, beating Boardman in the semi-final.

It looked at that point like they would be serious rivals for the rest of the nineties, but the UCI's targeting of Obree's technical innovations, and Obree's own character, meant that they seldom clashed directly after that. We were denied a rematch in the 1994 world pursuit championship when Obree was disqualified, in 1995 when Boardman was injured, and in 1996 when Obree was off form.

It's tempting to say that of the two, Boardman is the one whose legacy was most long-lasting. Obree carved his own path through elite cycling – a unique one, born of the innovative and imaginative way in which he approached aerodynamics, and of an almost frightening capacity to drive himself beyond normal limits. But it was all about him, and when he stopped racing there was nobody to pass the methods on to. In cycling terms, he was an evolutionary dead-end, although one with a compelling story. Boardman, on the other hand, is the spiritual forebear of the modern British cycling team and the first British Tour de France win. Keen and Boardman's extraordinary working relationship was a paradigm shift in training and physiology, and it had begun with the almost chance meeting of a scientist and a guinea pig, both of them willing to challenge norms. Would the shift have happened anyway? Possibly, although Keen met with most of the young elite cyclists of the late 1980s and early 1990s and none seemed to respond as well as Boardman.

Boardman and Keen didn't succeed in everything, but ultimately, the groundwork they laid led to others succeeding. When Peter Keen was employed as British Cycling's performance director, in charge of the new World Class Performance Plan, one of the first athletes on the programme was a young Bradley Wiggins. Wiggins went on to repeat Boardman's achievement of winning world and Olympic individual pursuit titles, but he also went on to do what Boardman could not, and win the Tour de France, with all the apparatus, money and expertise of Team Sky behind him.

But does it matter that one rider has a tangible legacy and the other does not? Obree's story is no poorer for having not led to other riders having success with the same methods. He was a one-off, his exploits unrepeatable. Boardman was also unique, but he and Keen always understood that while the rider was a one-off, the process could be universal.

In just a few decades British cycling has changed from being a small, deeply parochial, traditional sport into a big, cosmopolitan, fast-changing sport. Look back on that time trial war Obree and Boardman waged in the 1980s and 1990s. The battles they fought pulled them forward, making them faster than they might otherwise have been, and in doing so they pulled British cycling itself along with them. Two self-obsessed one-offs who wouldn't listen to received wisdom, and as a result started a revolution.

Major Race Wins and Results

Chris Boardman

1984
Winner, national schoolboy 10-mile championship
Second, junior best all-rounder competition

1985
Second, individual pursuit, national junior championship

1986
Winner, national junior 25-mile championship
Winner, junior best all-rounder competition
8th, national 25-mile championship

1987
Second, national hill climb championship
Third, national individual pursuit championship
14th, national 25-mile championship

1988
Winner, national hill climb championship
Second, national individual pursuit championship
15th, national 25-mile championship

1989
Winner, national 25-mile championship
Winner, national individual pursuit championship
Winner, national hill climb championship
Winner, GP de France
Third, Tour of Lancashire

1990
Winner, stage of Tour of Texas
Winner, national 25-mile championship
Winner, national hill climb championship
Second, national individual pursuit championship

1991
Winner, Tour of Lancashire
Winner, Hope Valley Classic
Winner, stage of Olympia Tour
Winner, national 25-mile championship
Winner, national 50-mile championship
Winner, national individual pursuit championship
Winner, national hill climb championship

1992
Winner, Olympic Games individual pursuit
Winner, stage of Circuit des Mines
Winner, national 25-mile championship
Winner, national 50-mile championship
Winner, national individual pursuit championship

1993
Winner, Tour of Lancashire
Winner, Grand Prix Eddy Merckx
Winner, national 25-mile championship

Set world hour record: 52.270km
Second, world individual pursuit championship
4th, Grand Prix des Nations

1994
Winner, stage of Tour de France
Winner, world individual pursuit championship
Winner, world time trial championship
Winner, two stages of Tour of Murcia
Winner, three stages of Critérium du Dauphiné Libéré
Winner, stage of Tour of Switzerland

1995
Winner, stage of Four Days of Dunkirk
Winner, stage of Tour de l'Oise
Winner, stage of Midi Libre
Winner, stage of Critérium du Dauphiné Libéré
Second overall, Critérium du Dauphiné Libéré

1996
Winner, world individual pursuit championship
Set world hour record: 56.375km
Winner, stage of Paris-Nice
Winner, Critérium International
Winner, stage of Critérium du Dauphiné Libéré
Winner, Grand Prix des Nations
Second, world time trial championship
Third, Olympic Games time trial
Third overall, Paris-Nice

1997
Winner, stage of Tour de France
Winner, stage of Tour of Romandy

Winner, stage of Critérium du Dauphiné Libéré
Winner, stage of Tour of Catalonia
Second overall, Tour of Romandy
Third, world time trial championship

1998
Winner, stage of Tour de France
Winner, two stages of PruTour
Winner, stage of Tour of Catalonia
Winner, stage of Tour de l'Ain

1999
Winner, stage of Paris-Nice
Winner, stage of Critérium International
Winner, stage of PruTour
Winner, Josef Vogeli TT
Second, Grand Prix des Nations
Third, world time trial championship

2000
Set world athlete's hour record: 49.441km

Major Race Wins and Results
Graeme Obree

1987
Second, Scottish 25-mile championship

1988
Second, Scottish 25-mile championship

1989
Winner, Scottish national pursuit championship
Winner, Scottish 10-mile championship
Set British hour record: 46.289km

1990
Winner, Clash of Champions 25-mile time trial
Set British hour record: 46.390km
Second, national 25-mile championship

1991
Winner, Scottish 25-mile championship

1992
Winner, Scottish 10-mile championship

Winner, Scottish 50-mile championship
Second, national 25-mile championship

1993
Winner, world individual pursuit championship
Winner, national 50-mile championship
Winner, national individual pursuit championship
Set British hour record: 49.383km
Set world hour record: 51.596km
Second, national 25-mile championship
10th, GP Eddy Merckx

1994
Set world hour record: 52.713km

1995
Winner, world individual pursuit championship
Winner, national individual pursuit championship

1996
Winner, national 25-mile championship

Acknowledgements

This book would not have been possible without the support and love of my wife Ellie and our two sons James and Tommy, who put up with the grumpy, unshaven eccentric who moved in for a few months and made occasional appearances at mealtimes. Thank you for your patience, tolerance and morale-lifting cake and coffee.

Thank you to my agent, Kevin Pocklington, who was an important motivating force from the very inception of this book. And to my publisher Giles Elliott at Transworld, who has been a voice of calm and encouragement throughout and whose flexibility with deadlines is a writer's dream, for seeing this book through from the original idea to its finished state. Thanks also to copy editor Dan Balado for his feedback and ideas.

I was lucky and thankful that both Chris Boardman and Graeme Obree agreed to be interviewed. Both were generous with their insight and time. Thanks also to Peter Keen, who made time for a thought-provoking interview despite having just seen Team GB through to a successful Olympic Games in London. That success was the culmination of the experiment that started when he met Chris Boardman, and I wish him luck in his return to academia at Loughborough University.

I'd like to express gratitude to everybody in the editorial

team at *Cycling Weekly*, whose archives were invaluable in the research process, and to Phil O'Connor for his memories of both riders and for showing me through his photo archive – the picture sections of this book showcase his work.

The interviews I conducted with Doug Dailey and Mike Burrows were fascinating and entertaining and overran by some time, for which I'm grateful. Both were happy to talk for hours, and I'd gladly have listened to both talk for hours more.

Thanks also to Tony Bell, Keith Bingham, Ned Boulting, Gregor Brown, Claudio Chiappucci, Gilbert Duclos-Lassalle, Alasdair Fotheringham, William Fotheringham, Adam Glasser, Vic Haines, Ed Hood, Michael Hutchinson, Matt Illingworth, Roger Legeay, Simon Lillistone, Richard Moore, Scott O'Brien, Colin Sturgess, Andy Sutcliffe, Dave Taylor, Kelvin Trott and Pete Woodworth, for their time, insight, help and memories. Also to two doctors – one aerodynamicist and one physiologist – for their advice and analysis of some of the scientific aspects of the story.

Lionel Birnie has been a voice of encouragement and source of humour, perspective and advice throughout and has provided expert feedback from the point of view of being a talented writer and knowledgeable historian of cycling. Thanks also to my good friends Mike and Lex Webb, who provided expert feedback from the real world.

The following books were extremely helpful in my research: *Fastest Man on Two Wheels* by Tony Bell; *The Complete Book of Cycling* by Chris Boardman; *Roule Britannia* by William Fotheringham; *Heroes, Villains and Velodromes* by Richard Moore; and *Flying Scotsman* by Graeme Obree. I also drew on the documentaries *The Final Hour* (VTV) and *Battle of the Bikes* (Independent Image Ltd). All these sources are recommended reading or viewing on the subject matter.

Index